Bayard Taylor

Northern Travel - Summer and Winter Pictures

Sweden, Denmark, and Lapland

Bayard Taylor

Northern Travel - Summer and Winter Pictures
Sweden, Denmark, and Lapland

ISBN/EAN: 9783337112271

Printed in Europe, USA, Canada, Australia, Japan

Cover: Foto ©Thomas Meinert / pixelio.de

More available books at **www.hansebooks.com**

Ever faithfully yours
Bayard Taylor.

NORTHERN TRAVEL.
BAYARD TAYLOR.

NORTHERN TRAVEL

SUMMER AND WINTER PICTURES

SWEDEN, DENMARK, AND LAPLAND

By BAYARD TAYLOR

NEW YORK:
G. P. PUTNAM AND SON, 661 BROADWAY
OPPOSITE BOND STREET.
1869.

Entered according to Act of Congress, in the year 1857, by
G. P. PUTNAM,
In the Clerk's Office of the District Court of the United States for the Southern
District of New York.

RIVERSIDE, CAMBRIDGE:
PRINTED BY H. O. HOUGHTON AND COMPANY.

PROSE WRITINGS OF BAYARD TAYLOR.

REVISED EDITION.

———◆———

NORTHERN TRAVEL: NORWAY, LAPLAND, ETC.

PREFACE.

This book requires no further words of introduction than those with which I have prefaced former volumes—that my object in travel is neither scientific, statistical, nor politico-economical; but simply artistic, pictorial,—if possible, panoramic. I have attempted to draw, with a hand which, I hope, has acquired a little steadiness from long practice, the people and the scenery of Northern Europe, to colour my sketches with the tints of the originals, and to invest each one with its native and characteristic atmosphere. In order to do this, I have adopted, as in other countries, a simple rule: to live, as near as possible, the life of the people among whom I travel. The history of Sweden and Norway, their forms of Government, commerce, productive industry, political condition, geology, botany, and agriculture, can be found in other works, and I have only touched upon such subjects where it was necessary to give completeness to my pictures. I have endeavoured to give photographs, instead of diagrams, or tables of figures ; and desire only that the untravelled reader, who is interested in the countries I visit, may find that he is able to see them by the aid of my eyes.

BAYARD TAYLOR.

LONDON: November, 1857.

CONTENTS.

CHAPTER I.
A WINTER VOYAGE ON THE BALTIC.

Embarking at Lübeck—Put into a Hut—The Company on Board—Night on the Baltic—Ystad—A Life Lost—Stopped by Ice—A Gale—The Swedish Coast—Arrival at Dalarö—Conscientious Custom-House Officer. . . . . Page 13

CHAPTER II.
STOCKHOLM—PREPARATIONS FOR THE NORTH.

Departure in Sleds—A Meteor—Winter Scenery—Swedish Post-Stations—View of Stockholm—Arrival—Stockholm Weather—Swedish Ignorance of the North—Funds—Equipment. 21

CHAPTER III.
FIRST EXPERIENCES OF NORTHERN TRAVEL.

A Swedish Diligence—Aspect of the Country—Upsala—A Fellow-Passenger—The Northern Gods—Scenery—Churches—Peasant's Houses—Arrival at Gefle—*Förbud* Papers—Speaking Swedish—Daylight at Gefle—A Cold Italian—Experience of *Skjuts* and *Förbud*—We reach Snow—Night Travel—An Arabic Landlord—A Midnight Chase—Quarters at Bro—The Second Day—We reach Sundsvall. . 27

CHAPTER IV.

A SLEIGH RIDE THROUGH NORRLAND.

Sundsvall and the Norrlanders—Purchase Sleighs—Start again—Driving on the Ice—Breakfast at Fjäl—Twilight Hymn—Angermannland—A Bleak Day—Scenery of Norrland—Postillions—Increase of Cold—Dark Travel—The Norrland People—The Country and its Products—Northern Thanks—Umeå—The Inn at Innertaflc. . Page 39

CHAPTER V.

PROGRESS NORTHWARD—A STORM.

Christmas Temperature—First Experience of intense Cold—Phenomena thereof—Arctic Travel—Splendour of the Scenery—The Northern Nature—Gross Appetites—My Nose and the Mercury Frozen—Dreary Travel—Skellefteå and its Temple—A Winter Storm—The Landlady at Abyn—Ploughing out—Travelling in a Tempest—Reach Piteå. 50

CHAPTER VI.

JOURNEY FROM PITEÅ TO HAPARANDA.

Torment—Under the Aurora Borealis—A Dismal Night—Around the Bothnian Gulf—Forest Scenery—Månsbyn—The Suspicious Iron-Master—Brother Horton and the Cold—A Trial of Languages—Another Storm—New Year's Day—Entrance into Finland—The Finns—Haparanda. 62

CHAPTER VII.

CROSSING THE ARCTIC CIRCLE.

Medical Treatment—The Kind Fredrika—Morals in the North—Our Quarters at Haparanda—Vain Questions—Start for Lapland—Arctic Daylight—Campbell's Torneå—A Finnish Inn—Colours of the Arctic Sky—Approach to Avasaxa—Crossing the Arctic Circle—An Afternoon Sunset—Reception at Juoxengi. 72

CHAPTER VIII.

ADVENTURES AMONG THE FINNS.

Journey up the Torneå—Wonders of the Winter Woods—Lapps and Reindeer—My Finnish Vocabulary—A Night Journey—Reception at Kengis—Continue the Journey—Finnish Sleds—A Hard Day—The Inn at Jokijalka—Its Inmates—Life in a Finnish Hut—An Arctic Picture—A Frozen Country—Kihlangi—A Polar Night—Parkajoki—We reach Muoniovara. . . . Page 83

CHAPTER IX.

LIFE IN LAPLAND.

Reception at Muoniovara—Mr. Wolley—Our Lapland Home—A Finnish Bath—Send for Reindeer—A Finnish House—Stables—The Reindeer Pulk—My first Attempt at driving Reindeer—Failure and Success—Muonioniska—View from the Hill—Fears of an old Finn—The Discovery of America—A Lapp Witch—Reindeer Accident. 98

CHAPTER X.

A REINDEER JOURNEY ACROSS LAPLAND.

Preparations for the Journey—Departure—A lazy Deer—"Long Isaac" —An Auroral Spectacle—A Night at Palajoki—The Table-Land of Lapland—Sagacity of the Deer—Driving a wild Reindeer—Polar Poetry—Lippajärvi—Picture of a Lapp—The Night—A Phantom Journey—The Track lost—A Lapp Encampment—Two Hours in a Lapp Tent—We start again—Descent into Norway—Heavy Travel—Lapp Hut in Siepe—A Fractious Reindeer—Drive to Kautokeino. 101

CHAPTER XI.

KAUTOKEINO—A DAY WITHOUT A SUN

Lapland Etiquette—The Inn—Quarters at the Länsman s—Situation of Kautokeino—Climate—Life—Habits of the Population—Approach of Sunrise—Church Service in Lapland—Cold Religion—Noonday without Sunrise—The North and the South—A Vision—Visits of the Lapps

—Lars Kaino—A Field for Portrait-painting—Character of the Lapp Race—Their present Condition—The religious Outbreak at Kautokeino—Pastor Hvoslef—A Piano in Lapland—The Schools—Visit to a *Gamme*. . . . . Page 126

CHAPTER XII.

THE RETURN TO MUONIOVARA.

Advantages of Lapp Costume—Turning Southward—Departure from Kautokeino—A Lapp Hut—Religion—The Reindeer—Their Qualities—Treatment by the Lapps—Annoyances of Reindeer Travel—Endurance of Northern Girls—The Table-Land—The "Roof of the World"—Journey to Lippajärvi—Descent to the Muonio—Female Curiosity—The Return to Muoniovara—Prosaic Life of the Lapps—Modern Prudery. 141

CHAPTER XIII.

ABOUT THE FINNS.

Change of Plans—Winter in Lapland—The Finns—Their Physical Appearance—Character—Drunkenness—A Spiritual Epidemic—Morality—Contradictory Customs—Family Names and Traditions—Apathy of Northern Life—The Polar Zone—Good Qualities of the Race—An English Naturalist. 154

CHAPTER XIV.

EXPERIENCES OF ARCTIC WEATHER.

Departure from Muoniovara—50° below Zero—A terrible Day—An Arctic Night—Jokijalka again—Travelling down the Torneå—A Night at Kardis—Increase of Daylight—Juoxengi—A Struggle for Life—Difficulty of keeping awake—Frozen Noses—The Norseman's Hell——Freezing Travellers—Full Daylight again—Safe Arrival at Haparanda—Comfort—The Doctor's Welcome—Drive to Torneå—The Weather. 164

CHAPTER XV.

INCIDENTS OF THE RETURN JOURNEY.

Mild Weather!—Miraculous Scenery—Näsby—Swedish Honesty—Ad-

ventures at Luleå—Northern Sleds—Piteå—Accident at Skellefteå—
The Norrland Climate—A damp Swede—Travelling in a Tempest—A
Norrland Inn—Character of the People—Their Houses.   Page 177

CHAPTER XVI.

CONCLUSION OF THE ARCTIC TRIP.

Warmth and Daylight—Swedish Linen—The Northern Women—Progress Southward—Quarrel with a Postillion—A Model Village—Rough Roads—Scarcity of Snow—Arrival at Stockholm—Remarks on Arctic Travel—Scale of Temperature—Record of Cold.   . .   187

CHAPTER XVII.

LIFE IN STOCKHOLM.

Stockholm—Its Position and Appearance—The Streets and Houses—Manner of Living—Swedish Diet—Stockholm in Spring—Swedish Gymnastics—A Grotesque Spectacle—Results of Gymnastics—Ling's System—The Swedish Language—Character of the Prose and Poetry—Songs—Life in Stockholm.   197

CHAPTER XVIII.

MANNERS AND MORALS OF STOCKHOLM.

Hospitality of the Swedes—Northern Frenchmen—Stockholm Manners—Dress—Conventionalism—Taking off the Hat—Courtesy of the Swedish—An Anecdote—King Oscar—The Royal Family—Tendency to Detraction—The King's Illness—Morals of Stockholm—Illegitimate Births—Sham Morality—Causes of Immorality—Drunkenness—An Incident. . . . . . . - . 210

CHAPTER XIX.

JOURNEY TO GOTTENBURG AND COPENHAGEN.

Appearance of Spring—Departure from Stockholm—The Gotha Canal—Vreta Kloster—Scenery of the Wener—European Ideas concerning America—A Democratic Nobleman—The Götha River—Gottenburg—

The Giant's Pots —The Cattegat—Elsinore—The Sound Dues—Copenhagen and its Inhabitants — Thorwaldsen— Interview with Hans Christian Andersen—Goldschmidt—Prof. Rafn. . . Page 222

CHAPTER XX.

RETURN TO THE NORTH.—CHRISTIANIA.

Visit to Germany and England—The Steamer at Hull—The North Sea —Fellow-Passengers—Christiansand—The Coast of Norway—Arrival at Christiania—Preparations for Travelling—The Carriole—Progress of Christiania—Beauty of its Environs. 235

CHAPTER XXI.

INCIDENTS OF CARRIOLE TRAVEL.

Disinterested Advice—Departure—Alarm—Descending the Hills—The *Skyds* System—Krogkleven—The King's View—Country and Country People—Summer Scenery—The Randsfjord—A Cow-Whale—The Miösen Lake—More than we bargained for—Astonishing Kindness— The Lake from a Steamer. 242

CHAPTER XXII.

GULDBRANDSDAL AND THE DOVRE FJELD.

Lillehammer—A Sabbath Morning—A Picture of Dahi—Guldbrandsdel —Annoyances of Norwegian Travel—The Lougen River—Cataracts— The Station at Viik—Sinclair's Defeat—Pass of the Rusten—The Upper Valley—Scenery of the Dovre Fjeld—Solitude of the Mountains —Jerkin—Summit of the Fjeld—Nature in the North—Defile of the Driv—A Silent Country—Valley of the Orkla—Park Scenery—A Cunning Hostess—Solidity of Norwegian Women. . 254

CHAPTER XXIII.

DRONTHEIM.—VOYAGE UP THE COAST OF NORWAY.

Panorama of Drontheim—Its Streets and Houses—Quarters at the Hotel —Protestant High Mass—Norwegian Steamers—Parting View of

CONTENTS. xiii

—Drontheim—The Namsen Fjord—Settlements on the Coast—The Rock of Torghätten—The Seven Sisters—Singular Coast Scenery—The Horseman—Crossing the Arctic Circle—Coasting Craft—Bodö—An Arctic Sunset. . . . . . . Page 269

CHAPTER XXIV.

THE LOFODEN ISLES.

Habits of the Arctic Summer—The Lofoden Islands—Mosköe—The Myth of the Maelström—The Lofoden Fishermen—Improvement in the People—Lofoden Scenery—The Rasksund—Disappearance of Daylight—Character of the Scenery—Tromsöe at Midnight. Page 281

CHAPTER XXV.

FINNARK AND HAMMERFEST.

Visit to the Lapps—Scenery of Tromsdal—Phenomena of the Arctic Summer—The Lapp *Gammes*—A Herd of Reindeer—The Midnight Sun and its Effect—Scenery of the Alten Fjord—Pastor Hvoslef—Mr. Thomas and his Home—Altengaard—A Polar Bishop—An Excited Discussion—Whales—Appearance of Hammerfest—Fishy Quarters.
289

CHAPTER XXVI.

THE MIDNIGHT SUN.

Plans of Travellers—Ship for the Varanger Fjord—Scenery of Magerõe—Miraculous Provision for human Life—Fisheries on the Coast—The Porsanger Fjord—Coast Scenery—Sværholtklub—Rousing the Sea Gulls—Picture of the Midnight Sun—Loss of a Night—The Church of the Lapps—Wonderful Rock-painting—Nordkyn. . . 300

CHAPTER XXVII.

THE VARANGER FJORD—ARCTIC LIFE.

The Tana Fjord—Another Midnight—Desolation—Arctic Life—The Varanger Fjord—The Fort of Vardöhuus—Arrival at Vadsö—Summer there—More of the Lapps—Climate and Delights of Living—Rich

B

Fishing—Jolly young Englishmen—Daylight Life—Its Effects, physical and Moral—Trees of Hammerfest—An astronomical Monument
Page 316

CHAPTER XXVIII.

THE RETURN TO DARKNESS—NORWEGIAN CHARACTER.

Splendour of the Northern Coast Scenery—Growth of Vegetation—Government of the Lapps—Pastor Lamers and his Secession—Religion in the North—An intelligent Clergyman—Discussions on Board—Starlight and Lamp-light—Character of the Norwegians—Their national Vanity—Jealousy of Sweden. 321

CHAPTER XXIX.

DRONTHEIM AND BERGEN.

Trouble at Drontheim—Valley of the Nid—The Lierfoss—Picture of Christiansund—Molde and Romsdal—The Vikings and their Descendants—The Rock of Hornelen—Rainy Bergen—A Group of Lepers—Norwegian Filth—Licentiousness—Picture of Bergen—Its Streets—Drunkenness—Days of Sunshine—Home-sick for Hammerfest—The Museum—Delays and dear Charges. 330

CHAPTER XXX.

A TRIP TO THE VÖRING-FOSS.

Parting View of Bergen—Lovely Scenery—Interested Kindness—The Roads of Norway—Uncomfortable Quarters—Voyage on the Oster fjord—Bolstadören—Swindling Postillions—Arrival at Vossevangen—Morning Scenery—Agriculture in Norway—Destruction of the Forests—Descent to Vasenden—A Captain on Leave—Crossing the Fjeld—The Shores of Ulvik—Hardanger Scenery—Angling and Anglers—Pedar Halstensen—National Song of Norway—Sæbö—A stupendous Defile—Ascent of the Fjeld—Plateau of the Hardanger—The Vöring-Foss—Its Grandeur—A Sæter Hut—Wonderful Wine. 341

CHAPTER XXXI.

SKETCHES FROM THE BERGENSTIFT.

Peder's Embarrassment—His Drowning—The Landlady—Morning at Ulvik—A Norwegian Girl—Female Ugliness—Return to Vossevangen—Indolence—Detention at Stalheim—Scenery of the Naerödal—Postillions—On the Gudvangen Fjord—The Sogne Fjord—Transparency of the Water—The Boatmen. . . . . Page 359

CHAPTER XXXII.

HALLINGDAL—THE COUNTRY-PEOPLE OF NORWAY.

Roads to Christiania—Southern Sunshine—Saltenaaset—The Church of Borgund—Top of the Fille Fjeld—Natives on Sunday—Peculiar Female Costume—Scarcity of Milk and Water—The Peak of Saaten—A Breakfast at Ekre—Hallingdal—Wages of Labourers—Valley Scenery—How *Förbuds* are sent—General Swindling—Character of the Norwegians for Honesty—Illustrations—Immorality—A " Cutty Sark"— Charms of Green. 370

CHAPTER XXXIII.

TELLEMARK AND THE RIUKAN-FOSS.

The Silver Mines of Kongsberg—Roads in Tellemark—Bargaining for Horses—The Inn at Bolkesjö—Sleeping Admonitions—Smashing Travel—Tinoset—The Tind Lake—A Norwegian Farm-House—The Westfjord-dal and its Scenery—Ole Torgensen's Daughter—The Valley—A Leper—Defile of the Maan Elv—Picture of the Riukan-Foss—Its Beauty—A Twilight View—Supper at Ole's—The Comprehension of Man—A singular Ravine—Hitterdal—How respectable People live—The old Church—Return to Christiania. . . 383

CHAPTER XXXIV.

NORWAY AND SWEDEN.

Norwegian Honesty—The Country People—Illicit Connections—The Icelandic Language—Professor Munck—The Storthing—The Norwe gian Constitution—The Farmer-State—Conversation between a German Author and a Swedish Statesman—Gottenburg—A Fire—Swedish Honesty and Courtesy—The Falls of Trollhätten. . Page 396

CHAPTER XXXV.

A TRAMP THROUGH WERMELAND AND DALECARLIA.

Our Route—Leaving Carlstad—The Scenery—Valley of the Klar Elv - Ohlsäter—Wedding Arches—Asplund—A Night Journey—Adventures in search of a Bed—Entrance into Dalecarlia—The Farmers at Tyngsjö—Journey through the Woods—The People at Westerdal—The Landlord at Rågsveden—The Landlady—Dalecarlian Morality—A Läsare—The Postillion—Poverty—A Dalecarlian Boy—Reception at Kettbo—Nocturnal Conversation—Little Pehr—The female Postillion—The *Läsare* in Dalecarlia—View of Mora Valley. . 407

CHAPTER XXXVI.

LAST DAYS IN THE NORTH.

Mora Scenery—"The Parsonage of Mora" The Magister—Peasants from Upper Elfdal—Scenery of the Siljan—Hymns on Board—Opinions of the Läsare—Their Increase—Conversation with the Peasants—Leksand—The Domprost Hvasser—Walk in the Garden—Dalecarlian Songs—Rainy Travel—Fahlun—Journey to Upsala—The Cholera—The Mound of Odin—*Skål* to the Gods—The End of Summer in Stockholm—Farewell to the North. 425

NORTHERN TRAVEL,

CHAPTER I.

A WINTER VOYAGE ON THE BALTIC.

WE went on board the little iron Swedish propeller, *Carl Johan*, at Lubeck, on the morning of December 1, A.D. 1856, having previously taken our passage for Stockholm What was our dismay, after climbing over hills of freight on deck, and creeping down a narrow companion-way, to find the cabin stowed full of bales of wool and barrels of butter. There was a little pantry adjoining it, with a friendly stewardess therein, who, in answer to my inquiries, assured us that we would probably be placed in a *hut*. After further search, I found the captain, who was superintending the loading of more freight, and who also stated that he would put us into a hut. "Let me see the hut, then," I demanded, and we were a little relieved when we found it to be a stateroom, containing two of the narrowest of bunks. There was another hut opposite, occupied by two more passengers, all that the steamer could carry and all we had, except a short deck-passenger, who disappeared at the commencement of the voyage, and was not seen again until its close.

The day was clear and cold, the low hills around Lubeck were covered with snow, and the Trave was already frozen over. We left at noon, slowly breaking our way down the narrow and winding river, which gradually widened and became clearer of ice as we approached the Baltic. When we reached Travemünde it was snowing fast, and a murky chaos beyond the sandy bar concealed the Baltic. The town is a long row of houses fronting the water. There were few inhabitants to be seen, for the bathing guests had long since flown, and all watering places have a funereal air after the season is over. Our fellow-passenger, a jovial Pole, insisted on going ashore to drink a last glass of Bavarian beer before leaving Germany; but the beverage had been so rarely called for that it had grown sharp and sour, and we hurried back unsatisfied.

A space about six feet square had been cleared out among the butter-kegs in the cabin, and we sat down to dinner by candle-light, at three o'clock. Swedish customs already appeared, in a preliminary decanter of lemon-colored brandy, a thimbleful of which was taken with a piece of bread and sausage, before the soup appeared. The taste of the liquor was sweet, unctuous and not agreeable. Our party consisted of the captain, the chief officer, who was his brother-in-law, the Pole, who was a second-cousin of Kosciusko, and had a name consisting of eight consonants and two vowels, a grave young Swede with a fresh Norse complexion, and our two selves. The steward, Hildebrand, and the silent stewardess, Marie, were our attendants and purveyors. The ship's officers were rather slow and opaque, and the Swede sublimely self-possessed and indifferent; but the Pole, who had been condemned to death at Cracow, and afterward invented cheap gas, was one of the jolliest fellows alive. His German was full of funny mistakes, but he rattled away with as much assurance as if it had been his native tongue. Before dinner was over, we were all perfectly well acquainted with each other.

Night had already set in on the Baltic; nothing was to be seen but snow; the deck was heaped with freight; the storm blew in our teeth; and the steamer, deeply laden, moved slowly and laboriously; so we stretched ourselves on the narrow bunks in our hut, and preserved a delicate regard for our equilibrium, even in sleep. In the morning the steep cliffs of Möen, a Danish island, were visible on our left. We looked for Rügen, the last stronghold of the worship of Odin in the Middle Ages, but a raw mist rolled down upon the sea, and left us advancing blindly as before. The wind was strong and cold, blowing the vapory water-smoke in long trails across the surface of the waves. It was not long, however, before some dim white gleams through the mist were pointed out as the shores of Sweden, and the *Carl Johan* slackened her speed to a snail's pace, snuffing at headland after headland, like a dog off the scent, in order to find her way into Ystad.

A lift of the fog favored us at last, and we ran into the little harbor. I walked the contracted hurricane deck at three o'clock, with the sunset already flushing the west, looked on the town and land, and thought of my friend Dr.

Kane. The mercury had fallen to 16°, a foot of snow covered the house-roofs, the low, undulating hills all wore the same monotonous no-color, and the yellow-haired people on the pier were buttoned up close, mittened and fur-capped. The captain telegraphed to Calmar, our next port, and received an answer that the sound was full of ice and the harbor frozen up. A custom-house officer, who took supper with us on board, informed us of the loss of the steam-ship Umeå, which was cut through by the ice near Sundsvall, and sunk, drowning fifteen persons—a pleasant prospect for our further voyage—and the Pole would have willingly landed at Ystad if he could have found a conveyance to get beyond it. We had twelve tons of coal to take on board, and the work proceeded so slowly that we caught another snow-storm so thick and blinding that we dared not venture out of the harbor.

On the third morning, nevertheless, we were again at sea, having passed Bornholm, and were heading for the southern end of the Island of Oland. About noon, as we were sitting huddled around the cabin stove, the steamer suddenly stopped. There was a hurried movement of feet overhead—a cry—and we rushed on deck. One of the sailors was in the act of throwing overboard a life buoy. "It is the Pole!" was our first exclamation. "No, no," said Hildebrand, with a distressed face, "it is the cabin-boy"—a sprightly, handsome fellow of fourteen. There he was struggling in the icy water, looking toward the steamer, which was every moment more distant. Two men were in the little boat, which had just been run down from the davits, but it seemed an eternity until their oars were shipped, and they pulled away on their errand of life or death. We urged the mate to put the steamer about, but he passively refused. The boy still swam, but the boat was not yet half-way, and headed too much to the left. There was no tiller, and the men could only guess at their course. We guided them by signs, watching the boy's head, now a mere speck, seen at intervals under the lowering sky. He struggled gallantly: the boat drew nearer, and one of the men stood up and looked around. We watched with breathless suspense for the reappearance of the brave young swimmer, but we watched in vain. Poor boy! who can know what was the agony of those ten minutes, while the icy waves gradually benumbed and dragged down the young life that struggled with such desperate energy to keep its place in the world! The men sat down and rowed back, bringing only his cap, which they had found floating on the sea. "Ah!" said Hildebrand, with tears in his eyes, "I did not want to take him this voyage, but his mother begged me so hard that I could not refuse, and this is the end!"

We had a melancholy party in the cabin that afternoon. The painful impression made by this catastrophe was heightened by the knowledge that it might have been prevented. The steamer amidships was filled up to her rail with coal, and the boy was thrown overboard by a sudden lurch while walking upon it. Immediately afterwards, lines were rove along the stanchions, to prevent the same thing happening again. The few feet of deck upon which we could walk were slippery with ice, and we kept below, smoking gloomily and saying little. Another violent snow-storm came on from the north, but in the afternoon we caught sight of some rocks off Carlscrona, and made the light on Oland in the evening. The wind had been blowing so freshly that our captain suspected Calmar Sound might be clear, and determined to try the passage. We felt our way slowly through the intricate sandbanks, in the midst of fog and snow, until after midnight, when only six miles from Calmar, we were stopped by fields of drift ice, and had to put back again.

The fourth morning dawned cold and splendidly clear. When I went on deck we were rounding the southern point of Oland, through long belts of floating ice. The low chalk cliffs were covered with snow, and looked bleak and desolate enough. The wind now came out of the west, enabling us to carry the foresail, so that we made eight or nine knots, in spite of our overloaded condition. Braisted and I walked the deck all day, enjoying the keen wind and clear, faint sunshine of the North. In the afternoon, however, it blew half a gale, with flurries of mingled rain and snow. The sea rose, and the steamer, lumbered as she was, could not be steered on her course, but had to be "conned," to keep off the strain. The hatches were closed, and an occasional sea broke over the bows. We sat below in the dark huts; the Pole, leaning against the bulkhead, silently awaiting his fate, as he afterwards confessed. I had faith enough in the timidity of our captain, not to feel the least alarm—and, true enough, two hours had not elapsed before we lay-to under the lee of the northern end of Oland. The Pole then sat down, bathed from head to foot in a cold sweat, and would have landed immediately, had it been possible. The Swede was as inexpressive as ever, with the same half-smile on his fair, serious face

I was glad to find that our captain did not intend to lose the wind, but would start again in an hour or two. We had a quieter night than could have been anticipated, followed by a brilliant morning. Such good progress had been made that at sunrise the lighthouse on the rocks of Landsort was visible, and the jagged masses of that archipelago of cloven isles which extends all the way to Tornea, began to stud the sea. The water became smoother as we ran into the sound between Landsort and the outer isles. A long line of bleak, black rocks, crusted with snow, stretched before us. Beside the lighthouse, at their southern extremity, there were two red frame-houses, and a telegraph station. A boat, manned by eight hardy sailors, came off with a pilot, who informed us that Stockholm was closed with ice, and that the other steamers had been obliged to stop at the little port of Dalarö, thirty miles distant. So for Dalarö we headed, threading the channels of the scattering islands, which gradually became higher and more picturesque, with clumps of dark fir crowning their snowy slopes. The midday sun hung low on the horizon, throwing a pale yellow light over the wild northern scenery; but there was life in the cold air, and I did not ask for summer.

We passed the deserted fortress of Dalarö, a square stone structure, which has long since outlived its purpose, on the summit of a rock in the sound. Behind it, opened a quiet bay, held in a projecting arm of the mainland, near the extremity of which appeared our port—a village of about fifty houses, scattered along the abrupt shore. The dark-red buildings stood out distinctly against the white background; two steamers and half a dozen sailing crafts were moored below them; about as many individuals were moving quietly about, and for all the life and animation we could see, we might have been in Kamtchatka.

As our voyage terminated here, our first business was to find means of getting to Stockholm by land. Our fellow-passengers proposed that we should join company, and engage five horses and three sleds for ourselves and luggage. The Swede willingly undertook to negotiate for us, and set about the work with his usual impassive semi-cheerfulness. The landlord of the only inn in the place promised to have everything ready by six o'clock the next morning, and our captain, who was to go on the same evening, took notices of our wants, to be served at the two intervening post-stations on the road. We then visited the custom-house, a cabin about ten feet square, and asked to have our luggage examined. "No," answered the official, "we have no authority to examine anything; you must wait until we send to Stockholm." This was at least a new experience. We were greatly vexed and annoyed, but at length, by dint of explanations and entreaties, prevailed upon the man to attempt an examination. Our trunks were brought ashore, and if ever a man did his duty conscientiously, it was this same Swedish official. Every article was taken out and separately inspected, with an honest patience which I could not but admire. Nothing was found contraband, however; we had the pleasure of re-packing, and were then pulled back to the *Carl Johan* in a profuse sweat, despite the intense cold.

CHAPTER II.

STOCKHOLM.—PREPARATIONS FOR THE NORTH.

On the following morning we arose at five, went ashore in fne darkness, and after waiting an hour, succeeded in getting our teams together. The horses were small, but spirited, the sleds rudely put together, but strong, and not uncomfortable, and the drivers, peasants of the neighborhood, patient, and good-humored. Climbing the steep bank, we were out of the village in two minutes, crossed an open common, and entered the forests of fir and pine. The sleighing was superb, and our little nags carried us merrily along, at the usual travelling rate of one Swedish mile (nearly seven English) per hour. Enveloped from head to foot in our fur robes, we did not feel the sharp air, and in comparing our sensations, decided that the temperature was about 20°. What was our surprise, on reaching the post-station, at learning that it was actually 2° below zero!

Slowly, almost imperceptibly, the darkness decreased, but the morning was cloudy, and there was little appearance of daybreak before nine o'clock. In the early twilight we were startled by the appearance of a ball of meteoric fire, nearly as large as the moon, and of a soft white lustre, which moved in a horizontal line from east to west, and disappeared without a sound. I was charmed by the forest scenery through which we passed. The pine, spruce, and fir trees, of the greatest variety of form, were completely coated with frozen snow, and stood as immovable as forests of bronze incrusted with silver. The delicate twigs of the weeping birch resembled sprays of crystal, of a thousand airy and exquisite patterns. There was no wind, except in the open glades between the woods, where the frozen lakes spread out like meadow intervals. As we approached the first station there were signs of cultivation—fields inclosed with stake fences, low red houses, low barns, and scanty patches of garden land. We occasionally met peasants with their sleds—hardy, red-faced fellows, and women solid enough to outweigh their bulk in pig-iron.

The post-station was a cottage in the little hamlet of Berga. We drove into the yard, and while sleds and horses were being changed, partook of some boiled milk and tough rye-bread, the only things to be had, but both good of their kind. The travellers' room was carpeted and comfortable, and the people seemed poor only because of their few wants. Our new sleds were worse than the former, and so were our horses, but we came to the second station in time, and found we must make still another arrangement. The luggage was sent ahead on a large sled, while each pair of us, seated in a one horse cutter, followed after it, driving ourselves. Swedish horses are stopped by a whistle, and encouraged by a smacking of the lips, which I found impossible to learn at once, and they considerately gave us no whips. We had now a broad, beaten road, and the many teams we met and passed gave evidence of our approach to Stockholm. The country, too, gently undulating all the way, was more thickly settled, and appeared to be under tolerable cultivation.

About one in the afternoon, we climbed a rising slope, and from its brow looked down upon Stockholm. The sky was dark-gray and lowering; the hills were covered with snow, and the roofs of the city resembled a multitude of tents, out of which rose half a dozen dark spires. On either side were arms of the Mälar Lake—white, frozen plains. Snow was already in the air, and presently we looked through a screen of heavy flakes on the dark, weird, wintry picture. The impression was perfect of its kind, and I shall not soon forget it.

We had passed through the southern suburb, and were descending to the lake, when one of our shafts snapped off. Resigning the cutter to the charge of a stout maiden, who acted as postillion, Braisted and I climbed upon the luggage, and in this wise, shaggy with snowy fur, passed through the city, before the House of Nobles and the King's Palace, and over the Northern Bridge, and around the northern suburb, and I know not where else, to the great astonishment of everybody we met, until our stupid driver found out where he was to go. Then we took leave of the Pole, who had engaged horses to Norrköping, and looked utterly disconsolate at parting; but the grave Swede showed his kind heart at last, for—neglecting his home, from which he had been absent seven years—he accompanied us to an hotel, engaged rooms, and saw us safely housed.

We remained in Stockholm a week, engaged in making

preparations for our journey to the North. During this time we were very comfortably quartered in Kahn's Hotel, the only one in the capital where one can get both rooms and meals. The weather changed so entirely, as completely to destroy our first impressions, and make the North, which we were seeking, once more as distant as when we left Germany. The day after our arrival a thaw set in, which cleared away every particle of snow and ice, opened the harbor, freed the Mälar Lake, and gave the white hills around the city their autumnal colors of brown and dark-green. A dense fog obscured the brief daylight, the air was close, damp, and oppressive, everybody coughed and snuffled, and the air-tight rooms, so comfortable in cold weather, became insufferable. My blood stagnated, my spirits decended as the mercury rose, and I grew all impatience to have zero and a beaten snow-track again.

We had more difficulty in preparing for this journey than I anticipated—not so much in the way of procuring the necessary articles, as the necessary information on the subject. I was not able to find a man who had made the journey in winter, or who could tell me what to expect, and what to do. The mention of my plan excited very general surprise, but the people were too polished and courteous to say outright that I was a fool, though I don't doubt that many of them thought so. Even the maps are only minute enough for the traveller as far as Torneå, and the only special maps of Lapland I could get dated from 1803. The Government, it is true, has commenced the publication of a very admirable map of the kingdom, in provinces, but these do not as yet extend beyond Jemteland, about Lat. 63°

north. Neither is there any work to be had, except some botanical and geological publications, which of course contain but little practical information. The English and German Handbooks for Sweden are next to useless, north of Stockholm. The principal assurances were, that we should suffer greatly from cold, that we should take along a supply of provisions, for nothing was to be had, and that we must expect to endure hardships and privations of all kinds. This prospect was not at all alarming, for I remembered that I had heard much worse accounts of Ethiopia while making similar preparations in Cairo, and have learned that all such bugbears cease to exist when they are boldly faced.

Our outfit, therefore, was restricted to some coffee, sugar, salt, gunpowder, lucifer-matches, lead, shot and slugs, four bottles of cognac for cases of extremity, a sword, a butcher-knife, hammer, screw-driver, nails, rope and twine, all contained in a box about eighteen inches square. A single valise held our stock of clothing, books, writing and drawing materials, and each of us carried, in addition, a double-barrelled musket. We made negotiations for the purchase of a handsome Norrland sleigh (numbers of which come to Stockholm, at this season, laden with wild-fowl), but the thaw prevented our making a bargain. The preparation of the requisite funds, however, was a work of some time. In this I was assisted by Mr. Moström, an excellent valet-de-place, whom I hereby recommend to all travellers. When, after three or four days' labor and diplomacy, he brought me the money, I thought I had suddenly come in possession of an immense fortune. There were hundreds of bank-notes, and thousands of silver pieces of all sizes—Swedish paper, silver and copper, Norwegian notes and dollars, Danish marks, and Russian gold, roubles and copecks. The value belied the quantity, and the vast pile melted away so fast that I was soon relieved of my pleasant delusion.

Our equipment should have been made in Germany, for, singularly enough, Stockholm is not half so well provided with furs and articles of winter clothing as Hamburg or Leipsic. Besides, everything is about fifty per cent dearer here. We were already provided with ample fur robes, I with one of gray bear-skin, and Braisted with yellow fox. To these we added caps of sea-otter, mittens of dog-skin, lined with the fur of the Arctic hare, knitted devil's caps, woollen sashes of great length for winding around the body, and, after long search, leather Russian boots lined with sheepskin and reaching halfway up the thigh. When rigged out in this costume, my diameter was about equal to half my height, and I found locomotion rather cumbrous; while Braisted, whose stature is some seven inches shorter, waddled along like an animated cotton-bale.

Everything being at last arranged, so far as our limited information made it possible, for a two months' journey, we engaged places in a diligence which runs as far as Gefle, 120 miles north of Stockholm. There we hoped to find snow and a colder climate. One of my first steps had been to engage a Swedish teacher, and by dint of taking double lessons every day, I flattered myself that I had made sufficient progress in the language to travel without an interpreter—the most inconvenient and expensive of persons. To be sure, a week is very little for a new language, but to one who speaks English and German, Swedish is already half acquired.

CHAPTER III.

FIRST EXPERIENCES OF NORTHERN TRAVEL.

THE diligence was a compact little vehicle, carrying four persons, but we two were so burdened with our guns, sword, money-bag, field-glass, over-boots and two-fathom-long sashes, that we found the space allotted to us small enough. We started at eight o'clock, and had not gone a hundred yards before we discovered that the most important part of our outfit—the maps—had been left behind. It was too late to return, and we were obliged to content ourselves with the hope of supplying them at Upsala or Gefle.

We rolled by twilight through the Northern suburb. The morning was sharp and cold, and the roads, which had been muddy and cut up the day before, were frozen terribly hard and rough. Our fellow-passengers were two Swedes, an unprepossessing young fellow who spoke a few words of English, and a silent old gentleman; we did not derive much advantage from their society, and I busied myself with observing the country through which we passed. A mile or two, past handsome country-seats and some cemeteries, brought us into the region of forests. The pines were tall and picturesque in their forms, and the grassy meadows between them, entirely clear of snow, were wonderfully green for the season. During the first stage we passed some inlets of the Baltic, highly picturesque with their irregular wooded shores. They had all been frozen over during the night. We were surprised to see, on a southern hill-side, four peasants at work ploughing. How they got their shares through the frozen sod, unless the soil was remarkably dry and sandy, was more than I could imagine. We noticed occasionally a large manor-house, with its dependent outbuildings, and its avenue of clipped beeches or lindens, looking grand and luxurious in the midst of the cold dark fields. Here and there were patches of wheat, which the early snow had kept green, and the grass in the damp hollows was still bright, yet it was the 15th of December, and we were almost in lat. 60° N.

The houses were mostly one-story wooden cottages, of a dull red color, with red roofs. In connection with the black-green of the pine and fir woods they gave the country a singularly sombre aspect. There was little variation in the scenery all the way to Upsala. In some places, the soil appeared to be rich and under good cultivation; here the red villages were more frequent, and squat church-towers showed themselves in the distance. In other places, we had but the rough hills, or rather knobs of gray gneiss, whose masses were covered with yellow moss, and the straggling fir forests. We met but few country teams on the road; nobody was to be seen about the houses, and the land seemed to be asleep or desolated. Even at noon, when the sun came out fairly, he was low on the horizon, and gave but an eclipsed light, which was more cheerless than complete darkness

The sun set about three o'clock, but we had a long, splendid twilight, a flush of orange, rose and amber-green, worthy of a Mediterranean heaven. Two hours afterwards, the lights of Upsala appeared, and we drove under the imposing front of the old palace, through clean streets, over the Upsala River, and finally stopped at the door of a court-yard. Here we were instantly hailed by some young fellows, who inquired if we did not want rooms. The place did not appear to be an inn, but as the silent old gentleman got out and went in, I judged it best to follow his example, and the diligence drove off with our baggage. We were right, after all: a rosy, handsome, good-humored landlady appeared, promised to furnish us with beds and a supper, to wake us betimes, and give us coffee before leaving.

The old gentleman kindly put on his coat and accompanied us to a bookstore on the public square, where I found Akrell's map of Northern Sweden, and thus partially replaced our loss. He sat awhile in our room trying to converse, but I made little headway. On learning that we were bound for Torneå, he asked: "Are you going to buy lumber?" "No," I answered; "we are merely going to see the country." He laughed long and heartily at such an absurd idea, got up in a hurry, and went to bed without saying another word. We had a supper of various kinds of sausage, tough rye bread, and a bowl of milk, followed by excellent beds—a thing which you are sure to find everywhere in Sweden.

We drove off again at half-past six in the morning moonlight, with a temperature of zero. Two or three miles from the town we passed the mounds of old Upsala, the graves of

Odin, Thor and Freya, rising boldly against the first glimmerings of daylight. The landscape was broad, dark and silent, the woods and fields confusedly blended together, and only the sepulchres of the ancient gods broke the level line of the horizon. I could readily have believed in them at that hour.

Passing over the broad rich plain of Upsala, we entered a gently undulating country, richer and better cultivated than the district we had traversed the previous day. It was splendidly wooded with thick fir forests, floored with bright green moss. Some of the views toward the north and west were really fine from their extent, though seen in the faded light and long shadows of the low northern sun. In the afternoon, we passed a large white church, with four little towers at the corners, standing in the midst of a village of low red stables, in which the country people shelter their horses while attending service. There must have been fifty or sixty of these buildings, arranged in regular streets In most of the Swedish country churches, the belfry stands apart, a squat, square tower, painted red, with a black upper story, and is sometimes larger than the church itself. The houses of the peasants are veritable western shanties, except in color and compactness. No wind finds a cranny to enter, and the roofs of thick thatch, kept down by long, horizontal poles, have an air of warmth and comfort. The stables are banked with earth up to the hay-loft, and the cattle enter their subterranean stalls through sloping doorways like those of the Egyptian tombs.

Notwithstanding we made good progress through the day, it was dark long before we reached the bridge over the Dal

Elv, and of the famous cascades we saw only a sloping white glimmer, between dark masses of forest, and heard the noise of the broken waters. At Elfkarleby we were allowed twenty minutes for dinner—boiled salmon and beefsteak, both bad. I slept after this, until aroused by the old Swede, as we entered Gefle. We drove across a broad bridge, looked over vessels frozen into the inlet of the Gulf, passed a large public square, and entered the yard of the diligence office. A boy in waiting conducted us to a private house, where furnished rooms were to be had, and here we obtained tea, comfortable beds, and the attendance of a rosy servant-girl, who spoke intelligible Swedish.

My first care the next morning, was to engage horses and send off my *förbud* papers. We were now to travel by "*skjuts*" (pronounced *shoos*), or post, taking new horses at each station on the road. The *förbud* tickets are simply orders for horses to be ready at an appointed time, and are sent in advance to all the stations on the road, either by mail or by a special messenger. Without this precaution, I was told, we might be subjected to considerable delay. This mode of travelling is peculiar to Sweden and Norway. It has been in existence for three or four centuries, and though gradually improved and systematized with the lapse of time, it is still sufficiently complex and inconvenient to a traveller coming from the railroad world.

Professor Retzius had referred me to the botanist Hartman, in case of need, but I determined to commence by helping myself. I had a little difficulty at first: the people are unused to speaking with foreigners, and if you ask them to talk slowly, they invariably rattle away twice as fast as before. I went into a variety shop on the public square, and asked where I could engage horses for Sundsvall. After making myself understood, as I supposed, the clerk handed me some new bridles. By dint of blundering, I gradually circumscribed the range of my inquiries, and finally came to a focus at the right place. Having ordered horses at six the next morning, and despatched the *förbud* tickets by the afternoon's mail, I felt that I had made a good beginning, and we set out to make the tour of Gefle.

This is a town of eight or ten thousand inhabitants, with a considerable shipping interest, and a naval school. It is a pretty place, well built, and with a neat, substantial air. The houses are mostly two stories high, white, and with spacious courts in the rear. The country around is low but rolling, and finely clothed with dark forests of fir and pine. It was a superb day—gloriously clear, with a south wind, bracing, and not too cold, and a soft, pale lustre from the cloudless sun. But such a day! Sunrise melting into sunset without a noon—a long morning twilight, a low, slant sun, shining on the housetops for an hour or so, and the evening twilight at three in the afternoon. Nothing seemed real in this strange, dying light—nothing but my ignorance of Swedish, whenever I tried to talk.

In the afternoon, we called on the Magister Hartman, whom we found poring over his plants. He spoke English tolerably, and having made a journey through Lapland from Torneå to the Lyngen Fiord, was able to give us some information about the country. He encouraged us in the belief that we should find the journey more rapid and easy in winter than in summer. He said the Swedes feared the

North and few of them ever made a winter journey thither, but nothing could stop the Americans and the English from going anywhere. He also comforted us with the assurance that we should find snow only six Swedish (forty English) miles further north. Lat. 60° 35′ N., the 17th of December, and no snow yet! In the streets, we met an organ-grinder playing the Marseillaise. There was no mistaking the jet-black hair, the golden complexion and the brilliant eyes o. the player, "*Siete Italiano?*" I asked. "*Sicuro!*" he answered, joyously: "*e lei anche?*" "Ah," he said, in answer to my questions, "*io non amo questo paese; è freddo ed oscuro; non si gagna niente—ma in Italia si vive.*" My friend Ziegler had already assured me: "One should see the North, but not *after* the South." Well, we shall see; but I confess that twenty degrees below zero would have chilled me less than the sight of that Italian.

We were at the inn punctually at six in the morning, but our horses were not ready. The *hållkarl*, or ostler, after hearing my remonstrances, went on splitting wood, and, as I did not know enough of Swedish to scold with any profit, I was obliged to remain wrathful and silent. He insisted on my writing something (I could not understand what) in the post-book, so I copied the affidavit of a preceding traveller and signed my name to it, which seemed to answer the purpose. After more than half an hour, two rough two-wheeled carts were gotten ready, and the farmers to whom they belonged, packed themselves and our luggage into one, leaving us to drive the other. We mounted, rolled ourselves in our furs, thrust our feet into the hay, and rattled out of Gefle in the frosty moonlight. Such was our first experience of travelling by *skjuts*.

The road went northward, into dark forests, over the same undulating, yet monotonous country as before. The ground was rough and hard, and our progress slow, so that we did not reach the end of the first station (10 miles) until nine o'clock. As we drove into the post-house, three other travellers, who had the start of us, and consequently the first right to horses, drove away. I was dismayed to find that my *förbud* had not been received, but the ostler informed me that by paying twelve skillings extra I could have horses at once. While the new carts were getting ready, the postman, wrapped in wolf-skin, and with a face reddened by the wind, came up, and handed out my *förbud* ticket. Such was our first experience of *förbud*.

On the next station, the peasant who was ahead with our luggage left the main road and took a rough track through the woods. Presently we came to a large inlet of the Bothnian gulf, frozen solid from shore to shore, and upon this we boldly struck out. The ice was nearly a foot thick, and as solid as marble. So we drove for at least four miles, and finally came to land on the opposite side, near a saw-mill. At the next post-house we found our predecessors just setting off again in sleds; the landlord informed us that he had only received my *förbud* an hour previous, and, according to law was allowed three hours to get ready his second instalment of horses, the first being exhausted. There was no help for it: we therefore comforted ourselves with breakfast. At one o'clock we set out again in low Norrland sleds, but there was little snow at first, and we were obliged to walk the first few miles. The station was a long one (twenty English miles), and our horses not the most promising. Coming upon solid snow at last, we travelled rather more swiftly, but with more risk. The sleds, although so low, rest upon narrow runners, and the shafts are attached by a hook, upon which they turn in all directions, so that the sled sways from side to side, entirely independent of them. In going off the main road to get a little more snow on a side track, I discovered this fact by overturning the sled, and pitching Braisted and myself out on our heads. There were lakes on either side, and we made many miles on the hard ice, which split with a dull sound under us. Long after dark, we reached the next station, Strätjära, and found our horses in readiness. We started again, by the gleam of a flashing aurora, going through forests and fields in the uncertain light, blindly following our leader, Braisted and I driving by turns, and already much fatigued. After a long time, we descended a steep hill, to the Ljusne River. The water foamed and thundered under the bridge, and I could barely see that it fell in a series of rapids over the rocks.

At Mo Myskie, which we reached at eight o'clock, our horses had been ready four hours, which gave us a dollar banco *väntapenningar* (waiting money) to pay. The landlord, a sturdy, jolly fellow, with grizzly hair and a prosperous abdomen, asked if we were French, and I addressed him in that language. He answered in English on finding that we were Americans. On his saying that he had learned English in Tripoli, I addressed him in Arabic. His eyes flashed, he burst into a roaring laugh of the profoundest delight, and at once answered in the majestic gutturals of the Orient. "*Allah akhbar!*" he cried; "I have been waiting twenty years for some one to speak to me in Arabic and you are the first!" He afterwards changed to Italian, which he spoke perfectly well, and preferred to any foreign language. We were detained half an hour by his delight, and went off forgetting to pay for a bottle of beer, the price of which I sent back by the *skjutsbonde*, or postillion.

This *skjutsbonde* was a stupid fellow, who took us a long, circuitous road, in order to save time. We hurried along in the darkness, constantly crying out "*Kör på!*" (Drive on!) and narrowly missing a hundred overturns. It was eleven at night before we reached the inn at Kungsgården, where, fortunately, the people were awake, and the pleasant old landlady soon had our horses ready. We had yet sixteen English miles to Bro, our lodging-place, where we should have arrived by eight o'clock. I hardly know how to describe the journey. We were half asleep, tired out, nearly frozen, (mercury below zero) and dashed along at haphazard, through vast dark forests, up hill and down, following the sleepy boy who drove ahead with our baggage. A dozen times the sled, swaying from side to side like a pendulum, tilted, hung in suspense a second, and then righted itself again. The boy fell back on the hay and slept, until Braisted, creeping up behind, startled him with terrific yells in his ears. Away then dashed the horse, down steep declivities, across open, cultivated valleys, and into the woods again. After midnight the moon rose, and the cold was intenser than ever. The boy having fallen asleep again, the horse took advantage of it to run off at full speed, we following at the same rate, sometimes losing sight of him and uncertain of our way, until, after a chase of a few miles, we found the boy getting his reins out from under the runners. Finally, after two in the morning, we reached Bro.

Here we had ordered a warm room, beds and supper, by *förbud*, but found neither. A sleepy, stupid girl, who had just got up to wait on a captain who had arrived before us and was going on, told us there was nothing to be had. "We *must* eat, if we have to eat *you*," I said, savagely, for we were chilled through and fierce with hunger; but I might as well have tried to hurry the Venus de Medici. At last we got some cold sausage, a fire, and two couches, on which we lay down without undressing, and slept. I had scarcely closed my eyes, it seemed, when the girl, who was to call us at half-past five o'clock, came into the room. "Is it half-past five?" I asked. "Oh, yes," she coolly answered, "it's much more." We were obliged to hurry off at once to avoid paying so much waiting money.

At sunrise we passed Hudiksvall, a pretty town at the head of a deep bay, in which several vessels were frozen up for the winter. There were some handsome country houses in the vicinity, better cultivation, more taste in building, and a few apple and cherry orchards. The mercury was still at zero, but we suffered less from the cold than the day previous, and began to enjoy our mode of travel. The horses were ready at all the stations on our arrival, and we were not delayed in changing. There was now plenty of snow, and the roads were splendid—the country undulating, with beautiful, deep valleys, separated by high, wooded hills, and rising to bold ridges in the interior. The houses were larger and better than we had yet seen—so were the people

—and there was a general air of progress and well-doing
In fact, both country and population improved in appearance
as we went northward.

The night set in very dark and cold, threatening snow.
We had an elephant of a horse, which kicked up his heels
and frisked like an awkward bull-pup, dashed down the hills
like an avalanche, and carried us forward at a rapid rate.
We coiled ourselves up in the hay, kept warm, and trusted
our safety to Providence, for it was impossible to see the
road, and we could barely distinguish the other sled, a dark
speck before us. The old horse soon exhausted his enthusiasm. Braisted lost the whip, and the zealous boy
ahead stopped every now and then to hurry us on. The
aurora gleamed but faintly through the clouds; we were
nearly overcome with sleep and fatigue, but took turns in
arousing and amusing each other. The sled vibrated continually from side to side, and finally went over, spilling
ourselves and our guns into a snow-bank. The horse stopped and waited for us, and then went on until the shafts
came off. Toward ten o'clock, the lights of Sundsvall
appeared, and we soon afterwards drove into the yard of the
inn, having made one hundred and fifty-five miles in two days.
We were wretchedly tired, and hungry as bears, but found
room in an adjoining house, and succeeded in getting a supper of reindeer steak. I fell asleep in my chair, before my
pipe was half-finished, and awoke the next morning to a sense
of real fatigue. I had had enough of travelling by *förbud*

CHAPTER IV.

A SLEIGH RIDE THROUGH NORRLAND.

SUNDSVALL is a pretty little town of two or three thousand inhabitants, situated at the head of a broad and magnificent bay. It is the eastern terminus of the only post-road across the mountains to Trondjem (Drontheim) in Norway, which passes through the extensive province of Jemteland. It is, consequently, a lively and bustling place, and has a considerable coasting trade. The day after our arrival was market-day, and hundreds of the Norrlanders thronged the streets and public square. They were all fresh, strong, coarse, honest, healthy people—the men with long yellow hair, large noses and blue eyes, the women with the rosiest of cheeks and the fullest development of body and limb. Many of the latter wore basques or jackets of sheepskin with the wool inside, striped petticoats and bright red stockings. The men were dressed in shaggy sheepskin coats, or garments of reindeer skin, with the hair outward. There was a vast collection of low Norrland sleds, laden with butter, cheese, hay, and wild game, and drawn by the rough and tough little horses of the country. Here was still plenty of life and animation, although we were already so far north that the sun did not shine upon Sundsvall the whole day, being hidden by a low hill to the south. The snowy ridges on the north, however, wore a bright roseate blush from his rays, from ten until two.

We called upon a merchant of the place, to whom I had a letter of introduction. He was almost the only man I met before undertaking the journey, who encouraged me to push on. "The people in Stockholm," said he, "know nothing about Northern Sweden." He advised me to give up travelling by *förbud*, to purchase a couple of sleds, and take our chance of finding horses: we would have no trouble in making from forty to fifty English miles per day. On returning to the inn, I made the landlord understand what we wanted, but could not understand him in return. At this juncture came in a handsome fellow, with a cosmopolitan air, whom Braisted recognised, by certain invisible signs, as the mate of a ship, and who explained the matter in very good English. I purchased two plain but light and strongly made sleds for 50 *rigs* (about $14), which seemed very cheap, but I afterwards learned that I paid much more than the current price.

On repacking our effects, we found that everything liquid was frozen—even a camphorated mixture, which had been carefully wrapped in flannel. The cold, therefore, must have been much more severe than we supposed. Our supplies, also, were considerably damaged—the lantern broken, a powder-flask cracked, and the salt, shot, nails, wadding, &c., mixed together in beautiful confusion. Everything was stowed in one of the sleds, which was driven by the postilion; the other contained only our two selves. We were off the next morning, as the first streaks of dawn appeared in the sky. The roads about Sundsvall were very much cut up, and even before getting out of the town we were pitched over head and ears into a snow-bank.

We climbed slowly up and darted headlong down the idges which descend from the west toward the Bothnian Gulf, dividing its tributary rivers; and toward sunrise, came to a broad bay, completely frozen over and turned into a snowy plain. With some difficulty the *skjutsbonde* made me understand that a shorter road led across the ice to the second post-station, Fjäl, avoiding one change of horses. The way was rough enough at first, over heaped blocks of ice, but became smoother where the wind had full sweep, and had cleared the water before it froze. Our road was marked out by a double row of young fir-trees, planted in the ice. The bay was completely land-locked, embraced by a bold sweep of wooded hills, with rich, populous valleys between. Before us, three or four miles across, lay the little port of Wifsta-warf, where several vessels—among them a ship of three or four hundred tuns—were frozen in for the winter. We crossed, ascended a long hill, and drove on through fir woods to Fjäl, a little hamlet with a large inn. Here we got breakfast; and though it may be in bad taste to speak of what one eats, the breakfast was in such good taste that I cannot pass over it without lingering to enjoy, in memory, its wonderful aroma. Besides, if it be true, as some shockingly gross persons assert, that the belly is a more important district of the human economy than the brain, a good meal deserves chronicling no less than an exalted impression. Certain it is, that strong digestive are to be preferred to strong thinking powers—better live unknown than die of dyspepsia. This was our first country meal in Norrland, of whose fare the Stockholmers have a horror, yet that stately capital never furnished a better. We had beefsteak and onions, delicious blood-puddings, the tenderest of pan-cakes (no *omelette soufflée* could be more fragile), with ruby raspberry jam, and a bottle of genuine English porter. If you think the bill of fare too heavy and solid, take a drive o. fifteen miles in the regions of Zero, and then let your delicate stomach decide.

In a picturesque dell near Fjål we crossed the rapid Indal River, which comes down from the mountains of Norway. The country was wild and broken, with occasional superb views over frozen arms of the Gulf, and the deep rich valleys stretching inland. Leaving Hernösand, the capital of the province, a few miles to our right, we kept the main northern road, slowly advancing from station to station with old and tired horses. There was a snow-storm in the afternoon, after which the sky came out splendidly clear, and gorgeous with the long northern twilight. In the silence of the hour and the deepening shadows of the forest through which we drove, it was startling to hear, all at once the sound of voices singing a solemn hymn. My first idea was, that some of those fanatical Dissenters of Norrland who meet, as once the Scotch Covenanters, among the hills, were having a refreshing winter meeting in the woods, but on proceeding further we found that the choristers were a company of peasants returning from market with their empty sleds.

It was already dark at four o'clock, and our last horses

were so slow that the postilion, a handsome, lively boy, whose pride was a little touched by my remonstrances, failed, in spite of all his efforts, to bring us to the station before seven. We stopped at Weda, on the Angermann River, the largest stream in Northern Sweden. Angermannland, the country which it drains, is said to be a very wild and beautiful region, where some traces of the old, original Asiatic type which peopled Scandinavia are yet to be traced in the features of its secluded population. At Weda, we found excellent quarters. A neat, quiet, old-fashioned little servant-girl, of twelve or fourteen, took charge of us, and attended to all our wants with the greatest assiduity. We had a good supper, a small but neat room, clean beds, and coffee in the morning, beside a plentiful provision for breakfast on the way, for a sum equal to seventy-five cents.

We left at half-past seven, the waning moon hanging on the horizon, and the first almost imperceptible signs of the morning twilight in the east. The Angermann River which is here a mile broad, was frozen, and our road led directly across its surface. The wind blew down it, across the snow-covered ice, making our faces tingle with premonitory signs of freezing, as the mercury was a little below zero. My hands were chilled inside the fur mittens, and I was obliged to rub my nose frequently, to prevent it from being nipped. The day was raw and chilly, and the temperature rose very little, although the hills occasionally sheltered us from the wind. The scenery, also, grew darker and wilder as we advanced. The fir-trees were shorter and stunted, and of a dark greenish-brown, which at a little distance appeared completely black. Nothing could exceed the bleak, inhospitable character of these landscapes. The inlets of the Bothnian Gulf were hard, snow-covered plains, inclosed by bold, rugged headlands, covered with ink-black forests. The more distant ridges faded into a dull indigo hue, flecked with patches of ghastly white, under the lowering, sullen, short-lived daylight.

Our road was much rougher than hitherto. We climbed long ridges, only to descend by as steep declivities on the northern side, to cross the bed of an inland stream, and then ascend again. The valleys, however, were inhabited and apparently well cultivated, for the houses were large and comfortable, and the people had a thrifty, prosperous and satisfied air. Beside the farmhouses were immense racks, twenty feet high, for the purpose of drying flax and grain, and at the stations the people offered for sale very fine and beautiful linen of their own manufacture. This is the staple production of Norrland, where the short summers are frequently insufficient to mature the grain crops. The inns were all comfortable buildings, with very fair accommodations for travellers. We had bad luck with horses this day, however, two or three travellers having been in advance and had the pick. On one stage our baggage-sled was driven by a *poike* of not more than ten years old—a darling fellow, with a face as round, fresh and sweet as a damask rose, the bluest of eyes, and a cloud of silky golden hair. His successor was a tall, lazy lout, who stopped so frequently to talk with the drivers of sleds behind us, that we lost all patience, drove past and pushed ahead in the darkness, trusting our horse to find the way. His horse followed, leaving him in the lurch, and we gave him a long-winded chase astern before we allowed him to overtake us. This so exasperated him that we had no trouble the rest of the way. *Mem.*—If you wish to travel with speed, make your postilion angry.

At Hörnäs they gave us a supper of ale and cold pig's feet, admirable beds, and were only deficient in the matter of water for washing. We awoke with headaches, on account of gas from the tight Russian stove. The temperature, at starting, was 22° below zero—colder than either of us had ever before known. We were a little curious, at first, to know how we should endure it, but, to our delight, found ourselves quite warm and comfortable. The air was still, dry, and delicious to inhale. My nose occasionally required friction, and my beard and moustache became a solid mass of ice, frozen together so that I could scarcely open my mouth, and firmly fastened to my fur collar. We travelled forty-nine miles, and were twelve hours on the way, yet felt no inconvenience from the temperature.

By this time it was almost wholly a journey by night, dawn and twilight, for full day there was none. The sun rose at ten and set at two. We skimmed along, over the black, fir-clothed hills, and across the pleasant little valleys, in the long, gray, slowly-gathering daybreak: then, heavy snow-clouds hid half the brief day, and the long, long, dusky evening glow settled into night. The sleighing was superb, the snow pure as ivory, hard as marble, and beautifully crisp and smooth. Our sleds glided over it without effort, the runners making music as they flew. With every day the country grew wilder, blacker and more rugged, with no change in the general character of the scenery. In the afternoon we passed the frontier of Norrland, and entered the province of West Bothnia. There are fewer horses at the stations, as we go north, but also fewer travellers, and we were not often detained. Thus far, we had no difficulty: my scanty stock of Swedish went a great way, and I began to understand with more facility, even the broad Norrland dialect.

The people of this region are noble specimens of th physical man—tall, broad-shouldered, large-limbed, ruddy and powerful; and they are mated with women who, I venture to say, do not even suspect the existence of a nervous system. The natural consequences of such health are: morality and honesty—to say nothing of the quantities of rosy and robust children which bless every household. If health and virtue cannot secure happiness, nothing can, and these Norrlanders appear to be a thoroughly happy and contented race. We had occasional reason to complain of their slowness; but, then, why should they be fast? It is rather we who should moderate our speed. Braisted, however, did not accept such a philosophy. "Charles XII. was the boy to manage the Swedes," said he to me one day; "he always kept them in a hurry."

We reached Lefwar, our resting-place for the night, in good condition, notwithstanding the 22° below, and felt much colder in the house, after stripping off our furs, than out of doors with them on. They gave us a supper consisting of *smörgås* ("buttergoose"—the Swedish prelude to a meal, consisting usually of bread, butter, pickled anchovies, and caviar flavored with garlic), sausages, potatoes, and milk, and made for us sumptuous beds of the snowiest and sweetest linen. When we rose next morning it was snowing About an inch had fallen during the night, and the mercury had risen to 6° below zero. We drove along in the dusky half-twilight toward Angesjö, over low, broad hills, covered with forests of stunted birch and fir. The scenery continued the same, and there is no use in repeating the description, except to say that the land became more cold and barren, and there seemed to be few things cultivated except flax, barley and potatoes. Still the same ridges sweeping down to the Gulf, on one hand, the same frozen bays and inlets on the other, and villages at intervals of eight or ten miles, each with its great solid church, low red belfry and deserted encampment of red frame stables. Before reaching the second station, we looked from a wooded height over the open expanse of the Gulf,—a plain of snow-covered ice, stretching eastward as far as the eye could reach.

The day gradually became still and cold, until the temperature reached—22° again, and we became comfortable in the same proportion. The afternoon twilight, splendid with its hues of amber, rose and saffron, died away so gradually, that it seemed scarcely to fade at all, lighting our path for at least three hours after sunset. Our postilions were all boys—ruddy, hardy young fellows of fourteen or fifteen, who drove well and sang incessantly, in spite of the cold. They talked much with us, but to little purpose, as I found it very difficult to understand the humming dialect they spoke. Each, as he received his *drickpenningar* (drink-money, or gratuity), at the end of the station, expressed his thanks by shaking hands with us. This is a universal custom throughout the north of Sweden: it is a part of the simple natural habits of the people; and though it seemed rather odd at first to be shaking hands with everybody, from the landlord down to the cook and the ostler, we soon came to take it as a matter of course. The frank, unaffected way in which the hand was offered, oftener made the custom a pleasant one.

At Stocksjö we decided to push on to a station beyond Umeå, called Innertaflc, and took our horses accordingly. The direct road, however, was unused on account of the drifts, so we went around through Umeå, after all. We had nearly a Swedish mile, and it was just dark when we descended to the Umeå River, across whose solid surface we drove, and up a steep bank into the town. We stopped a few moments in the little public square, which was crowded with people, many of whom had already commenced their Christmas sprees. The shops were lighted, and the little town looked very gay and lively. Passing through, we kept down the left bank of the river for a little distance, and then struck into the woods. It was night by this time; all at once the boy stopped, mounted a snow-bank, whirled around three or four times, and said something to me which I could not understand. "What's the matter?" I asked; "is not this the road to Innertafle?" "I don't know—I think not," he said. "Don't you know the way, then?" I asked again. "No!" he yelled in reply, whirled around several times more, and then drove on. Presently we overtook a pedestrian, to whom he turned for advice, and who willingly acted as guide for the sake of a ride. Away we went again, but the snow was so spotless that it was impossible to see the track. Braisted and I ran upon a snow-bank, were over turned and dragged some little distance, but we righted ourselves again, and soon afterwards reached our destination.

In the little inn the guests' room lay behind the large family kitchen, through which we were obliged to pass. We were seized with a shivering fit on stripping off our furs, and it seemed scarcely possible to get warm again. This was followed by such intense drowsiness that we were obliged to lie down and sleep an hour before supper. After the cold weather set in, we were attacked with this drowsy fit every day, toward evening, and were obliged to take turns in arousing and stimulating each other. This we generally accomplished by singing "From Greenland's icy mountains," and other appropriate melodies. At Innertafle we were attended by a tall landlady, a staid, quiet, almost grim person, who paid most deliberate heed to our wants After a delay of more than two hours, she furnished us with a supper consisting of some kind of fresh fish, with a sauce composed of milk, sugar and onions, followed by *gryngröt*, a warm mush of mixed rice and barley, eaten with milk. Such was our fare on Christmas eve; but hunger is the best sauce, and our dishes were plentifully seasoned with it.

CHAPTER V.

PROGRESS NORTHWARDS.—A STORM.

WE arose betimes on Christmas morn, but the grim and deliberate landlady detained us an hour in preparing our coffee. I was in the yard about five minutes, wearing only my cloth overcoat and no gloves, and found the air truly sharp and nipping, but not painfully severe. Presently, Braisted came running in with the thermometer, exclaiming, with a yell of triumph, "*Thirty*, by Jupiter!" (30° of Reaumur, equal to $35\frac{1}{2}$° below zero of Fahrenheit.) We were delighted with this sign of our approach to the Arctic circle.

The horses were at last ready; we muffled up carefully, and set out. The dawn was just streaking the East, the sky was crystal-clear, and not a breath of air stirring. My beard was soon a solid mass of ice, from the moisture of my breath, and my nose required constant friction. The day previous, the ice which had gathered on my fur collar lay against my face so long that the flesh began to freeze over my cheek bones, and thereafter I was obliged to be particularly cautious. As it grew lighter, we were surprised to find that our postilion was a girl. She had a heavy sheepskin over her knees, a muff for her hands, and a shawl around her head, leaving only the eyes visible. Thus accoutred, she drove on merrily, and, except that the red of her cheeks became scarlet and purple, showed no signs of the weather. As we approached Sörmjöle, the first station, we again had a broad view of the frozen Bothnian Gulf, over which hovered a low cloud of white ice-smoke. Looking down into the snowy valley of Sörmjöle, we saw the straight pillars of smoke rising from the houses high into the air, not spreading, but gradually breaking off into solid masses which sank again and filled the hollow, almost concealing the houses. Only the white, handsome church, with its tall spire, seated on a mound, rose above this pale blue film and shone softly in the growing flush of day.

We ordered horses at once, after drinking a bowl of hot milk, flavored with cinnamon. This is the favourite winter drink of the people, sometimes with the addition of brandy. But the *finkel*, or common brandy of Sweden, is a detestable beverage, resembling a mixture of turpentine, train oil, and bad molasses, and we took the milk unmixed, which admirably assisted in keeping up the animal heat. The mercury by this time had fallen to 38° below zero. We were surprised and delighted to find that we stood the cold so easily, and prided ourselves not a little on our powers of endurance. Our feet gradually became benumbed, but, by walking up the hills, we prevented the circulation from coming to a stand-still.

The cold, however, played some grotesque pranks with us. My beard, moustache, cap, and fur collar were soon one undivided lump of ice. Our eye-lashes became snow-white and heavy with frost, and it required constant motion to keep them from freezing together. We saw everything through visors barred with ivory. Our eyebrows and hair were as hoary as those of an octogenarian, and our cheeks a mixture of crimson and orange, so that we were scarcely recognizable by each other. Every one we met had snow-white locks, no matter how youthful the face, and, whatever was the colour of our horses at starting, we always drove milk-white steeds at the close of the post. The irritation of our nostrils occasioned the greatest inconvenience, and as the handkerchiefs froze instantly, it soon became a matter of pain and difficulty to use them. You might as well attempt to blow your nose with a poplar chip. We could not bare our hands a minute, without feeling an iron grasp of cold which seemed to squeeze the flesh like a vice, and turn the very blood to ice. In other respects we were warm and jolly, and I have rarely been in higher spirits. The air was exquisitely sweet and pure, and I could open my mouth (as far as its icy grating permitted) and inhale full draughts into the lungs with a delicious sensation of refreshment and exhilaration. I had not expected to find such freedom of respiration in so low a temperature. Some descriptions of severe cold in Canada and Siberia, which I have read, state that at such times the air occasions a tingling, smarting sensation in the throat and lungs, but I experienced nothing of the kind.

This was arctic travel at last. By Odin, it was glorious! The smooth, firm road, crisp and pure as alabaster, over which our sleigh-runners talked with the rippling, musical murmur of summer brooks; the sparkling, breathless firmament; the gorgeous rosy flush of morning, slowly deepening until the orange disc of the sun cut the horizon; the golden blaze of the tops of the bronze firs; the glittering of the glassy birches; the long, dreary sweep of the landscape; the icy nectar of the perfect air; the tingling of the roused blood in every vein, all alert to guard the outposts of life against the besieging cold—it was superb! The natives themselves spoke of the cold as being unusually severe, and we congratulated ourselves all the more on our easy endurance of it. Had we judged only by our own sensations we should not have believed the temperature to be nearly so low.

The sun rose a little after ten, and I have never seen anything finer than the spectacle which we then saw for the first time, but which was afterwards almost daily repeated—the illumination of the forests and snow-fields in his level orange beams, for even at midday he was not more than eight degrees above the horizon. The tops of the trees, only, were touched: still and solid as iron, and covered with sparkling frost-crystals, their trunks were changed to blazing gold, and their foliage to a fiery orange-brown The delicate purple sprays of the birch, coated with ice, glittered like wands of topaz and amethyst, and the slopes of virgin snow, stretching towards the sun, shone with the fairest saffron gleams. There is nothing equal to this in the South—nothing so transcendently rich, dazzling, and glorious. Italian dawns and twilights cannot surpass those we saw every day, not, like the former, fading rapidly into the ashen hues of dusk, but lingering for hour after hour with scarce a decrease of splendour. Strange that Nature should repeat these lovely aërial effects in such widely different zones and seasons. I thought to find in the winter landscapes of the far North a sublimity of death and desolation—a wild, dark, dreary, monotony of expression—but I had, in reality, the constant enjoyment of the rarest, the tenderest, the most enchanting beauty.

The people one meets along the road harmonise with these unexpected impressions. They are clear eyed and rosy as the morning, straight and strong as the fir saplings in their forests, and simple, honest, and unsophisticated beyond any class of men I have ever seen. They are no milksops either. Under the serenity of those blue eyes and smooth, fair faces, burns the old Berserker rage, not easily kindled, but terrible as the lightning when once loosed. "I would like to take all the young men north of Sundsvall," says Braisted, "put them into Kansas, tell them her history, and then let them act for themselves." "The cold in clime are cold in blood," sings Byron, but they are only cold through superior self-control and freedom from perverted passions. Better is the assertion of Tennyson:

> "That bright, and fierce, and fickle is the South,
> And dark, and true, and tender is the North."

There are tender hearts in the breasts of these northern men and women, albeit they are as undemonstrative as the English—or we Americans, for that matter. It is exhilarating to see such people—whose digestion is sound, whose nerves are tough as whipcord, whose blood runs in a strong full stream, whose impulses are perfectly natural, who are good without knowing it, and who are happy without trying to be so. Where shall we find such among our restless communities at home?

We made two Swedish miles by noon, and then took a breakfast of fried reindeer meat and pancakes, of which we ate enormously, to keep up a good supply of fuel. Braisted and I consumed about a pound of butter between us. Shriek not, young ladies, at our vulgar appetites—you who sip a spoonful of ice-cream, or trifle with a diminutive *meringue*, in company, but make amends on cold ham and pickles in the pantry, after you go home—I shall tell the truth, though it disgust you. This intense cold begets a necessity for fat, and with the necessity comes the taste—a wise provision of Nature! The consciousness now dawned upon me that I might be able to relish train-oil and tallow-candles before we had done with Lapland.

I had tough work at each station to get my head out of my wrappings, which were united with my beard and hair in one solid lump. The cold increased instead of diminishing, and by the time we reached Gumboda, at dusk, it was 40° below zero. Here we found a company of Finns travelling southward, who had engaged five horses, obliging us to wait a couple of hours. We had already made forty miles, and were satisfied with our performance, so we stopped for the night. When the thermometer was brought in, the mercury was frozen, and on unmuffling I found the end of my nose seared as if with a hot iron. The inn was capital; we had a warm carpeted room, beds of clean, lavendered linen, and all civilised appliances. In the evening we sat down to a Christmas dinner of sausages, potatoes, pancakes, raspberry jam, and a bottle of Barclay and Perkin's best porter, in which we drank the health of all dear relatives and friends in the two hemispheres. And this was in West Bothnia, where we had been told in Stockholm that we should starve! At bedtime, Braisted took out the thermometer again, and soon brought it in with the mercury frozen below all the numbers on the scale.

In the morning, the landlord came in and questioned us, in order to satisfy his curiosity. He took us for Norwegians, and was quite surprised to find out our real character. We had also been taken for Finns, Russians and Danes, since leaving Stockholm. "I suppose you intend to buy lumber?" said the landlord. "No," said I, "we travel merely for the pleasure of it." "*Ja so-o-o!*" he exclaimed, in a tone of the greatest surprise and incredulity. He asked if it was necessary that we should travel in such cold weather, and seemed reluctant to let us go. The mercury showed 25° below zero when we started, but the sky was cloudy, with a raw wind from the north-west. We did not feel the same hard, griping cold as the day previous, but a more penetrating chill. The same character of scenery continued, but with a more bleak and barren aspect, and the population became more scanty. The cloudy sky took away what little green there was in the fir-trees, and they gloomed as black as Styx on either side of our road. The air was terribly raw and biting as it blew across the hollows and open plains. I did not cover my face, but kept up such a lively friction on my nose, to prevent it from freezing, that in the evening I found the skin quite worn away.

At Daglösten, the third station, we stopped an hour for

breakfast. It was a poverty-stricken place, and we could only get some fish-roes and salt meat. The people were all half-idiots, even to the postilion who drove us. We had some daylight for the fourth station, did the fifth by twilight, and the sixth in darkness. The cold (—30°) was so keen that our postilions made good time, and we reached Sunnanå on the Skeleftéa River, 52 miles, soon after six o'clock. Here we were lodged in a large, barn-like room, so cold that we were obliged to put on our overcoats and sit against the stove. I began to be troubled with a pain in my jaw, from an unsound tooth—the commencement of a martyrdom from which I suffered for many days afterwards. The existence of nerves in one's teeth has always seemed to me a superfluous provision of Nature, and I should have been well satisfied if she had omitted them in my case.

The handmaiden called us soon after five o'clock, and brought us coffee while we were still in bed. This is the general custom here in the North, and is another point of contact with the South. The sky was overcast, with raw violent wind—mercury 18° below zero. We felt the cold very keenly; much more so than on Christmas day. The wind blew full in our teeth, and penetrated even beneath our furs. On setting out, we crossed the Skeleftéa River by a wooden bridge, beyond which we saw, rising duskily in the uncertain twilight, a beautiful dome and lantern, crowning a white temple, built in the form of a Greek cross. It was the parish church of Skeleftéa. Who could have expected to find such an edifice, here, on the borders of Lapland? The village about it contains many large and handsome houses. This is one of the principal points of trade and intercourse between the coast and the interior.

The weather became worse as we advanced, traversing the low, broad hills, through wastes of dark pine forests. The wind cut like a sharp sword in passing the hollows, and the drifting snow began to fill the tracks. We were full two hours in making the ten miles to Frostkage, and the day seemed scarcely nearer at hand. The leaden, lowering sky gave out no light, the forests were black and cold, the snow a dusky grey—such horribly dismal scenery I have rarely beheld. We warmed ourselves as well as we could, and started anew, having for postilions two rosy boys, who sang the whole way and played all sorts of mad antics with each other to keep from freezing. At the next station we drank large quantities of hot milk, flavored with butter, sugar and cinnamon, and then pushed on, with another chubby hop-o'-my-thumb as guide and driver. The storm grew worse and worse: the wind blew fiercely over the low hills, loaded with particles of snow, as fine as the point of a needle and as hard as crystal, which struck full on our eyeballs and stung them so that we could scarcely see. I had great difficulty in keeping my face from freezing, and my companion found his cheek touched.

By the time we reached Abyn, it blew a hurricane, and we were compelled to stop. It was already dusk, and our cosy little room was doubly pleasant by contrast with the wild weather outside. Our cheerful landlady, with her fresh complexion and splendid teeth, was very kind and attentive, and I got on very well in conversation, notwithstanding her broad dialect. She was much astonished at my asking for a bucket of cold water, for bathing. "Why," said she, "I always thought that if a person put his feet into cold water, in winter, he would die immediately." However, she supplied it, and was a little surprised to find me none the worse in the morning. I passed a terrible night from the pain in my face, and was little comforted, on rising, by the assurance that much snow had fallen. The mercury had risen to zero, and the wind still blew, although not so furiously as on the previous day. We therefore determined to set out, and try to reach Piteå. The landlady's son, a tall young Viking, with yellow locks hanging on his shoulders, acted as postilion, and took the lead. We started at nine, and found it heavy enough at first. It was barely light enough to see our way, and we floundered slowly along through deep drifts for a mile, when we met the snow-plows, after which our road became easier. These plows are wooden frames, shaped somewhat like the bow of a ship—in fact, I have seen very fair clipper models among them—about fifteen feet long by ten feet wide at the base, and so light that, if the snow is not too deep, one horse can manage them. The farmers along the road are obliged to turn out at six o'clock in the morning whenever the snow falls or drifts, and open a passage for travellers. Thus, in spite of the rigorous winter, communication is never interrupted, and the snow-road, at last, from frequent plowing, becomes the finest sleighing track in the world.

The wind blew so violently, however, that the furrows were soon filled up, and even the track of the baggage-sled, fifty yards in advance, was covered. There was one hollow where the drifts of loose snow were five or six feet deep, and here we were obliged to get out and struggle across, sinking to our loins at every step. It is astonishing how soon one becomes hardened to the cold. Although the mercury stood at zero, with a violent storm, we rode with our faces fully exposed, frost-bites and all, and even drove with bare hands, without the least discomfort. But of the scenery we saw this day, I can give no description. There was nothing but long drifts and waves of spotless snow, some dim, dark, spectral fir-trees on either hand, and beyond that a wild chaos of storm. The snow came fast and blinding, beating full in our teeth. It was impossible to see; the fine particles so stung our eyeballs, that we could not look ahead. My eyelashes were loaded with snow, which immediately turned to ice and froze the lids together, unless I kept them in constant motion. The storm hummed and buzzed through the black forests; we were all alone on the road, for even the pious Swedes would not turn out to church on such a day. It was terribly sublime and desolate, and I enjoyed it amazingly. We kept warm, although there was a crust of ice a quarter of an inch thick on our cheeks, and the ice in our beards prevented us from opening our mouths. At one o'clock, we reached the second station, Gefre, unrecognisable by our nearest friends. Our eyelashes were weighed down with heavy fringes of frozen snow, there were icicles an inch long hanging to the eaves of our moustaches, and the handkerchiefs which wrapped our faces were frozen fast to the flesh. The skin was rather improved by this treatment, but it took us a great while to thaw out.

At Gefre, we got some salt meat and hot milk, and then started on our long stage of fifteen miles to Pitea. The wind had moderated somewhat, but the snow still fell fast and thick. We were again blinded and frozen up more firmly than ever, cheeks and all, so that our eyes and lips were the only features to be seen. After plunging along for more than two hours through dreary woods, we came upon the estuary of the Pitea River, where our course was marked out by young fir-trees, planted in the ice. The world became a blank; there was snow around, above and below, and but for these marks a man might have driven at random until he froze. For three miles or more, we rode over the solid gulf, and then took the woods on the opposite shore. The way seemed almost endless. Our feet grew painfully cold, our eyes smarted from the beating of the fine snow, and my swollen jaw tortured me incessantly. Finally lights appeared ahead through the darkness, but another half hour elapsed before we saw houses on both sides of us. There was a street, at last, then a large mansion, and to our great joy the *skjutsbonde* turned into the court-yard of an inn.

4

CHAPTER VI.

JOURNEY FROM PITEÅ TO HAPARANDA.

My jaw was so painful on reaching Piteå, that I tossed about in torment the whole night, utterly unable to sleep. The long northern night seemed as if it would never come to an end, and I arose in the morning much more fatigued and exhausted than when I lay down. It was 6° below zero, and the storm still blowing, but the cold seemed to relieve my face a little, and so we set out. The roads were heavy, but a little broken, and still led over hills and through interminable forests of mingled fir and pine, in the dark, imperfect day. I took but little note of the scenery, but was so drowsy and overcome, that Braisted at last filled the long baggage-sled with hay, and sat at the rear, so that I could lie stretched out, with my head upon his lap. Here, in spite of the cold and wind, I lay in a warm, stupid half-sleep.

It was dark when we reached Ersnäs, whence we had twelve miles to Old Luleå, with tired horses, heavy roads, and a lazy driver. I lay down again, dosed as usual, and tried to forget my torments. So passed three hours; the night had long set in, with a clear sky, 13° below zero, and a sharp wind blowing. All at once an exclamation from Braisted aroused me. I opened my eyes, as I lay in his lap, looked upward, and saw a narrow belt or scarf of silver fire stretching directly across the zenith, with its loose, frayed ends slowly swaying to and fro down the slopes of the sky. Presently it began to waver, bending back and forth, sometimes slowly, sometimes with a quick, springing motion, as if testing its elasticity. Now it took the shape of a bow, now undulated into Hogarth's line of beauty, brightening and fading in its sinuous motion, and finally formed a shepherd's crook, the end of which suddenly began to separate and fall off, as if driven by a strong wind, until the whole belt shot away in long, drifting lines of fiery snow. It then gathered again into a dozen dancing fragments, which alternately advanced and retreated, shot hither and thither, against and across each other, blazed out in yellow and rosy gleams or paled again, playing a thousand fantastic pranks, as if guided by some wild whim.

We lay silent, with upturned faces, watching this wonderful spectacle. Suddenly, the scattered lights ran together, as by a common impulse, joined their bright ends, twisted them through each other, and fell in a broad, luminous curtain straight downward through the air until its fringed hem swung apparently but a few yards over our heads. This phenomenon was so unexpected and startling, that for a moment I thought our faces would be touched by the skirts of the glorious auroral drapery. It did not follow the spheric curve of the firmament, but hung plumb from the zenith, falling, apparently, millions of leagues through the air, its folds gathered together among the stars and its embroidery of flame sweeping the earth and shedding a pale, unearthly radiance over the wastes of snow. A moment afterwards and it was again drawn up, parted, waved its flambeaux and shot its lances hither and thither, advancing and retreating as before. Anything so strange, so capricious, so wonderful, so gloriously beautiful, I scarcely hope to see again.

By this time we came upon the broad Luleå River, and were half an hour traversing its frozen surface, still watching the snow above us, which gradually became fainter and less active. Finally we reached the opposite shore, drove up a long slope, through a large village of stables, and past the imposing church of Old Luleå to the inn. It was now nearly eight o'clock, very cold, and I was thoroughly exhausted. But the inn was already full of travellers, and there was no place to lay our heads. The landlord, a sublimely indifferent Swede, coolly advised us to go on to Persö, ten miles distant. I told him I had not slept for two nights, but he merely shrugged his shoulders, repeated his advice, and offered to furnish horses at once, to get us off. It was a long, cold, dreary ride, and I was in a state of semi-consciousness the whole time. We reached Persö about eleven, found the house full of travellers, but procured two small beds in a small room with another man in it, and went to sleep without supper. I was so thoroughly worn out that I got about three hours' rest, in spite of my pain.

We took coffee in bed at seven, and started for Rånbyn, on the Råneå River. The day was lowering, temperature $8\frac{1}{2}°$ below zero. The country was low, slightly undulating, with occasional wide views to the north, over the inlets of the gulf, and vast wide tracts of forest. The settlements were still as frequent as ever, but there was little apparent cultivation, except flax. Rånbyn is a large village, with a stately church. The people were putting up booths for a fair (a fair in the open air, in lat. 65° N., with the mercury freezing!), which explained the increased travel on the road. We kept on to Hvitå for breakfast, thus getting north of the latitude of Tornea; thence our road turned eastward at right angles around the head of the Bothnian Gulf. Much snow had fallen, but the road had been ploughed, and we had a tolerable track, except when passing sleds, which sometimes gave us an overturn.

We now had uninterrupted forest scenery between the stations—and such scenery! It is almost impossible to paint the glory of those winter forests. Every tree, laden with the purest snow, resembles a Gothic fountain of bronze, covered with frozen spray, through which only suggestive glimpses of its delicate tracery can be obtained. From every rise we looked over thousands of such mimic fountains, shooting, low or high, from their pavements of ivory and alabaster. It was an enchanted wilderness—white, silent, gleaming, and filled with inexhaustible forms of beauty. To what shall I liken those glimpses under the boughs, into the depths of the forest, where the snow destroyed all perspective, and brought the remotest fairy nooks and coverts, too lovely and fragile to seem cold, into the glittering foreground? "Wonderful!" "glorious!" I could only exclaim, in breathless admiration. Once, by the roadside, we saw an Arctic ptarmigan, as white as the snow, with ruby eyes that sparkled like jewels as he moved slowly and silently along, not frightened in the least.

The sun set a little after one o'clock and we pushed on to reach the Kalix River the same evening. At the last station we got a boy postilion and two lazy horses, and were three hours and a half on the road, with a temperature of 20° below zero. My feet became like ice, which increased the pain in my face, and I began to feel faint and sick with so much suffering and loss of rest. The boy aggravated us so much by his laziness, that Braisted ran ahead and cuffed his ears, after which he made better speed. After a drive through interminable woods, we came upon the banks of the Kalix, which were steep and fringed with splendid firs. Then came the village of Månsbyn, where, thank Heaven, we got something to eat, a warm room, and a bed.

While we were at supper, two travellers arrived, one of whom, a well-made, richly-dressed young fellow, was ushered into our room. He was a *bruk-patron* (iron-master), so the servant informed us, and from his superfine broad-cloth, rings, and the immense anchor-chain which attached him to his watch, appeared to be doing a thriving business. He had the Norse bloom on his face, a dignified nose, and English whiskers flanking his smoothly-shaven chin. His air was flushed and happy; he was not exactly drunk, but comfortably within that gay and cheerful vestibule beyond which lies the chamber of horrors. He listened to our conversation for some time, and finally addressed me in imperfect English. This led to mutual communications, and a declaration of our character, and object in travel—nothing of which would he believe. "Nobody can possibly come here for pleasure," said he; "I know better; you have a secret political mission." Our amusement at this only strengthened him in his suspicions. Nevertheless he called for a bottle of port wine, which, when it came, turned out to be bad Malaga, and insisted on drinking a welcome. "You are in latitude 66° north," said he; "on the Kalix, where no American has ever been before, and I shall call my friend to give a *skål* to your country. We have been to the church, where my friend is stationed."

With that he went out, and soon returned with a short, stout, broad-faced, large-headed man of forty or thereabouts. His manner was perfectly well-bred and self-possessed, and I took him to be a clergyman, especially as the iron-master addressed him as "Brother Horton." "Now," said he, "welcome to 66° north, and prosperity to free America! Are you for Buchanan or Fremont?" Brother Horton kept a watchful eye upon his young friend, but cheerfully joined in the sentiment. I gave in return: "*Skål* to Sweden and the Swedish people," and hoped to get rid of our jolly acquaintance; but he was not to be shaken off. "You don't know me," he said; "and I don't know you—but you are something more than you seem to be; you are a political character." Just then Braisted came in with the thermometer, and announced 24° of cold (Reaumur). "Thousand devils!" exclaimed Brother Horton (and now I was convinced that he was not a clergyman), "what a thermometer! How cold it makes the weather! Would you part with it if I were to give you money in return?" I declined, stating that it was impossible for us to procure so cold a thermometer in the north, and we wanted to have as low a temperature as could be obtained.

This seemed to puzzle the iron-master, who studied awhile

upon it, and then returned to the subject of my political mission. "I suppose you speak French," said he; "it is necessary in diplomacy. I can speak it also"—which he began to do, in a bungling way. I answered in the same language, but he soon gave up the attempt and tried German. I changed also, and, finding that he had exhausted his philology, of which he was rather proud, especially as Brother Horton knew nothing but Swedish, determined to have a little fun. "Of course you know Italian," said I; "it is more musical than German," and forthwith addressed him in that language. He reluctantly confessed his ignorance. "Oh, well," I continued, "Spanish is equally agreeable to me;" and took up that tongue before he could reply. His face grew more and more blank and bewildered. "The Oriental languages are doubtless familiar to you;" I persisted, "I have had no practice in Arabic for some time," and overwhelmed him with Egyptian salutations. I then tried him with Hindustanee, which exhausted my stock, but concluded by giving him the choice of Malay, Tartar, or Thibetan. "Come, come,' said Brother Horton, taking his arm as he stood staring and perplexed—"the horses are ready." With some difficulty he was persuaded to leave, after shaking hands with us, and exclaiming, many times, "You are a very seldom man!"

When we awoke, the temperature had risen to 2° above zero, with a tremendous snow-storm blowing. As we were preparing to set out, a covered sled drove in from the north, with two Swedish naval officers, whose vessel had been frozen in at Cronstadt, and who had been obliged to return home through Finland, up the eastern coast of the Bothnian Gulf.

The captain, who spoke excellent English, informed me that they were in about the same latitude as we, on Christmas day, on the opposite side of the gulf, and had experienced the same degree of cold. Both of them had their noses severely frozen. We were two hours and a half in travelling to the first station, seven miles, as the snow was falling in blinding quantities, and the road was not yet ploughed out. All the pedestrians we met were on runners, but even with their snow skates, five feet long, they sank deep enough to make their progress very slow and toilsome.

By the time we reached Näsby my face was very much swollen and inflamed, and as it was impossible to make the next stage by daylight, we wisely determined to stop there. The wind blew a hurricane, the hard snow-crystals lashed the windows and made a gray chaos of all out-of-doors, but we had a warm, cosy, carpeted room within, a capital dinner in the afternoon, and a bottle of genuine London porter with our evening pipe. So we passed the last day of A. D. 1856, grateful to God for all the blessings which the year had brought us, and for the comfort and shelter we enjoyed, in that Polar wilderness of storm and snow.

On New Year's morning it blew less, and the temperature was comparatively mild, so, although the road was very heavy, we started again. Näsby is the last Swedish station, the Finnish frontier, which is an abrupt separation of races and tongues, being at the north-western corner of the Bothnian Gulf. In spite of the constant intercourse which now exists between Norrland and the narrow strip of Finnish soil which remains to Sweden, there has been no perceptible assimilation of the two races. At Näsby, all is pure Swe-

4*

dish; at Sängis, twelve miles distant, everything is Finnish The blue eyes and fair hair, the lengthened oval of the face, and slim, straight form disappear. You see, instead, square faces, dark eyes, low foreheads, and something of an Oriental fire and warmth in the movements. The language is totally dissimilar, and even the costume, though of the same general fashion, presents many noticeable points of difference. The women wear handkerchiefs of some bright color bound over the forehead and under the chin, very similar to those worn by the Armenian women in Asia Minor. On first coming among them, the Finns impressed me as a less frank and open hearted, but more original and picturesque, race than the Swedes. It is exceedingly curious and interesting to find such a flavour of the Orient on the borders of the Frigid Zone.

The roads were very bad, and our drivers and horses provokingly slow, but we determined to push on to Haparanda the same night. I needed rest and medical aid, my jaw by this time being so swollen that I had great difficulty in eating—a state of things which threatened to diminish my supply of fuel, and render me sensitive to the cold. We reached Nickala, the last station, at seven o'clock. Beyond this, the road was frightfully deep in places. We could scarcely make any headway, and were frequently overturned headlong into the drifts. The driver was a Finn, who did not understand a word of Swedish, and all our urging was of no avail. We went on and on, in the moonlight, over arms of the gulf, through forests, and then over ice again— a flat, monotonous country, with the same dull features repeated again and again. At half-past nine, a large white church announced our approach to Haparanda, and soon afterwards we drove up to the inn, which was full of New-Year carousers. The landlord gave us quarters in the same room with an old Norrlander, who was very drunk, and annoyed us not a little until we got into bed and pretended to sleep. It was pretence nearly the whole night, on my part, for my torture was still kept up. The next morning I called upon Dr. Wretholm, the physician of the place,—not without some misgivings,—but his prescription of a poultice of mallow leaves, a sudorific and an opiate, restored my confidence, and I cheerfully resigned myself to a rest of two or three days, before proceeding further northward.

CHAPTER VII.

CROSSING THE ARCTIC CIRCLE.

I was obliged to remain three days in Haparanda, applying poultices, gargles, and liniments, according to the doctor's instructions. As my Swedish was scarcely sufficient for the comprehension of prescriptions, or medical technicalities in general, a written programme of my treatment was furnished to Fredrika, the servant-maid, who was properly impressed with the responsibility thereby devolving upon her. Fredrika, no doubt, thought that my life was in her hands, and nothing could exceed the energy with which she undertook its preservation. Punctually to the minute appeared the prescribed application, and, if she perceived or suspected any dereliction on my part, it was sure to be reported to the doctor at his next visit. I had the taste of camomile and mallows in my mouth from morning till night; the skin of my jaw blistered under the scorching of ammonia; but the final result was, that I was cured, as the doctor and Fredrika had determined.

This good-hearted girl was a genuine specimen of the Northern Swedish female. Of medium height, plump, but not stout, with a rather slender waist and expansive hips, and a foot which stepped firmly and nimbly at the same time, she was as cheerful a body as one could wish to see. Her hair was of that silky blonde so common in Sweden; her eyes a clear, pale blue, her nose straight and well formed, her cheeks of the delicate pink of a wild-rose leaf, and her teeth so white, regular and perfect that I am sure they would make her fortune in America. Always cheerful, kind and active, she had, nevertheless, a hard life of it; she was alike cook, chambermaid, and hostler, and had a cross mistress to boot. She made our fires in the morning darkness, and brought us our early coffee while we yet lay in bed, in accordance with the luxurious habits of the Arctic zone. Then, until the last drunken guest was silent, towards midnight, there was no respite from labour. Although suffering from a distressing cough, she had the out-door as well as the in-door duties to discharge, and we saw her in a sheepskin jacket harnessing horses, in a temperature 30° below zero. The reward of such a service was possibly about *eight* American dollars a year. When, on leaving, I gave her about as much as one of our hotel servants would expect for answering a question, the poor girl was overwhelmed with gratitude, and even the stern landlady was so impressed by my generosity that she insisted on lending us a sheepskin for our feet, saying we were "good men."

There is something exceedingly primitive and unsophisticated in the manners of these Northern people—a straightforward honesty, which takes the honesty of others for granted—a latent kindness and good-will which may at first be overlooked, because it is not demonstrative, and a total unconsciousness of what is called, in highly civilized circles, "propriety." The very freedom of manners which, in some countries, might denote laxity of morals, is here the evident stamp of their purity. The thought has often recurred to me—which is the most truly pure and virginal nature, the fastidious American girl, who blushes at the sight of a pair of boots outside a gentleman's bedroom door, and who requires that certain unoffending parts of the body and articles of clothing should be designated by delicately circumlocutious terms, or the simple-minded Swedish women, who come into our bedrooms with coffee, and make our fires while we get up and dress, coming and going during all the various stages of the toilet, with the frankest unconsciousness of impropriety? This is modesty in its healthy and natural development, not in those morbid forms which suggest an imagination ever on the alert for prurient images. Nothing has confirmed my impression of the virtue of the Northern Swedes more than this fact, and I have rarely felt more respect for woman or more faith in the inherent purity of her nature.

We had snug quarters in Haparanda, and our detention was therefore by no means irksome. A large room, carpeted, protected from the outer cold by double windows, and heated by an immense Russian stove, was allotted to us. We had two beds, one of which became a broad sofa during the day, a backgammon table, the ordinary appliances for washing, and, besides a number of engravings on the walls, our window commanded a full view of Torneå, and the ice-track across the river, where hundreds of persons daily passed to and fro. The eastern window showed us the Arctic dawn, growing and brightening through its wonderful gradations of color, for four hours, when the pale orange sun appeared above the distant houses, to slide along their roofs for two hours, and then dip again. We had plentiful meals, consisting mostly of reindeer meat, with a sauce of Swedish cranberries, potatoes, which had been frozen, but were still palatable, salmon roes, soft bread in addition to the black shingles of *fladbröd*, English porter, and excellent Umeå beer. In fact, in no country inn of the United States could we have been more comfortable. For the best which the place afforded, during four days, with a small provision for the journey, we paid about seven dollars.

The day before our departure, I endeavored to obtain some information concerning the road to Lapland, but was disappointed. The landlord ascertained that there were *skjuts*, or relays of post-horses, as far as Muonioniski, 210 English miles, but beyond this I could only learn that the people were all Finnish, spoke no Swedish, were miserably poor, and could give us nothing to eat. I was told that a certain official personage at the apothecary's shop spoke German, and hastened thither; but the official, a dark-eyed, olive-faced Finn, could not understand my first question. The people even seemed entirely ignorant of the geography of the country beyond Upper Torneå, or Matarengi, forty miles off. The doctor's wife, a buxom, motherly lady, who seemed to feel quite an interest in our undertaking and was as kind and obliging as such women always are, procured for us a supply of *fladbröd* made of rye, and delightfully crisp and hard—and this was the substance of our preparations. Reindeer mittens were not to be found, nor a reindeer skin to cover our feet, so we relied, as before, on plenty of hay and my Scotch plaid. We might, perhaps, have had better success in Torneå, but I knew no one there who would be likely to assist us, and we did not even visit the old place. We had taken the precaution of getting the Russian *visé*, together with a small stock of roubles, at Stockholm, but found that it was quite unnecessary. No passport is required for entering Torneå, or travelling on the Russian side of the frontier.

Trusting to luck, which is about the best plan after all, we started from Haparanda at noon, on the 5th of January. The day was magnificent, the sky cloudless, and resplendent as polished steel, and the mercury 31° below zero. The sun, scarcely more than the breadth of his disc above the horizon, shed a faint orange light over the broad, level snow-plains, and the bluish-white hemisphere of the Bothnian Gulf, visible beyond Torneå. The air was perfectly still, and exquisitely cold and bracing, despite the sharp grip it took upon my nose and ears. These Arctic days, short as they are, have a majesty of their own—a splendor, subdued though it be; a breadth and permanence of hue, imparted alike to the sky and to the snowy earth, as if tinted glass was held before your eyes. I find myself at a loss how to describe these effects, or the impression they produce upon the traveller's mood. Certainly, it is the very reverse of that depression which accompanies the Polar night, and which even the absence of any real daylight might be considered sufficient to produce.

Our road was well beaten, but narrow, and we had great difficulty in passing the many hay and wood teams which met us, on account of the depth of the loose snow on either side. We had several violent overturns at such times, one of which occasioned us the loss of our beloved pipe—a loss which rendered Braisted disconsolate for the rest of the day. We had but one between us, and the bereavement was not slight. Soon after leaving Haparanda, we passed a small white obelisk, with the words "Russian Frontier" upon it. The town of Torneå, across the frozen river, looked really imposing, with the sharp roof and tall spire of its old church rising above the line of low red buildings. Campbell, I remember, says,

"Cold as the rocks on Torneo's hoary brow,"

with the same disregard of geography which makes him grow palm trees along the Susquehanna River. There was Torneå; but I looked in vain for the "hoary brow." Not a hill within sight, nor a rock within a circuit of ten miles, but one unvarying level, like the western shore of the Adriatic, formed by the deposits of the rivers and the retrocession of the sea.

Our road led up the left bank of the river, both sides of which were studded with neat little villages. The country was well cleared and cultivated, and appeared so populous and flourishing that I could scarcely realise in what part of the world we were. The sun set at a quarter past one, but for two hours the whole southern heaven was superb in its hues of rose and orange. The sheep-skin lent us by our landlady kept our feet warm, and we only felt the cold in our faces; my nose, especially, which, having lost a coat of skin, was very fresh and tender, requiring unusual care.

At three o'clock, when we reached Kuckula, the first station, the northern sky was one broad flush of the purest violet, melting into lilac at the zenith, where it met the fiery skirts of sunset.

We refreshed ourselves with hot milk, and pushed ahead, with better horses. At four o'clock it was bright moonlight, with the stillest air. We got on bravely over the level beaten road, and in two hours reached Korpikylä, a larg new inn, where we found very tolerable accommodations. Our beds were heaps of reindeer skins; a frightfully ugly Finnish girl, who knew a few words of Swedish, prepared us a supper of tough meat, potatoes, and ale. Everything was now pure Finnish, and the first question of the girl, " *Hvarifrån kommar du ?*" (Where dost thou come from?) showed an ignorance of the commonest Swedish form of address. She awoke us with a cup of coffee in the morning, and negotiated for us the purchase of a reindeer skin, which we procured for something less than a dollar. The *husbonde* (house-peasant, as the landlord is called here) made no charge for our entertainment, but said we might give what we pleased. I offered, at a venture, a sum equal to about fifty cents, whereupon he sent the girl to say that he thanked us most heartily.

The next day was a day to be remembered: such a glory of twilight splendors for six full hours was beyond all the charms of daylight in any zone. We started at seven, with a temperature of 20° below zero, still keeping up the left bank of the Torneå. The country now rose into bold hills, and the features of the scenery became broad and majestic. The northern sky was again pure violet, and a pale red

tinge from the dawn rested on the tops of the snowy hills
The prevailing color of the sky slowly brightened into lilac,
then into pink, then rose color, which again gave way to a
flood of splendid orange when the sun appeared. Every
change of color affected the tone of the landscape. The
woods, so wrapped in snow that not a single green needle
was to be seen, took by turns the hues of the sky, and
seemed to give out, rather than to reflect, the opalescent
lustre of the morning. The sunshine brightened instead of
dispelling these effects. At noon the sun's disc was not
more than 1° above the horizon, throwing a level golden
light on the hills. The north, before us, was as blue as the
Mediterranean, and the vault of heaven, overhead, canopied
us with pink. Every object was glorified and transfigured
in the magic glow.

At the first station we got some hot milk, with raw
salmon, shingle bread and frozen butter. Our horses were
good, and we drove merrily along, up the frozen Torneå.
The roads were filled with people going to church, probably
to celebrate some religious anniversary. Fresh ruddy faces
had they, firm features, strong frames and resolute carriage,
but the most of them were positively ugly, and, by contrast
with the frank Swedes, their expression was furtive and
sinister. Near Packilä we passed a fine old church of red
brick, with a very handsome belfry. At Niemis we changed
horses in ten minutes, and hastened on up the bed of the
Torneå to Matarengi, where we should reach the Arctic
Circle. The hills rose higher, with fine sweeping outlines,
and the river was still half a mile broad—a plain of solid
snow, with the track marked out by bushes. We kept a

sharp look-out for the mountain of Avasaxa, one of the stations of Celsius, Maupertius, and the French Academicians, who came here in 1736, to make observations determining the exact form of the earth. Through this mountain, it is said, the Arctic Circle passes, though our maps were neither sufficiently minute nor correct to determine the point. We took it for granted, however, as a mile one way or the other could make but little difference; and as Matarengi lies due west of Avasaxa, across the river, we decided to stop there and take dinner on the Arctic Circle.

The increase of villages on both banks, with the appearance of a large church, denoted our approach to Matarengi, and we saw at once that the tall, gently-rounded, isolated hill opposite, now blazing with golden snow, could be none other than Avasaxa. Here we were, at last, entering the Arctic Zone, in the dead of winter—the realization of a dream which had often flashed across my mind, when lounging under the tropical palms; so natural is it for one extreme to suggest the opposite. I took our bearings with a compass-ring, as we drove forward, and as the summit of Avasaxa bore due east we both gave a shout which startled our postilion and notably quickened the gait of our horses. It was impossible to toss our caps, for they were not only tied upon our heads, but frozen fast to our beards. So here we were at last, in the true dominions of Winter. A mild ruler he had been to us, thus far, but he proved a despot before we were done with him.

Soon afterwards, we drove into the inn at Matarengi, which was full of country people, who had come to attend church. The landlord, a sallow, watery-eyed Finn, who knew a few words of Swedish, gave us a room in an adjoining house, and furnished a dinner of boiled fish and barley mush, to which was added a bottle labelled "Dry Madeira," brought from Haparanda for the occasion. At a shop adjoining, Braisted found a serviceable pipe, so that nothing was wanting to complete our jubilee. We swallowed the memory of all who were dear to us, in the dubious beverage, inaugurated our Arctic pipe, which we proposed to take home as a *souvenir* of the place, and set forward in the most cheery mood.

Our road now crossed the river and kept up the Russian side to a place with the charming name of Torakankorwa. The afternoon twilight was even more wonderful than that of the forenoon. There were broad bands of purple, pure crimson, and intense yellow, all fusing together into fiery orange at the south, while the north became a semi-vault of pink, then lilac, and then the softest violet. The dazzling Arctic hills participated in this play of colors, which did not fade, as in the South, but stayed, and stayed, as if God wished to compensate by this twilight glory for the loss of the day. Nothing in Italy, nothing in the Tropics, equals the magnificence of the Polar skies. The twilight gave place to a moonlight scarcely less brilliant. Our road was hardly broken, leading through deep snow, sometimes on the river, sometimes through close little glens, hedged in with firs drooping with snow—fairy Arctic solitudes, white, silent and mysterious

By seven o'clock we reached a station called Juoxengi. The place was wholly Finnish, and the landlord, who did not understand a word of Swedish, endeavoured to make us go on to the next station. We pointed to the beds and quietly carried in our baggage. I made the usual signs for eating, which speedily procured us a pail of sour milk, bread and butter, and two immense tin drinking-horns of sweet milk. The people seemed a little afraid of us, and kept away. Our postilion was a silly fellow, who could not understand whether his money was correct. In the course of our stenographic conversation, I learned that "*cax*" signified two. When I gave him his drink-money he said "*ketox!*" and on going out the door, "*hüweste!*"—so that I at least discovered the Finnish for "Thank you!" and "Good-bye!" This, however, was not sufficient to order horses the next morning. We were likewise in a state of delightful uncertainty as to our future progress, but this very uncertainty gave a zest to our situation, and it would have been difficult to find two jollier men with frozen noses.

CHAPTER VIII.

ADVENTURES AMONG THE FINNS.

We drank so much milk (for want of more solid food) at Juoxengi, that in spite of sound sleep under our sheepskin blankets, we both awoke with headaches in the morning. The Finnish landlord gave me to understand, by holding up his fore-finger, and pronouncing the word "*ax*," that I was to pay one *rigsdaler* (about 26 cents), for our entertainment, and was overcome with grateful surprise when I added a trifle more. We got underway by six o'clock, when the night was just at its darkest, and it was next to impossible to discern any track on the spotless snow. Trusting to good luck to escape overturning, we followed in the wake of the *skjutsbonde*, who had mounted our baggage sled upon one of the country sledges, and rode perched upon his lofty seat. Our horses were tolerable, but we had eighteen miles to Pello, the next station, which we reached about ten o'clock.

Our road was mostly upon the Torneå River, sometimes taking to the woods on either side, to cut off bends. The morn was hours in dawning, with the same splendid transitions of colour. The forests were indescribable in their silence, whiteness, and wonderful variety of snowy adornment. The weeping birches leaned over the road, and formed white fringed arches; the firs wore mantles of ermine, and ruffs and tippets of the softest swan's down. Snow, wind, and frost had worked the most marvellous transformations in the forms of the forest. Here were kneeling nuns, with their arms hanging listlessly by their sides, and the white cowls falling over their faces; there lay a warrior's helmet; lace curtains, torn and ragged, hung from the points of little Gothic spires; caverns, lined with sparry incrustations, silver palm-leaves, doors, loop-holes, arches and arcades were thrown together in a fantastic confusion and mingled with the more decided forms of the larger trees, which, even, were trees but in form, so completely were they wrapped in their dazzling disguise. It was an enchanted land, where you hardly dared to breathe, lest a breath might break the spell.

There was still little change in the features of the country, except that it became wilder and more rugged, and the settlements poorer and further apart. There were low hills on either side, wildernesses of birch and fir, and floors of level snow over the rivers and marshes. On approaching Pello, we saw our first rein-deer, standing beside a hut. He was a large, handsome animal; his master, who wore a fur dress, we of course set down for a Lapp. At the inn a skinny old hag, who knew a dozen words of Swedish, got us some bread, milk, and raw frozen salmon, which, with the aid of a great deal of butter, sufficed us for a meal. Our next stage was to Kardis, sixteen miles, which we made in four hours. While in the midst of a forest on the Swedish side, we fell in with a herd of rein-deer, attended by half-a-dozen Lapps

They came tramping along through the snow, about fifty in number, including a dozen which ran loose. The others were harnessed to *pulks*, the canoe-shaped rein-deer sledges, many of which were filled with stores and baggage. The Lapps were rather good-looking young fellows, with a bright, coppery, orange complexion, and were by no means so ill-favoured, short, and stunted as I had imagined. One of them was, indeed, really handsome, with his laughing eyes, sparkling teeth, and a slender, black moustache.

We were obliged to wait a quarter-of-an-hour while the herd passed, and then took to the river again. The effect of sunset on the snow was marvellous—the spotless mounds and drifts, far and near, being stained with soft rose colour, until they resembled nothing so much as heaps of strawberry ice. At Kardis the people sent for an interpreter, who was a young man, entirely blind. He helped us to get our horses, although we were detained an hour, as only one horse is kept in readiness at these stations, and the neighbourhood must be scoured to procure another. I employed the time in learning a few Finnish words—the whole travelling-stock, in fact, on which I made the journey to Muonioniska. That the reader may see how few words of a strange language will enable him to travel, as well as to give a sample of Finnish, I herewith copy my whole vocabulary:

one	üx	eight	kahexa
two	cax	nine	öhexa
three	kolma	ten	kiumene
four	nelia	a half	puoli
five	viis	horses	hevorsto
six	oos'	immediately	varsin
seven	settima	ready	walmis

drive on!	ayò perli!	butter	voy
how much?	guinga palıa?	fire	valkär
a mile	peligorma	a bed	sängu (Swedish)
bread	leba	good	hüva
meat	liha	bad	páhá
milk	maito		

We kept on our way up the river, in the brilliant afternoon moonlight. The horses were slow; so were the two *skjutsbonder*, to whom I cried in vain: "Ayò perli!" Braisted with difficulty restrained his inclination to cuff their ears. Hour after hour went by, and we grew more and more hungry, wrathful and impatient. About eight o'clock they stopped below a house on the Russian side, pitched some hay to the horses, climbed the bank, and summoned us to follow. We made our way with some difficulty through the snow, and entered the hut, which proved to be the abode of a cooper—at least the occupant, a rough, shaggy, dirty Orson of a fellow, was seated upon the floor, making a tub, by the light of the fire. The joists overhead were piled with seasoned wood, and long bundles of thin, dry fir, which is used for torches during the winter darkness. There was neither chair nor table in the hut; but a low bench ran around the walls, and a rough bedstead was built against one corner. Two buckets of sour milk, with a wooden ladle, stood beside the door. This beverage appears to be generally used by the Finns for quenching thirst, instead of water. Our postilions were sitting silently upon the bench, and we followed their example, lit our pipes, and puffed away, while the cooper, after the first glance, went on with his work; and the other members of his family, clustered together in the dusky corner behind the fire-place, were equally silent. Half an hour passed, and the spirit moved no one to open his mouth. I judged at last that the horses had been baited sufficiently, silently showed my watch to the postilions, who, with ourselves, got up and went away without a word having been said to mar the quaint drollery of the incident.

While at Haparanda, we had been recommended to stop at Kingis Bruk, at the junction of the Torneå and Muonio. "There," we were told, "you can get everything you want: there is a fine house, good beds, and plenty to eat and drink." Our blind interpreter at Kardis repeated this advice. "Don't go on to Kexisvara;" (the next station) said he, "stop at Kengis, where everything is good." Toward Kengis, then, this oasis in the arctic desolation, our souls yearned. We drove on until ten o'clock in the brilliant moonlight and mild, delicious air—for the temperature had actually risen to 25° above zero!—before a break in the hills announced the junction of the two rivers. There was a large house on the top of a hill on our left, and, to our great joy, the postilions drove directly up to it. "Is this Kengis?" I asked, but their answers I could not understand, and they had already unharnessed their horses.

There was a light in the house, and we caught a glimpse of a woman's face at the window, as we drove up. But the light was immediately extinguished, and everything became silent. I knocked at the door, which was partly open, but no one came. I then pushed: a heavy log of wood, which was leaning against it from the inside, fell with a noise which reverberated through the house. I waited awhile, and then, groping my way along a passage to the door of the room which had been lighted, knocked loudly. After a little delay, the door was opened by a young man, who ushered me into a warm, comfortable room, and then quietly stared at me, as if to ask what I wanted. " We are travellers and strangers," said I, " and wish to stop for the night." " This is not an inn," he answered ; " it is the residence of the *patron* of the iron works." I may here remark that it is the general custom in Sweden, in remote districts, for travellers to call without ceremony upon the parson, magistrate, or any other prominent man in a village, and claim his hospitality. In spite of this doubtful reception, considering that our horses were already stabled and the station three or four miles further, I remarked again: " But perhaps we may be allowed to remain here until morning ?" " I will ask," he replied, left the room, and soon returned with an affirmative answer.

We had a large, handsomely furnished room, with a sofa and curtained bed, into which we tumbled as soon as the servant-girl, in compliance with a hint of mine, had brought up some bread, milk, and cheese. We had a cup of coffee in the morning, and were preparing to leave when the *patron* appeared. He was a short, stout, intelligent Swede, who greeted us courteously, and after a little conversation, urged us to stay until after breakfast. We were too hungry to need much persuasion, and indeed the table set with *tjäde*, or capercailie (one of the finest game birds in the world), potatoes, cranberries, and whipped cream, accompanied with excellent Umeå ale, and concluded with coffee, surpassed anything we had sat down to for many a day. The *patron* gave me considerable information about the country, and quieted a little anxiety I was beginning to feel, by assuring me that we should find post-horses all the way to Muonioniska, still ninety-five miles distant. He informed me that we had already got beyond the daylight, as the sun had not yet risen at Kengis. This, however, was in consequence of a hill to the southward, as we afterwards found that the sun was again above the horizon.

We laid in fuel enough to last us through the day, and then took leave of our host, who invited us to visit him on our return. Crossing the Torneå, an hour's drive over the hills brought us to the village of Kexisvara, where we were obliged to wait some time for our horses. At the inn there was a well forty feet deep, with the longest sweep-pole I ever saw. The landlady and her two sisters were pleasant bodies, and sociably inclined, if we could have talked to them. They were all spinning tow, their wheels purring like pleased lionesses. The sun's disc came in sight at a quarter past eleven, and at noon his lower limb just touched the horizon. The sky was of a splendid saffron hue, which changed into a burning brassy yellow.

Our horses promised little for speed when we set out, and their harness being ill adapted to our sleds increased the difficulty. Instead of hames there were wide wooden yokes, the ends of which passed through mortices in the ends of the shafts, and were fastened with pins, while, as there was no belly-bands, the yokes rose on going down hill, bringing our sleds upon the horses' heels. The Finnish sleds have excessively long shafts, in order to prevent this. Our road all day was upon the Muonio River, the main branch of the Torneå, and the boundary between Sweden and Russia, above the junction. There had been a violent wind during the night, and the track was completely filled up. The Torneå and Muonio are both very swift rivers, abounding in dangerous rapids, but during the winter, rapids and all, they are solid as granite from their sources to the Bothnian Gulf. We plunged along slowly, hour after hour, more than half the time clinging to one side or the other, to prevent our sled from overturning—and yet it upset at least a dozen times during the day. The scenery was without change: low, black fir forests on either hand, with the decorative snow blown off them; no villages, or signs of life, except the deserted huts of the wood-cutters, nor did we meet but one sled during the whole day. Here and there, on the banks, were sharp, canoe-like boats, twenty or thirty feet long, turned bottom upward. The sky was overcast, shutting out the glorious coloring of the past days. The sun set before one o'clock, and the dull twilight deepened apace into night. Nothing could be more cheerless and dismal: we smoked and talked a little, with much silence between, and I began to think that one more such day would disgust me with the Arctic Zone.

It was four o'clock, and our horses were beginning to stagger, when we reached a little village called Jokijalka, on the Russian side. The postilion stopped at a house, or rather a quadrangle of huts, which he made me comprehend was an inn, adding that it was 4 *polàn* and 3 *belikor* (a fearfully unintelligible distance!) to the next one. We entered, and found promise enough in the thin, sallow, sandy-haired, and most obsequious landlord, and a whole herd of rosy children, to decide us to stop. We were ushered into the milk-room, which was warm and carpeted, and had a single narrow bed. I employed my vocabulary with good effect, the quick-witted children helping me out, and in due time we got a supper of fried mutton, bread, butter, and hot milk. The children came in every few minutes to stare at our writing, an operation which they probably never saw before. They would stand in silent curiosity for half an hour at a time, then suddenly rush out, and enjoy a relief of shouts and laughter on the outside Since leaving Matarengi we had been regarded at all the stations with much wonder, not always unmixed with mistrust. Whether this was simply a manifestation of the dislike which the Finns have for the Swedes, for whom they probably took us, or of other suspicions on their part, we could not decide.

After a time one of the neighbors, who had been sent for on account of his knowing a very few words of Swedish, was ushered into the room. Through him I ordered horses, and ascertained that the next station, Kihlangi, was three and a half Swedish miles distant, but there was a place on the Russian side, one mile off, where we could change horses. We had finished writing, and were sitting by the stove, consulting how we should arrange the bed so as to avoid contact with the dirty coverlet, when the man returned and told us we must go into another house. We crossed the yard to the opposite building, where, to our great surprise, we were ushered into a warm room, with two good beds, which had clean though coarse sheets, a table, looking-glass, and a bit of carpet on the floor. The whole male household congregated to see us take possession and ascertain whether our wants were supplied. I slept luxuriously until awakened by the sound of our landlord bringing in wood to light the fire. He no sooner saw that my eyes were open than he snatched off his cap and threw it upon the floor, moving about with as much awe and silence as if it were the Emperor's bedroom. His daughter brought us excellent coffee betimes. We washed our faces with our tumblers of drinking water, and got under way by half-past six.

The temperature had changed again in the night, being 28° below zero, but the sky was clear and the morning moonlight superb. By this time we were so far north that the moon did not set at all, but wheeled around the sky, sinking to within eight degrees of the horizon at noonday. Our road led across the river, past the church of Kolare, and through a stretch of the Swedish forests back to the river again. To our great surprise, the wind had not blown here, the snow still hung heavy on the trees, and the road was well beaten. At the Russian post-house we found only a woman with the usual troop of children, the eldest of whom, a boy of sixteen, was splitting fir to make torches. I called out *"hevorste!"* (horses), to which he made a deliberate answer, and went on with his work. After some consultation with the old woman, a younger boy was sent off somewhere, and we sat down to await the result. I called for meat, milk, bread, and butter, which procured us in course of time a pitcher of cold milk, some bread made of ground barley straw, horribly hard and tough, and a lump of sour frozen butter. There was some putrid fish in a wooden bowl, on which the family had breakfasted, while an immense pot of sour milk, butter, broken bread, and straw meal, hanging over the fire, contained their dinner. This was testimony enough to the accounts we had heard in Stockholm, of the year's famine in Finland; and we seemed likely to participate in it.

I chewed the straw bread vigorously for an hour, and succeeded in swallowing enough to fill my stomach, though not enough to satisfy my hunger. The younger children occupied themselves in peeling off the soft inner bark of the fir, which they ate ravenously. They were handsome, fair-skinned youngsters, but not so rosy and beautiful as those of the Norrland Swedes. We were obliged to wait more than two hours before the horses arrived, thus losing a large part of our daylight. The postilions fastened our sleds behind their own large sledges, with flat runners, which got through the snow more easily than ours. We lay down in the sledge, stretched ourselves at full length upon a bed of hay, covered our feet with the deerskin, and set off. We had gone about a Swedish mile when the postilions stopped to feed the horses before a house on the Russian side. There was nobody within, but some coals among the ashes on the hearth showed that it had been used, apparently, as a place of rest and shelter. A tall, powerful Finn, who was travelling alone, was there, smoking his pipe. We all sat down and did likewise, in the bare, dark hut. There were the three Finns, in complete dresses of reindeer skin, and ourselves, swaddled from head to foot, with only a small segment of scarlet face visible between our frosted furs and icy beards. It was a true Arctic picture, as seen by the pale dawn which glimmered on the wastes of snow outside.

We had a poor horse, which soon showed signs of breaking

down, especially when we again entered a belt of country
where the wind had blown, the trees were clear, and the
track filled up. At half-past eleven we saw the light of the
sun on the tops of the hills, and at noon about half his disc
was visible. The cold was intense; my hands became so stiff
and benumbed that I had great difficulty in preventing them
from freezing, and my companion's feet almost lost all feeling. It was well for us that we were frequently obliged to
walk, to aid the horse. The country was a wilderness of
mournful and dismal scenery—low hills and woods, stripped
bare of snow, the dark firs hung with black, crape-like moss,
alternating with morasses. Our Finnish postilions were
pleasant, cheerful fellows. who insisted on our riding when
there was the least prospect of a road. Near a solitary hut
(the only one on the road) we met a man driving a reindeer.
After this we lost all signs of our way, except the almost
obliterated track of his pulk. The snow was deeper than
ever, and our horses were ready to drop at every step. We
had been five hours on the road; the driver said Kihlangi
was "*ûx verst*" distant, and at three, finally, we arrived.
We appreciated rather better what we had endured when we
found that the temperature was 44° below zero.

I at once ordered horses, and a strapping young fellow was
sent off in a bad humor to get them. We found it impossible, however, to procure milk or anything to eat, and as the
cold was not to be borne else, we were obliged to resort to a
bottle of cognac and our Haparanda bread. The old woman
sat by the fire smoking, and gave not the least attention to
our demands. I paid our postilions in Norwegian *orts*,
which they laid upon a chair and counted, with the assist-

ance of the whole family. After the reckoning was finished they asked me what the value of each piece was, which gave rise to a second general computation. There was, apparently, more than they had expected, for they both made me a formal address of thanks, and took my hand. Seeing that I had produced a good effect I repeated my demand for milk. The old woman refused, but the men interfered in my behalf; she went out and presently returned with a bowl full, which she heated for us. By this time our horses had arrived, and one of our new postilions prepared himself for the journey, by stripping to the loins and putting on a clean shirt. He was splendidly built, with clean, firm muscle, a white glossy skin, and no superfluity of flesh. He then donned a reindeer of *pösk*, leggings and boots, and we started again.

It was nearly five o'clock, and superb moonlight. This time they mounted our sleds upon their own sledges, so that we rode much higher than usual. Our way lay up the Muonio River: the track was entirely snowed up, and we had to break a new one, guided by the fir-trees stuck in the ice. The snow was full three feet deep, and whenever the sledge got a little off the old road, the runners cut in so that we could scarcely move. The milk and cognac had warmed us tolerably, and we did not suffer much from the intense cold. My nose, however, had been rubbed raw, and I was obliged to tie a handkerchief across my face to protect it.

While journeying along in this way, the sledge suddenly tilted over, and we were flung head foremost into the snow. Our drivers righted the sledge, we shook ourselves and got in again, but had not gone ten yards before the same thing happened again. This was no joke on such a night, but we took it good-humouredly, to the relief of the Finns, who seemed to expect a scolding. Very soon we went over a third time, and then a fourth, after which they kept near us and held on when there was any danger. I became very drowsy, and struggled with all my force to keep awake, for sleeping was too hazardous. Braisted kept his senses about him by singing, for our encouragement, the mariner's hymn:—

> "Fear not, but trust in Providence,
> Wherever thou may'st be."

Thus hour after hour passed away. Fortunately we had good, strong horses, which walked fast and steadily. The scenery was always the same—low, wooded hills on either side of the winding, snowy plain of the river. We had made up our minds not to reach Parkajoki before midnight, but at half-past ten our track left the river, mounted the Swedish bank, and very soon brought us to a quadrangle of low huts, having the appearance of an inn. I could scarcely believe my eyes when we stopped before the door. "Is this Parkajoki?" I asked. "*Ja!*" answered the postilion. Braisted and I sprang out instantly, hugged each other in delight, and rushed into the warm inn. The thermometer still showed—44°, and we prided ourselves a little on having travelled for seventeen hours in such a cold with so little food to keep up our animal heat. The landlord, a young man, with a bristly beard of three weeks' growth, showed us into the milk room, where there was a bed of reindeer skins. His wife brought us some fresh hay, a quilt and a sheepskin coverlet, and we soon forgot both our hunger and our frozen blood.

In the morning coffee was brought to us, and as nothing else was to be had, we drank four cups apiece. The landlord asked half a *rigs* (13 cents) for our entertainment, and was overcome with gratitude when I gave him double the sum. We had the same sledges as the previous night, but new postilions and excellent horses. The temperature had risen to 5° below zero, with a cloudy sky and a light snow falling. We got off at eight o'clock, found a track partly broken, and went on at a merry trot up the river. We took sometimes one bank and sometimes the other, until, after passing the rapid of Eyanpaika (which was frozen solid, although large masses of transparent ice lay piled like rocks on either side), we kept the Swedish bank. We were in excellent spirits, in the hope of reaching Muonioniska before dark, but the steady trot of our horses brought us out of the woods by noon, and we saw before us the long, scattering village, a mile or two distant, across the river. To our left, on a gentle slope, stood a red, two-story building, surrounded by out-houses, with a few humbler habitations in its vicinity. This was Muoniovara, on the Swedish side—the end of our Finnish journey.

CHAPTER IX.

LIFE IN LAPLAND.

As we drove up to the red two-story house, a short man with dark whiskers and a commercial air came forward to meet us. I accosted him in Swedish, asking him whether the house was an inn. He replied in the negative, adding that the only inn was in Muonioniska, on the Russian side, a mile or more distant. I then asked for the residence of Mr. Wolley, the English naturalist, whose name had been mentioned to me by Prof. Retzius and the botanist Hartman. He thereupon called to some one across the court, and presently appeared a tall, slender man dressed in the universal gray suit which travelling Englishmen wear, from the Equator to the Poles. He came up with extended hand, on hearing his own language; a few words sufficed for explanation, and he devoted himself to our interests with the cordiality of an old acquaintance. He lived with the Swede, Herr Forström, who was the merchant of the place; but the wife of the latter had just been confined, and there was no room in his house. Mr. Wolley proposed at first to send to the inn in Muonioniska, and engage a room, but afterwards arranged with a Norsk carpenter, who lived on the hill above, to give us quarters in his house, so that we might be near enough to take our meals together. Nothing could have suited us better. We took possession at once, and then descended the hill to a dinner — I had ventured to hint at our famished condition—of capercailie, cranberries, soft bread, whipped cream, and a glass of genuine port.

Warmed and comforted by such luxurious fare, we climbed the hill to the carpenter's house, in the dreary Arctic twilight, in the most cheerful and contented frame of mind. Was this, indeed, Lapland? Did we, indeed, stand already in the dark heart of the polar Winter? Yes; there was no doubt of it. The imagination could scarcely conceive a more desolate picture than that upon which we gazed—the plain of sombre snow, beyond which the black huts of the village were faintly discernible, the stunted woods and bleak hills, which night and the raw snow clouds had half obscured, and yonder fur-clad figure gliding silently along beside his reindeer. Yet, even here, where Man seemed to have settled out of pure spite against Nature, were comfort and hospitality and kindness. We entered the carpenter's house, lit our candles and pipes, and sat down to enjoy at ease the unusual feeling of shelter and of home. The building was of squared fir-logs, with black moss stuffed in the crevices, making it very warm and substantial. Our room contained a loom, two tables, two beds with linen of voluptuous softness and cleanness, an iron stove (the first we had seen in Sweden), and the usual washing apparatus, besides a piece of carpet on the floor. What more could any man desire? The carpenter, Herr Knoblock, spoke some German; his son, Ludwig, Mr. Wolley's servant, also looked after our needs; and the daughter, a fair, blooming girl of about nineteen, brought us coffee before we were out of bed, and kept our fire in order. Why, Lapland was a very Sybaris in comparison with what I had expected.

Mr. Wolley proposed to us another luxury, in the shape of a vapour-bath, as Herr Forström had one of those bathing-houses which are universal in Finland. It was a little wooden building without windows. A Finnish servant-girl who had been for some time engaged in getting it in readiness, opened the door for us. The interior was very hot and moist, like an Oriental bathing-hall. In the centre was a pile of hot stones, covered with birch boughs, the leaves of which gave out an agreeable smell, and a large tub of water. The floor was strewn with straw, and under the roof was a platform extending across one end of the building. This was covered with soft hay, and reached by means of a ladder, for the purpose of getting the full effect of the steam Some stools, and a bench for our clothes, completed the arrangements. There was also in one corner a pitcher of water, standing in a little heap of snow to keep it cool.

The servant-girl came in after us, and Mr. W. quietly proceeded to undress, informing us that the girl was bathing-master, and would do the usual scrubbing and shampooing. This, it seems, is the general practice in Finland, and is but another example of the unembarrassed habits of the people in this part of the world. The poorer families go into their bathing-rooms together—father, mother, and children—and take turns in polishing each other's backs. It would have been ridiculous to have shown any hesitation under the circumstances—in fact, an indignity to the honest simple-hearted, virtuous girl—and so we deliberately undressed also. When at last we stood, like our first parents in Paradise, "naked and not ashamed," she handed us bunches of birch-twigs with the leaves on, the use of which was suggested by the leaf of sculpture. We mounted to the platform and lay down upon our backs, whereupon she increased the temperature by throwing water upon the hot stones, until the heat was rather oppressive, and we began to sweat profusely. She then took up a bunch of birch-twigs which had been dipped in hot water, and switched us smartly from head to foot. When we had become thoroughly parboiled and lax, we descended to the floor, seated ourselves upon the stools, and were scrubbed with soap as thoroughly as propriety permitted. The girl was an admirable bather, the result of long practice in the business. She finished by pouring hot water over us, and then drying us with warm towels. The Finns frequently go out and roll in the snow during the progress of the bath. I ventured so far as to go out and stand a few seconds in the open air. The mercury was at zero, and the effect of the cold on my heated skin was delightfully refreshing.

I dressed in a violent perspiration, and then ran across to Herr Forström's house, where tea was already waiting for us. Here we found the *lansman* or magistrate of the Russian district opposite, a Herr Bràxen, who was decorated with the order of Stanislaus for his services in Finland during the recent war. He was a tall, dark-haired man, with a restless light in his deep-set eyes, and a gentleman in his demeanor. He entered into our plans with interest, and the evening was spent in consultation concerning them.

Finally, it was decided that Herr Forström should send a messenger up the river to Palajoki (forty miles off), to engage Lapps and reindeer to take us across the mountains to Kautokeino, in Norway. As the messenger would be absent three or four days, we had a comfortable prospect of rest before us, and I went to bed with a light heart, to wake to the sixth birthday I have passed in strange lands.

In the morning, I went with Mr. Wolley to call upon a Finn, one of whose children was suffering from inflamed eyes, or snowthalmia, as it might be called. The family were prolific, as usual—children of all sizes, with a regular gradation of a year between. The father, a short, shock-headed fellow, sat in one corner; the mother, who, like nine-tenths of all the matrons we had seen between Lapland and Stockholm, gave promise of additional humanity, greeted us with a comical, dipping courtesy—a sudden relaxing and stiffening again of the muscles of the knees—which might be introduced as a novelty into our fashionable circles. The boy's eyes were terribly blood-shot, and the lids swollen, but a solution of nitrate of silver, which Mr. W. applied, relieved him greatly in the course of a day or two. We took occasion to visit the stable, where half a dozen cows lay in darkness, in their warm stalls, on one side, with two bulls and some sheep on the other. There was a fire in one corner, over which hung a great kettle filled with a mixture of boiled hay and reindeer moss. Upon this they are fed, while the sheep must content themselves with bunches of birch, willow and aspen twigs, gathered with the leaves on. The hay is strong and coarse, but nourishing, and the reindeer moss, a delicate white lichen, contains a glutinous ingredient, which probably increases the secretion of milk. The stable, as well as Forström's, which we afterwards inspected, was kept in good order. It was floored, with a gutter past each row of stalls, to carry off the manure. The cows were handsome white animals, in very good condition.

Mr. Wolley sent for his reindeer in the course of the morning, in order to give us a lesson in driving. After lunch, accordingly, we prepared ourselves for the new sensation. I put on a poesk of reindeer skin, and my fur-lined Russian boots. Ludwig took a pulk also, to assist us in case of need. These pulks are shaped very much like a canoe; they are about five feet long, one foot deep, and eighteen inches wide, with a sharp bow and a square stern. You sit upright against the stern-board, with your legs stretched out in the bottom. The deer's harness consists only of a collar of reindeer skin around the neck, with a rope at the bottom, which passes under the belly, between the legs, and is fastened to the bow of the pulk. He is driven by a single rein, attached to the base of the left horn, and passing over the back to the right hand of the driver, who thrusts his thumb into a loop at the end, and takes several turns around his wrist. The rein is held rather slack, in order that it may be thrown over to the right side when it slips to the left, which it is very apt to do.

I seated myself, took proper hold of the rein, and awaited the signal to start. My deer was a strong, swift animal, who had just shed his horns. Ludwig set off first; my deer gave a startling leap, dashed around the corner of the house, and made down the hill. I tried to catch the breath which had been jerked out of me, and to keep my balance, as the pulk, swaying from side to side, bounced over the snow. It was too late; a swift presentiment of the catastrophe flashed across my mind, but I was powerless to avert it. In another second I found myself rolling in the loose snow, with the pulk bottom upward beside me. The deer, who was attached to my arm, was standing still, facing me, with an expression of stupid surprise (but no sympathy) on his face. I got up, shook myself, righted the pulk, and commenced again. Off we went, like the wind, down the hill, the snow flying in my face and blinding me. My pulk made tremendous leaps, bounding from side to side, until, the whirlwind suddenly subsiding, I found myself off the road, deep overhead in the snow, choked and blinded, and with small snow-drifts in my pockets, sleeves and bosom. My beard and eyebrows became instantly a white, solid mass, and my face began to tingle from its snow-bath; but, on looking back, I saw as white a beard suddenly emerge from a drift, followed by the stout body of Braisted, who was gathering himself up after his third shipwreck.

We took a fresh start, I narrowly missing another overturn, as we descended the slope below the house, but on reaching the level of the Muonio, I found no difficulty in keeping my balance, and began to enjoy the exercise. My deer struck out, passed the others, and soon I was alone on the track. In the grey Arctic twilight, gliding noiselessly and swiftly over the snow, with the low huts of Muonioniska dimly seen in the distance before me, I had my first true experience of Lapland travelling. It was delightfully novel and exhilarating; I thought of "Afraja," and the song of

"Kulnasatz, my reindeer!" and Bryant's "Arctic Lover," and whatever else there is of Polar poetry, urged my deer with shouts, and never once looked behind me until I had climbed the opposite shore and reached the village. My companions were then nowhere to be seen. I waited some time before they arrived, Braisted's deer having become fractious and run back with him to the house. His crimson face shone out from its white frame of icy hair, as he shouted to me, "There is nothing equal to this, except riding behind a right whale when he drives to windward, with every man trimming the boat, and the spray flying over your bows!"

We now turned northward through the village, flying around many sharp corners, but this I found comparatively easy work. But for the snow I had taken in, which now began to melt, I got on finely in spite of the falling flakes, which beat in our faces. Von Buch, in his journey through Lapland in 1807, speaks of Muonioniska as "a village with an inn where they have silver spoons." We stopped at a house which Mr. Wolley stated was the very building, but it proved to be a more recent structure on the site of the old inn. The people looked at us with curiosity on hearing we were Americans. They had heard the name of America, but did not seem to know exactly where it was. On leaving the house, we had to descend the steep bank of the river. I put out my feet to steady the pulk, and thereby ploughed a cataract of fine snow into my face, completely blinding me. The pulk gave a flying leap from the steepest pitch, flung me out, and the deer, eager to make for home, dragged me by the arm for about twenty yards before I could arrest him. This was the worst upset of all, and far from pleasant, although the temperature was only zero. I reached home again without further mishap, flushed, excited, soaked with melted snow, and confident of my ability to drive reindeer with a little more practice.

During the first three days, the weather was raw, dark, and lowering, with a temperature varying from 9° above to 13° below zero. On the morning of the 14th, however, the sky finally cleared, with a cold south wind, and we saw, for the first time, the range of snowy mountains in the east. The view from our hill, before so dismally bleak and dark, became broad and beautiful, now that there was a little light to see it by. Beyond the snowy floor of the lake and the river Muonio stretched the scattering huts of Muonioniska, with the church overlooking them, and the round, white peak of Ollastyntre rising above his belt of black woods to the south. Further to the east extended alternate streaks of dark forest and frozen marsh for eighteen miles, to the foot of the mountain range of Palastyntre, which stood like a line of colossal snow-drifts against the soft violet sky, their sides touched by the rosily-golden beams of the invisible sun. This and the valley of the Torneå, at Avasaxa, are two of the finest views in Lapland.

I employed part of my time in making some sketches of characteristic faces. Mr. Wolley, finding that I wished to procure good types of the Finns and Lapps, kindly assisted me—his residence of three years in Muoniovara enabling him to know who were the most marked and peculiar personages. Ludwig was despatched to procure an old fellow by the name of Niemi, a Finn, who promised to comply with my wishes; but his ignorance made him suspicious, and it was necessary to send again. "I know what travellers are," said he, "and what a habit they have of getting people's skulls to carry home with them. Even if they are arrested for it, they are so rich, they always buy over the judges. Who knows but they might try to kill me for the sake of my skull?" After much persuasion, he was finally induced to come, and, seeing that Ludwig supposed he was still afraid, he said, with great energy: "I have made up my mind to go, even if a shower of knives should fall from heaven!" He was seventy-three years old, though he did not appear to be over sixty—his hair being thick and black, his frame erect and sturdy, and his colour crimson rather than pale. His eyebrows were jet-black and bushy, his eyes large and deep set, his nose strong and prominent, and the corners of his long mouth drawn down in a settled curve, expressing a melancholy grimness. The high cheek-bones, square brow, and muscular jaw belonged to the true Finnish type. He held perfectly still while I drew, scarcely moving a muscle of his face, and I succeeded in getting a portrait which everybody recognised.

I gave him a piece of money, with which he was greatly delighted; and, after a cup of coffee, in Herr Knoblock's kitchen, he went home quite proud and satisfied. "They do not at all look like dangerous persons," said he to the carpenter; "perhaps they do not collect skulls. I wish they spoke our language, that I might ask them how people live in their country. America is a very large, wild place. I know all about it, and the discovery of it. I was not there myself at the time, but Jenis Lampi, who lives in Kittila, was one of the crew of the ship, and he told me how it happened. Jenis Lampi said they were going to throw the captain overboard, but he persuaded them to give him three days, and on the third day they found it. Now I should like to know whether these people, who come from that country, have laws as we have, and whether they live as comfortably." So saying, Isaaki Anderinpoika Niemi departed.

No sooner had he gone than the old Lapp woman, Elsa, who had been sent for, drove up in her pulk, behind a fast reindeer. She was in complete Lapp costume—a blue cloth gown with wide sleeves, trimmed with scarlet, and a curious pear-shaped cap of the same material, upon her head. She sat upon the floor, on a deer-skin, and employed herself in twisting reindeer sinews, which she rolled upon her cheek with the palm of her hand, while I was sketching her. It was already dark, and I was obliged to work by candle light, but I succeeded in catching the half-insane, witch-like expression of her face. When I took the candle to examine her features more closely, she cried out, "Look at me, O son of man!" She said that I had great powers, and was capable of doing everything, since I had come so far, and could make an image of her upon paper. She asked whether we were married, saying we could hardly travel so much if we were; yet she thought it much better to be married and stay at home. I gave her a rigsdaler, which she took with joyful surprise, saying "What! am I to get my coffee and tobacco, and be paid too? Thanks, O son of man, for your great goodness!" She chuckled very much over the drawing, saying that the dress was exactly right.

In the afternoon we took another reindeer drive to Muonioniska, paying a visit to Pastor Fali, the clergyman whom we had met at Forström's. This time I succeeded very well, making the trip without a single overturn, though with several mishaps. Mr. Wolley lost the way, and we drove about at random for some time. My deer became restive, and whirled me around in the snow, filling my pulk. It was so dark that we could scarcely see, and, without knowing the ground, one could not tell where the ups and down were. The pastor received us courteously, treated us to coffee and pipes, and conversed with us for some time. He had not, as he said, a Swedish tongue, and I found it difficult to understand him. On our way back, Braisted's and Ludwig's deers ran together with mine, and, while going at full speed, B.'s jumped into my pulk. I tried in vain either to stop or drive on faster; he trampled me so violently that I was obliged to throw myself out to escape his hoofs. Fortunately the animals are not heavy enough to do any serious harm. We reached Forström's in season for a dinner of fat reindeer steak, cranberries, and a confect of the Arctic raspberry.

After an absence of three days Salomon, the messenger who had been sent up the river to engage reindeer for us, returned, having gone sixty miles before he could procure them. He engaged seven, which arrived the next evening, in the charge of a tall, handsome Finn, who was to be our conducter. We had, in the meantime, supplied ourselves with reindeer *poesks*, such as the Lapps wear,—our own furs being impracticable for pulk travelling—reindeer mittens, and boas of squirrel tails strung on reindeer sinews. The carpenter's second son, Anton, a lad of fifteen, was engaged to accompany us as an interpreter.

CHAPTER X.

A REINDEER JOURNEY ACROSS LAPLAND.

WE left Muoniovara at noon on the 15th, fully prepared for a three days' journey across the wilds of Lapland. We were about to traverse the barren, elevated table-land, which divides the waters of the Bothnian Gulf from those of the Northern Ocean,—a dreary, unfriendly region, inhabited only by a few wandering Lapps. Even without the prevalence of famine, we should have had difficulty in procuring food from them, so we supplied ourselves with a saddle of reindeer, six loaves of rye bread, sugar, and a can of coffee. The carpenter lent us a cup and saucer, and Anton, who felt all the responsibility of a boy who is employed for the first time, stowed everything away nicely in the broad baggage pulk. We found it impossible to procure Lapp leggings and shoes at Muonivara, but our Russian boots proved an admirable substitute. The *poesk* of reindeer skin is the warmest covering for the body which could be devised. It is drawn over the head like a shirt, fitting closely around the neck and wrists, where it is generally trimmed with ermine, and reaching half-way below the knee. A thick woollen sash, wrapped first around the neck, the ends then twisted together down to the waist, where they are passed tightly around the body and tied in front, not only increases the warmth and convenience of the garment, but gives it a highly picturesque air. Our sea-otter caps, turned down so as to cover the ears and forehead, were fastened upon our heads with crimson handkerchiefs, and our boas, of black and red squirrel tails, passed thrice around the neck, reached to the tips of our noses. Over our dog-skin mittens we drew gauntlets of reindeer skin, with which it was difficult to pick up or take hold of anything; but as the deer's rein is twisted around one's wrist, their clumsiness does not interfere with the facility of driving. It would seem impossible for even Arctic cold to penetrate through such defences—and yet it did.

Herr Forström prepared us for the journey by a good breakfast of reindeer's marrow, a justly celebrated Lapland delicacy, and we set out with a splendidly clear sky and a cold of 12° below zero. The Muonio valley was superb, towards sunrise, with a pale, creamy, saffron light on the snow, the forests on the tops of the hills burning like jagged masses of rough opal, and the distant range of Palastyntre bathed in pink light, with pure sapphire shadows on its northern slopes. These Arctic illuminations are transcendent; nothing can equal them, and neither pen nor pencil can describe them. We passed through Muonioniska, and kept up the Russian side, over an undulating, wooded country. The road was quite good, but my deer, in spite of his size and apparent strength, was a lazy beast, and gave me much trouble. I was obliged to get out of the pulk frequently and punch him in the flanks, taking my chance to tumble in headlong as he sprang forward again. I soon became disgusted with reindeer travelling, especially when, after we had been on the road two hours and it was nearly dark, we reached Upper Muonioniska, only eight miles. We there took the river again, and made better progress to Kyrkesuando, the first station, where we stopped an hour to feed the deer. Here there was a very good little inn, with a bed for travellers.

We had seven reindeer, two of which ran loose, so that we could change occasionally on the road. I insisted on changing mine at once, and received in return a smaller animal, which made up in spirit what he lacked in strength. Our conductor was a tall, handsome Finn, with blue eyes and a bright, rosy complexion. His name was Isaac, but he was better known by his nickname of *Pitka Isaaki*, or Long Isaac. He was a slow, good-humoured, prudent, careful fellow, and probably served our purpose as well as anybody we could have found. Anton, however, who made his first journey with us, was invaluable. His father had some misgivings on account of his timidity, but he was so ambitious to give satisfaction that we found him forward enough.

I have already described the country through which we passed, as it was merely a continuation of the scenery below Muonioniska — low, wooded hills, white plains, and everywhere snow, snow, snow, silence and death. The cold increased to 33° below zero, obliging me to bury my nose in my boa and to keep up a vigorous exercise of my toes to prevent them from freezing, as it is impossible to cover one's boots in a pulk. The night was calm, clear, and starry; but after an hour a bank of auroral light gradually arose in the north, and formed a broad arch, which threw its lustre over the snow and lighted up our path. Almost stationary at first, a restless motion after a time agitated the gleaming bow; it shot out broad streamers of yellow fire, gathered them in and launched them forth again, like the hammer of Thor, which always returned to his hand, after striking the blow for which it had been hurled. The most wonderful appearance, however, was an immense square curtain, which fell from all the central part of the arch. The celestial scene-shifters were rather clumsy, for they allowed one end to fall lower than the other, so that it over-lapped and doubled back upon itself in a broad fold. Here it hung for probably half an hour, slowly swinging to and fro, as if moved by a gentle wind. What new spectacle was in secret preparation behind it we did not learn, for it was hauled up so bunglingly that the whole arch broke and fell in, leaving merely a pile of luminous ruins under the Polar Star.

Hungry and nearly frozen, we reached Palajoki at half-past nine, and were at once ushered into the guests' room, a little hut separated from the main building. Here, barring an inch of ice on the windows and numerous windy cracks in the floor, we felt a little comfort before an immense fire kindled in the open chimney. Our provisions were already adamantine; the meat was transformed into red Finland granite, and the bread into mica-slate. Anton and the old Finnish landlady, the mother of many sons, immediately commenced the work of thawing and cooking, while I, by the light of fir torches, took the portrait of a dark-haired, black-eyed, olive-skinned, big-nosed, thick-lipped youth, who gave his name as Eric Johan Sombasi. When our meal of meat, bread, and coffee had been despatched, the old woman made a bed of reindeer skins for us in one corner, covered with a coarse sheet, a quilt, and a sheepskin blanket. She then took her station near the door, where several of the sons were already standing, and all appeared to be waiting in silent curiosity to see us retire. We undressed with genuine Finnish freedom of manner, deliberately enough for them to understand the peculiarities of our apparel, and they never took their eyes from us until we were stowed away for the night in our warm nest.

It was snowing and blowing when we arose. Long Isaac had gone to the woods after the reindeer, and we employed the delay in making a breakfast off the leavings of our supper. Crossing the Muonio at starting, we entered the Russian territory and drove up the bed of the Palajok, a tributary stream which comes down from the north. The sky became clearer as the dawn increased; the road was tolerably broken, and we sped merrily along the windings of the river, under its tall banks fringed with fir trees, which, loaded with snow, shone brilliantly white against the rosy sky. The temperature was 8° below zero, which felt unpleasantly warm, by contrast with the previous evening.

After a time we left the river and entered a rolling upland—alternate thickets of fir and birch, and wastes of frozen marsh, where our path was almost obliterated. After more than two hours' travel we came upon a large lake, at the further end of which, on the southern side of a hill, was the little hamlet of Suontajärvi. Here we stopped to bait the deer, Braisted's and mine being nearly fagged out. We entered one of the huts, where a pleasant woman was taking charge of a year-old baby. There was no fire on the hearth, and the wind whistled through the open cracks of the floor, Long Isaac and the woman saluted each other by placing their right arms around each other's waists, which is the universal manner of greeting in Finland. They only shake hands as a token of thanks for a favour.

We started again at noon, taking our way across a wilderness of lakes and snow-covered marshes, dotted with stunted birch-thickets. The road had entirely disappeared, but Eric of Palajoki, who accompanied us as an extra guide, went ahead with a strong reindeer and piloted us. The sagacity with which these animals find the track under a smooth covering of loose snow, is wonderful. They follow it by the feet, of course, but with the utmost ease and rapidity, often while going at full speed. I was struck by the sinuous, mazy character of our course, even where the ground was level, and could only account for it by the supposition that the first track over the light snow had followed the smoothest and firmest ridges of the marshes. Our progress was now slow and toilsome, and it was not long before my deer gave up entirely. Long Isaac, seeing that a change must be made, finally decided to give me a wild, powerful animal, which he had not yet ventured to intrust to either of us.

The deer was harnessed to my pulk, the rein carefully secured around my wrist, and Long Isaac let go his hold A wicked toss of the antlers and a prodigious jump followed, and the animal rushed full tilt upon Braisted, who was next before me, striking him violently upon the back. The more I endeavored to rein him in, the more he plunged and tore, now dashing against the led deer, now hurling me over the baggage pulk, and **now leaping off the** track **into bottomless beds of loose snow.** Long Isaac at last shouted to me to go ahead and follow Eric, **who was about half a** mile in advance. **A few furious plunges carried me past our** little **caravan, with** my **pulk full of snow, and** my face likewise. **Now,** lowering his neck **and** thrusting **out** his **head, with open mouth and glaring eyes, the deer set off** at the top of **his speed.**

Away I went, like a lance shot out from the auroral **armoury;** the **pulk slid over the snow with** the swiftness of **a fish** through the **water; a torrent of snow-spray poured into my lap and showered against my face, until** I was com**pletely blinded. Eric was overtaken so quickly that** he had **no time to give me the track, and as I was not in a** condi**tion to see or hear anything, the deer, with** the stupidity of **his race, sprang directly upon him, trampled** him **down, and** dragged **me and my pulk over him. We came to a** stand **in the deep snow, while Eric shook himself and** started **again. My deer now turned and made for the** caravan, but **I succeeded in pulling his head around, when** he charged a **second time upon Eric, who threw himself out** of his pulk **to escape. My strength was fast giving way,** when we came **to a ridge of deep, loose snow, in which the** animals sank **above their bellies, and up which they could** hardly drag us. **My deer was so exhausted when we reached the** top, that I **had no further difficulty in controlling him.**

Before us stretched a trackless plain, bounded by a low **mountain ridge. Eric set off at a fast trot,** winding hither **and thither, as his deer followed the invisible path.** I kept close behind him, white as a Polar bear, but glowing like a volcano under my furs. The temperature was 10° below zero, and I could have wished it ten degrees colder. My deer, although his first savage strength was spent, was still full of spirit, and I began to enjoy this mode of travel. We soon entered the hills, which were covered with thickets of frozen birch, with here and there a tall Scotch fir, completely robed in snow. The sun, which had showed about half his disc at noon, was now dipping under the horizon, and a pure orange glow lighted up the dazzling masses of the crystal woods. All was silver-clear, far and near, shining, as if by its own light, with an indescribable radiance. We had struck upon a well-beaten track on entering the hills, and flew swiftly along through this silent splendour, this jewelled solitude, under the crimson and violet mode of the sky. Here was true Northern romance; here was poetry beyond all the Sagas and Eddas that ever were written.

We passed three Lapps, with heavy hay-sleds, drawn by a reindeer apiece, and after a time issued from the woods upon a range of hills entirely bare and white. Before us was the miserable hamlet of Lippajärvi, on the western side of the barren mountain of Lippivara, which is the highest in this part of Lapland, having an altitude of 1900 feet above the sea. I have rarely seen anything quite so bleak and God-forsaken as this village. A few low black huts, in a desert of snow—that was all. We drove up to a sort of station-house, where an old, white-headed Finn received me kindly, beat the snow off my poesk with a birch broom, and hung my boa near the fire to dry. There was a wild, fierce-looking Lapp in the room, who spoke some Norwegian,

6*

and at once asked who and what I was. His head was covered with a mop of bright brown hair, his eyes were dark blue and gleamed like polished steel, and the flushed crimson of his face was set off by the strong bristles of a beard of three weeks growth. There was something savage and ferocious in his air, as he sat with his clenched fists planted upon his knees, and a heavy knife in a wooden scabbard hanging from his belt. When our caravan arrived I transferred him to my sketch-book. He gave me his name as Ole Olsen Thore, and I found he was a character well known throughout the country.

Long Isaac proposed waiting until midnight, for moonrise, as it was already dark, and there was no track beyond Lippajärvi. This seemed prudent, and we therefore, with the old woman's help, set about boiling our meat, thawing bread, and making coffee. It was necessary to eat even beyond what appetite demanded, on account of the long distances between the stations. Drowsiness followed repletion, as a matter of course, and they gave us a bed of skins in an inner-room. Here, however, some other members of the family were gathered around the fire, and kept up an incessant chattering, while a young married couple, who lay in one corner, bestowed their endearments on each other, so that we had but little benefit of our rest. At midnight all was ready, and we set out. Long Isaac had engaged a guide and procured fresh deer in place of those which were fatigued. There was a thick fog, which the moon scarcely brightened, but the temperature had risen to zero, and was as mild as a May morning. For the first time in many days our beards did not freeze.

We pursued our way in complete silence. Our little caravan, in single file, presented a strange, shadowy, mysterious appearance as it followed the winding path, dimly seen through the mist, first on this side and then on that; not a sound being heard, except the crunching of one's own pulk over the snow. My reindeer and myself seemed to be the only living things, and we were pursuing the phantoms of other travellers and other deer, who had long ago perished in the wilderness. It was impossible to see more than a hundred yards; some short, stunted birches, in their spectral coating of snow, grew along the low ridges of the deep, loose snow, which separated the marshes, but nothing else interrupted the monotony of the endless grey ocean through which we went floundering, apparently at hap-hazard. How our guides found the way was beyond my comprehension, for I could discover no distinguishable landmarks. After two hours or more we struck upon a cluster of huts called Palajärvi, seven miles from Lippajärvi, which proved that we were on the right track.

The fog now became thicker than ever. We were upon the water-shed between the Bothnian Gulf and the Northern Ocean, about 1400 feet above the sea. The birches became mere shrubs, dotting the low mounds which here and there arose out of the ocean of snow. The pulks all ran in the same track and made a single furrow, so that our gunwales were generally below the sea-level. The snow was packed so tight, however, that we rarely shipped any. Two hours passed, and I was at length roused from a half-sleep by the evidence of our having lost the way. Long Isaac and the guide stopped and consulted every few minutes, striking sometimes in one direction and sometimes in another, but without any result. We ran over ridges of heavy, hard tussocks, blown bare of snow, which pitched our pulks right and left, just as I have bumped over the coral reefs of Loo-Choo in a ship's cutter. Then followed deep beds of snow-drifts, which tasked the utmost strength of our deer, low birch thickets and hard ridges again, over which we plunged in the wildest way possible.

After wandering about for a considerable time, we suddenly heard the barking of a dog at some distance on our left. Following the welcome sound, we reached a scrubby ridge, where we were saluted with a whole chorus of dogs, and soon saw the dark cone of a Lapp tent. Long Isaac aroused the inmates, and the shrill cry of a baby proclaimed that there was life and love, even here. Presently a clumsy form, enveloped in skins, waddled out and entered into conversation with our men. I proposed at once to engage a Lapp to guide us as far as Eitajärvi, which they informed us was two Norwegian (fourteen English) miles farther. The man agreed, but must first go off to the woods for his deer, which would detain us two hours. He put on his snow-skates and started, and I set about turning the delay to profit by making acquaintance with the inmates of the tents. We had now reached the middle of the village; the lean, wolfish dogs were yelling on all sides, and the people began to bestir themselves. Streams of sparks issued from the open tops of the tents, and very soon we stood as if in the midst of a group of volcanic cones.

The Lapps readily gave us permission to enter. We lifted the hanging door of reindeer hide, crept in, stumbling over a confused mixture of dogs and deer-skins, until we found room to sit down. Two middle-aged women, dressed in poesks, like the men, were kindling a fire between some large stones in the centre, but the air inside was still as cold as outside. The damp birch sticks gave out a thick smoke, which almost stifled us, and for half an hour we could scarcely see or breathe. The women did not appear to be incommoded in the least, but I noticed that their eyes were considerably inflamed. After a time our company was increased by the arrival of two stout, ruddy girls of about seventeen, and a child of two years old, which already wore a complete reindeer costume. They were all very friendly and hospitable in their demeanour towards us, for conversation was scarcely possible. The interior of the tent was hung with choice bits of deer's hide, from the inside of the flanks and shoulders, designed, apparently, for mittens. Long Isaac at once commenced bargaining for some of them, which he finally purchased. The money was deposited in a rather heavy bag of coin, which one of the women drew forth from under a pile of skins. Our caps and Russian boots excited their curiosity, and they examined them with the greatest minuteness.

These women were neither remarkably small nor remarkably ugly, as the Lapps are generally represented. The ground-tone of their complexion was rather tawny, to be sure, but there was a glowing red on their cheeks, and their eyes were a dark bluish-grey. Their voices were agreeable, and the language (a branch of the Finnish) had none of that barbaric harshness common to the tongues of nomadic tribes. These favorable features, nevertheless, were far from reconciling me to the idea of a trial of Lapp life. When I saw the filth, the poverty, and discomfort in which they lived, I decided that the present experience was all-sufficient. Roasting on one side and freezing on the other, with smarting eyes and asphyxiated lungs, I soon forgot whatever there was of the picturesque in my situation, and thought only of the return of our Lapp guide. The women at last cleared away several dogs, and made room for us to lie down—a more tolerable position, in our case; though how a whole family, with innumerable dogs, stow themselves in the compass of a circle eight feet in diameter, still remains a mystery.

The Lapp returned with his reindeer within the allotted time, and we took our leave of the encampment. A strong south wind had arisen, but did not dissipate the fog, and for two hours we had a renewal of our past experiences, in thumping over hard ridges and ploughing through seas of snow. Our track was singularly devious, sometimes doubling directly back upon itself without any apparent cause. At last, when a faint presentiment of dawn began to glimmer through the fog, the Lapp halted and announced that he had lost the way. Bidding us remain where we were, he struck off into the snow and was soon lost to sight. Scarcely a quarter of an hour had elapsed, however, before we heard his cries at a considerable distance. Following, as we best could, across a plain nearly a mile in diameter, we found him at last in a narrow dell between two hills. The ground now sloped rapidly northward, and I saw that we had crossed the water-shed, and that the plain behind us must be the lake Jedeckejaure, which, according to Von Buch, is 1370 feet above the sea.

On emerging from the dell we found a gentle slope before us, covered with hard ice, down which our pulks flew like the wind. This brought us to another lake, followed by a similar slope, and so we descended the icy terraces, until, in a little more than an hour, some covered haystacks gave evidence of human habitation, and we drew up at the huts of Eitajärvi, in Norway. An old man, who had been watching our approach, immediately climbed upon the roof and removed a board from the chimney, after which he ushered us into a bare, cold room, and kindled a roaring fire on the hearth. Anton unpacked our provisions, and our hunger was so desperate, after fasting for twenty hours, that we could scarcely wait for the bread to thaw and the coffee to boil. We set out again at noon, down the frozen bed of a stream which drains the lakes, but had not proceeded far before both deers and pulks began to break through the ice, probably on account of springs under it. After being almost swamped, we managed to get up the steep snow-bank and took to the plain again, making our own road over ridge and through hollow. The caravan was soon stopped, that the pulks might be turned bottom upwards and the ice scraped off, which, like the barnacles on a ship's hull, impeded their progress through the snow. The broad plain we were traversing stretched away to the north without a break or spot of color to relieve its ghastly whiteness; but toward the south-west, where the sunset of an unrisen sun spread its roseate glow through the mist, arose some low mounds, covered with drooping birches, which shone against the soft, mellow splendor, like sprays of silver embroidered on rose-colored satin.

Our course, for about fifteen miles, lay alternately upon the stream (where the ice was sufficiently strong) and the wild plain. Two or three Lapp tents on the bank exhibited the usual amount of children and dogs, but we did not think it worth while to extend the circle of our acquaintance in that direction. At five o'clock, after it had long been dark, we reached half a dozen huts called Siepe, two Norwegian miles from Kautokeino. Long Isaac wished to stop here for the night, but we resolutely set ourselves against him. The principal hut was filthy, crowded with Lapps, and filled with a disagreeable smell from the warm, wet poesks hanging on the rafters. In one corner lay the carcases of two deer-calves which had been killed by wolves. A long bench, a table, and a rude frame covered with deerskins, and serving as a bed, comprised all the furniture. The usual buckets of sour milk, with wooden ladles, stood by the door. No one appeared to have any particular occupation, if we except the host's wife, who was engaged with an infant in reindeer breeches. We smoked and deliberated while the deers ate their balls of moss, and the result was, that a stout yellow-haired Lapp youngster was engaged to pilot us to Kautokeino.

Siepe stands on a steep bank, down which our track led to the stream again. As the caravan set off, my deer, which had behaved very well through the day, suddenly became fractious, sprang off the track, whirled himself around on his hind legs, as if on a pivot, and turned the pulk completely over, burying me in the snow. Now, I had come from Muoniovara, more than a hundred miles, without being once overturned, and was ambitious to make the whole journey with equal success. I therefore picked myself up, highly disconcerted, and started afresh. The very same thing happened a second and a third time, and I don't think I shall be considered unreasonable for becoming furiously angry. I should certainly have committed cervicide had any weapon been at hand. I seized the animal by the horns, shook, cuffed, and kicked him, but all to no purpose. Long Isaac, who was passing in his pulk, made some remark, which Anton, with all the gravity and conscientiousness of his new position of interpreter, immediately translated.

"Long Isaac says," he shouted, "that the deer will go well enough, if you knew how to drive him." "Long Isaac may go to the devil!" was, I am sorry to say, my profane reply, which Anton at once translated to him.

Seating myself in the pulk again, I gave the deer the rein, and for a time kept him to the top of his speed, following the Lapp, who drove rapidly down the windings of the stream. It was quite dark, but our road was now somewhat broken, and for three hours our caravan swiftly and silently sped on its way. Then, some scattered lights appeared in the distance; our tired deers leaped forward with fresher spirit, and soon brought us to the low wooden huts of Kautokeino. We had travelled upwards of sixty miles since leaving Lippajärvi, breaking our own road through deep snow for a great part of the way. During this time our deers had not been changed. I cannot but respect the provoking animals after such a feat.

CHAPTER XI.

KAUTOKEINO.—A DAY WITHOUT A SUN.

WHILE in Dresden, my friend Ziegler had transferred to me a letter of introduction from Herr Berger, a merchant of Hammerfest, to his housekeeper in Kautokeino. Such a transfer might be considered a great stretch of etiquette in those enlightened regions of the world where hospitality requires certificates of character; but, in a benighted country like Lapland, there was no danger of very fine distinctions being drawn, and Ziegler judged that the house which was to have been placed at his disposal had he made the journey, would as readily open its doors to me. At Muoniovara, I learned that Berger himself was now in Kautokeino, so that I needed only to present him with his own letter. We arrived so late, however, that I directed Long Isaac to take us to the inn until morning. He seemed reluctant to do this, and I could not fathom the reason of his hesitation, until I had entered the hovel to which we were conducted. A single room, filled with smoke from a fire of damp birch sticks, was crammed with Lapps of all sizes, and of both sexes. There was scarcely room to spread a deerskin on the floor while the smell exhaled from their greasy garments and their unwashed bodies was absolutely stifling. I have travelled too much to be particularly nice in my choice of lodgings, but in this instance I instantly retreated, determined to lie on the snow, under my overturned pulk, rather than pass the night among such bed-fellows.

We drove on for a short distance, and drew up before a large, substantial log-house, which Long Isaac informed me was the residence of the *Länsman*, or magistrate of the district. I knocked at the door, and inquired of the Norwegian servant girl who opened it, where Herr Berger lived. Presently appeared a stout, ruddy gentleman—no less than Herr Berger himself—who addressed me in fluent English. A few words sufficed to explain everything, and in ten minutes our effects were deposited in the guest's room of the Länsman's house, and ourselves, stripped of our Polar hides, were seated on a sofa, in a warm, carpeted room, with a bountiful supper-table before us. Blessed be civilization! was my inward ejaculation. Blessed be that yearning for comfort in Man, which has led to the invention of beds, of sofas, and easy chairs; which has suggested cleanliness of body and of habitation, and which has developed the noble art of cooking! The dreary and perilous wastes over which we had passed were forgotten. With hearts warmed in both senses, and stomachs which reacted gratefully upon our hearts, we sank that night into a paradise of snowy linen, which sent a consciousness of pleasure even into the oblivion of sleep.

The Länsman, Herr Lie, a tall handsome man of twenty-three, was a native of Altengaard, and spoke tolerable English. With him and Herr Berger, we found a third person, a theological student, stationed at Kautokeino to learn the Lapp tongue. Pastor Hvoslef, the clergyman, was the only other Norwegian resident. The village, separated from the Northern Ocean, by the barren, uninhabited ranges of the Kiölen Mountains, and from the Finnish settlements on the Muonio by the swampy table-lands we had traversed, is one of the wildest and most forlorn places in all Lapland. Occupying, as it does, the centre of a large district, over which the Lapps range with their reindeer herds during the summer, it is nevertheless a place of some importance, both for trade and for the education, organization, and proper control of the barely-reclaimed inhabitants. A church was first built here by Charles XI. of Sweden, in 1660, although, in the course of subsequent boundary adjustments, the district was made over to Norway. Half a century afterwards, some families of Finns settled here; but they appear to have gradually mixed with the Lapps, so that there is little of the pure blood of either race to be found at present. I should here remark that throughout Norwegian Lapland the Lapps are universally called *Finns*, and the Finns, *Quäns*. As the change of names, however, might occasion some confusion, I shall adhere to the more correct Swedish manner of designating them, which I have used hitherto.

Kautokéino is situated in a shallow valley, or rather basin, opening towards the north-east, whither its river flows to join the Alten. Although only 835 feet above the sea, and consequently below the limits of the birch and the fir in this latitude, the country has been stripped entirely bare for miles around, and nothing but the scattering groups of low, dark huts, breaks the snowy monotony. It is with great difficulty that vegetables of any kind can be raised. Potatoes have once or twice been made to yield eight-fold, but they are generally killed by the early autumn frosts before maturity. On the southern bank of the river, the ground remains frozen the whole year round, at a depth of only nine feet. The country furnishes nothing except reindeer meat, milk, and cheese. Grain, and other supplies of all kinds, must be hauled up from the Alten Fiord, a distance of 112 miles. The carriage is usually performed in winter, when, of course, everything reaches its destination in a frozen state. The potatoes are as hard as quartz pebbles, sugar and salt become stony masses, and even wine assumes a solid form. In this state they are kept until wanted for use, rapidly thawed, and immediately consumed, whereby their flavour is but little impaired. The potatoes, cabbage, and preserved berries on the Länsman's table were almost as fresh as if they had never been frozen.

Formerly, the place was almost entirely deserted during the summer months, and the resident missionary and Länsman returned to Alten until the Lapps came back to their winter huts; but, for some years past, the stationary population has increased, and the church is kept open the whole year. Winter, however, is the season when the Lapps are found at home, and when their life and habits are most characteristic and interesting. The population of Kautokeino is then, perhaps, about 800; in summer it is scarcely one-tenth of this number. Many of the families — especially those of mixed Finnish blood — live in wooden huts, with the luxury of a fireplace and chimney, and a window or two;

but the greater part of them burrow in low habitations of earth, which resemble large mole-hills raised in the crust of the soil. Half snowed over and blended with the natural inequalities of the earth, one would never imagine, but for the smoke here and there issuing from holes, that human beings existed below. On both sides of the stream are rows of storehouses, wherein the Lapps deposit their supplies and household articles during their summer wanderings. These structures are raised upon birch posts, each capped with a smooth, horizontal board, in order to prevent the rats and mice from effecting an entrance. The church is built upon a slight eminence to the south, with its low red belfry standing apart, as in Sweden, in a small grove of birches, which have been spared for a summer ornament to the sanctuary.

We awoke at eight o'clock to find a clear twilight and a cold of 10° below zero. Our stay at Muoniovara had given the sun time to increase his altitude somewhat, and I had some doubts whether we should succeed in beholding a day of the Polar winter. The Länsman, however, encouraged us by the assurance that the sun had not yet risen upon his residence, though nearly six weeks had elapsed since his disappearance, but that his return was now looked for every day, since he had already begun to shine upon the northern hills. By ten o'clock it was light enough to read; the southern sky was a broad sea of golden orange, dotted with a few crimson cloud-islands, and we set ourselves to watch with some anxiety the gradual approach of the exiled god. But for this circumstance, and two other drawbacks, I should have gone to church to witness the Lapps at their religious exercises. Pastor Hvoslef was ill, and the service consisted only of the reading of some prayers by the Lapp schoolmaster; added to which, the church is never warmed, even in the coldest days of winter. One cause of this may, perhaps, be the dread of an accidental conflagration; but the main reason is, the inconvenience which would arise from the thawing out of so many antiquated reindeer garments, and the effluvia given out by the warmed bodies within them. Consequently, the temperature inside the church is about the same as outside, and the frozen moisture of the worshippers' breath forms a frosty cloud so dense as sometimes to hide the clergyman from the view of his congregation. Pastor Hvoslef informed me that he had frequently preached in a temperature of 35° below zero. "At such times," said he, "the very words seem to freeze as they issue from my lips, and fall upon the heads of my hearers like a shower of snow." "But," I ventured to remark, "our souls are controlled to such a degree by the condition of our bodies, that I should doubt whether any true devotional spirit could exist at such a time. Might not even religion itself be frozen?" "Yes," he answered, "there is no doubt that all the better feelings either disappear, or become very faint, when the mercury begins to freeze." The pastor himself was at that time suffering the penalty of indulging a spirit of reverence which for a long time led him to officiate with uncovered head.

The sky increased in brightness as we watched. The orange flushed into rose, and the pale white hills looked even more ghastly against the bar of glowing carmine which fringed the horizon. A few long purple streaks of cloud hung over the sun's place, and higher up in the vault floated some loose masses, tinged with fiery crimson on their lower edges. About half-past eleven, a pencil of bright red light shot up—a signal which the sun uplifted to herald his coming. As it slowly moved westward along the hills, increasing in height and brilliancy until it became a long tongue of flame, playing against the streaks of cloud we were apprehensive that the near disc would rise to view When the Länsman's clock pointed to twelve, its base had become so bright as to shine almost like the sun itself; but after a few breathless moments the unwelcome glow began to fade. We took its bearing with a compass, and after making allowance for the variation (which is here very slight) were convinced that it was really past meridian, and the radiance, which was that of morning a few minutes before, belonged to the splendours of evening now. The colours of the firmament began to change in reverse order, and the dawn, which had almost ripened to sunrise, now withered away to night without a sunset. We had at last seen a day without a sun.

The snowy hills to the north, it is true, were tinged with a flood of rosy flame, and the very next day would probably bring down the tide-mark of sunshine to the tops of the houses. One day, however, was enough to satisfy me. You, my heroic friend*, may paint with true pencil, and still truer pen, the dreary solemnity of the long Arctic night: but, greatly as I enjoy your incomparable pictures, much as

---

* This was written in Lapland; and at the same time my friend Dr. Elisha Kent Kane, of immortal memory, lay upon his death-bed, in Havana. I retain the words, which I then supposed would meet his eye, that I may add my own tribute of sorrow for the untimely death of one of the truest, bravest, and noblest-hearted men I ever knew.

I honour your courage and your endurance, you shall never tempt me to share in the experience. The South is a cup which one may drink to inebriation; but one taste from the icy goblet of the North is enough to allay curiosity and quench all further desire. Yet the contrast between these two extremes came home to me vividly but once during this journey. A traveller's mind must never stray too far from the things about him, and long habit has enabled me to throw myself entirely into the conditions and circumstances of each separate phase of my wandering life, thereby preserving distinct the sensations and experiences of each, and preventing all later confusion in the memory. But one day, at Muoniovara, as I sat before the fire in the afternoon darkness, there flashed across my mind a vision of cloudless Egypt—palm-trees rustling in the hot wind, yellow mountain-walls rising beyond the emerald plain of the Nile, the white pencils of minarets in the distance, the creamy odour of bean-blossoms in the air—a world of glorious vitality, where Death seemed an unaccountable accident. Here, Life existed only on sufferance, and all Nature frowned with a robber's demand to give it up. I flung my pipe across the room and very soon, behind a fast reindeer, drove away from the disturbing reminiscence.

I went across the valley to the schoolmaster's house to make a sketch of Kautokeino, but the frost was so thick on the windows that I was obliged to take a chair in the open air and work with bare hands. I soon learned the value of rapidity in such an employment. We spent the afternoon in the Länsman's parlor, occasionally interrupted by the visits of Lapps, who, having heard of our arrival, were very curious to behold the first Americans who ever reached this part of the world. They came into the room with the most perfect freedom, saluted the Länsman, and then turned to stare at us until they were satisfied, when they retired to give place to others who were waiting outside. We were obliged to hold quite a levee during the whole evening. They had all heard of America, but knew very little else about it, and many of them questioned us, through Herr Berger, concerning our religion and laws. The fact of the three Norwegian residents being able to converse with us astonished them greatly. The Lapps of Kautokeino have hitherto exalted themselves over the Lapps of Karasjok and Karessuando, because the Länsman, Berger, and Pastor Hvoslef could speak with English and French travellers in their own language, while the merchants and pastors of the latter places are acquainted only with Norwegian and Swedish; and now their pride received a vast accession. "How is it possible?" said they to Herr Berger, "these men come from the other side of the world, and you talk with them as fast in their own language as if you had never spoken any other!" The schoolmaster, Lars Kaino, a one-armed fellow, with a more than ordinary share of acuteness and intelligence, came to request that I would take his portrait, offering to pay me for my trouble. I agreed to do it gratuitously, on condition that I should keep it myself, and that he should bring his wife to be included in the sketch.

He assented, with some sacrifice of vanity, and came around the next morning, in his holiday suit of blue cloth, trimmed with scarlet and yellow binding. His wife, a short woman of about twenty-five, with a face as flat and round as a platter, but a remarkably fair complexion, accompanied him, though with evident reluctance, and sat with eyes modestly cast down while I sketched her features. The circumstance of my giving Lars half a dollar at the close of the sitting was immediately spread through Kautokeino, and before night all the Lapps of the place were ambitious to undergo the same operation. Indeed, the report reached the neighboring villages, and a Hammerfest merchant, who came in the following morning from a distance of seven miles, obtained a guide at less than the usual price, through the anxiety of the latter to arrive in time to have his portrait taken. The shortness of the imperfect daylight, however, obliged me to decline further offers, especially as there were few Lapps of pure, unmixed blood among my visitors.

Kautokeino was the northern limit of my winter journey. I proposed visiting Altengaard in the summer, on my way to the North Cape, and there is nothing in the barren tract between the two places to repay the excursion. I had already seen enough of the Lapps to undeceive me in regard to previously-formed opinions respecting them, and to take away the desire for a more intimate acquaintance. In features, as in language, they resemble the Finns sufficiently to indicate an ethnological relationship. I could distinguish little, if any, trace of the Mongolian blood in them. They are fatter, fairer, and altogether handsomer than the nomadic offshoots of that race, and resemble the Esquimaux (to whom they have been compared) in nothing but their rude, filthy manner of life. Von Buch ascribes the difference in stature and physical stamina between them and the Finns to the use of the vapor bath by the latter and the aversion to water of the former. They are a race of Northern gipsies, and it is the restless blood of this class rather than any want of natural capacity which retards their civilisation. Although the whole race has been converted to Christianity, and education is universal among them—no Lapp being permitted to marry until he can read—they have but in too many respects substituted one form of superstition for another. The spread of temperance among them, however, has produced excellent results, and, in point of morality, they are fully up to the prevailing standard in Sweden and Norway. The practice, formerly imputed to them, of sharing their connubial rights with the guests who visited them, is wholly extinct,—if it ever existed. Theft is the most usual offence, but crimes of a more heinous character are rare.

Whatever was picturesque in the Lapps has departed with their paganism. No wizards now ply their trade of selling favorable winds to the Norwegian coasters, or mutter their incantations to discover the concealed grottoes of silver in the Kiölen mountains. It is in vain, therefore, for the romantic traveller to seek in them the materials for weird stories and wild adventures. They are frightfully pious and commonplace. Their conversion has destroyed what little of barbaric poetry there might have been in their composition, and, instead of chanting to the spirits of the winds, and clouds, and mountains, they have become furious ranters, who frequently claim to be possessed by the Holy Ghost. As human beings, the change, incomplete as it is. is nevertheless to their endless profit; but as objects of interest to the traveller, it has been to their detriment. It would be far more picturesque to describe a sabaoth of Lapland witches than a prayer-meeting of shouting converts, yet no friend of his race could help rejoicing to see the latter substituted for the former. In proportion, therefore, as the Lapps have become enlightened (like all other savage tribes), they have become less interesting. Retaining nearly all that is repulsive in their habits of life, they have lost the only peculiarities which could persuade one to endure the inconveniences of a closer acquaintance.

I have said that the conversion of the Lapps was in some respects the substitution of one form of superstition for another. A tragic exemplification of this fact, which produced the greatest excitement throughout the North, took place in Kautokeino four years ago. Through the preaching of Lestadius and other fanatical missionaries, a spiritual epidemic, manifesting itself in the form of visions, trances, and angelic possessions, broke out among the Lapps. It infected the whole country, and gave rise to numerous disturbances and difficulties in Kautokeino. It was no unusual thing for one of the congregation to arise during church service, declare that he was inspired by the Holy Ghost, and call upon those present to listen to his revelations. The former Länsman arrested the most prominent of the offenders, and punished them with fine and imprisonment. This begat feelings of hatred on the part of the fanatics, which soon ripened into a conspiracy. The plot was matured during the summer months, when the Lapps descended towards the Norwegian coast with their herds of reindeer.

I have the account of what followed from the lips of Pastor Hvoslef, who was then stationed here, and was also one of the victims of their resentment. Early one morning in October, when the inhabitants were returning from their summer wanderings, he was startled by the appearance of the resident merchant's wife, who rushed into his house in a frantic state, declaring that her husband was murdered. He fancied that the woman was bewildered by some sudden fright, and, in order to quiet her, walked over to the merchant's house. Here he found the unfortunate man lying dead upon the floor, while a band of about thirty Lapps headed by the principal fanatics, were forcing the house of the Länsman, whom they immediately dispatched with their knives and clubs. They then seized the pastor and his wife, beat them severely with birch-sticks, and threatened them with death unless they would acknowledge the divine mission of the so-called prophets.

The greater part of the day passed in uncertainty and terror, but towards evening appeared a crowd of friendly Lapps from the neighbouring villages, who, after having received information, through fugitives, of what had happened, armed themselves and marched to the rescue. A fight ensued, in which the conspirators were beaten, and the prisoners delivered out of their hands. The friendly Lapps, unable to take charge of all the criminals, and fearful lest some of them might escape during the night, adopted the alternative of beating every one of them so thoroughly that they were all found the next morning in the same places where they had been left the evening before. They were tried at Alten, the two ringleaders executed, and a number of the others sent to the penitentiary at Christiania. This summary justice put a stop to all open and violent manifestations of religious frenzy, but it still exists to some extent, though only indulged in secret.

We paid a visit to Pastor Hvoslef on Monday, and had the pleasure of his company to dinner in the evening. He is a Christian gentleman in the best sense of the term, and though we differed in matters of belief, I was deeply impressed with his piety and sincerity. Madame Hvoslef and two rosy little Arctic blossoms shared his exile—for this is nothing less than an exile to a man of cultivation and intellectual tastes. In his house I saw—the last thing one would have expected to find in the heart of Lapland—a piano. Madame Hvoslef, who is an accomplished performer, sat down to it, and gave us the barcarole from Massaniello. While in the midst of a maze of wild Norwegian melodies, I saw the Pastor whisper something in her ear. At once, to our infinite amazement, she boldly struck up "Yankee Doodle!" Something like an American war-whoop began to issue from Braisted's mouth, but was smothered in time to prevent an alarm. "How on earth did that air get into Lapland!" I asked. "I heard Ole Bull play it at Christiania," said Madame Hvoslef, "and learned it from memory afterwards."

The weather changed greatly after our arrival. From 23° below zero on Sunday evening, it rose to 8½° above, on Monday night, with a furious hurricane of snow from the north. We sent for our deer from the hills early on Tuesday morning, in order to start on our return to Muoniovara. The Lapps, however, have an Oriental disregard of time, and as there was no chance of our getting off before noon, we improved part of the delay in visiting the native schools and some of the earthen huts, or, rather, dens, in which most of the inhabitants live. There were two schools, each containing about twenty scholars—fat, greasy youngsters, swaddled in reindeer skins, with blue eyes, light brown or yellow hair, and tawny red cheeks, wherever the original colour could be discerned. As the rooms were rather warm, the odour of Lapp childhood was not quite as fresh as a cowslip, and we did not tarry long among them.

Approaching the side of a pile of dirt covered with snow, we pushed one after another, against a small square door, hung at such a slant that it closed of itself, and entered an ante-den used as a store-room. Another similar door ushered us into the house, a rude, vaulted space, framed with poles, sticks and reindeer hides, and covered compactly with earth, except a narrow opening in the top to let out the smoke from a fire kindled in the centre. Pieces of reindeer hide, dried flesh, bags of fat, and other articles, hung from the frame and dangled against our heads as we entered. The den was not more than five feet high by about eight feet in diameter. The owner, a jolly, good-humoured Lapp, gave me a low wooden stool, while his wife, with a pipe in her mouth, squatted down on the hide which served for a bed and looked at me with amiable curiosity. I contemplated them for a while with my eyes full of tears (the smoke being very thick,) until finally both eyes and nose could endure no more, and I sought the open air again.

CHAPTER XII.

THE RETURN TO MUONIOVARA.

WHILE at Kautokeino I completed my Lapp outfit by purchasing a scarlet cap, stuffed with eider down, a pair of *bœllinger*, or reindeer leggings, and the *komager*, or broad, boat-shaped shoes, filled with dry soft hay, and tightly bound around the ankles, which are worn by everybody in Lapland. Attired in these garments, I made a very passable Lapp, barring a few superfluous inches of stature, and at once realized the prudence of conforming in one's costume to the native habits. After the first feeling of awkwardness is over, nothing can be better adapted to the Polar Winter than the Lapp dress. I walked about at first with the sensation of having each foot in the middle of a large feather bed, but my blood preserved its natural warmth even after sitting for hours in an open pulk. The *bœllinger*, fastened around the thighs by drawing-strings of reindeer sinew, are so covered by the poesk that one becomes, for all practical purposes, a biped reindeer, and may wallow in the snow as much as he likes without the possibility of a particle getting through his hide.

The temperature was, nevertheless, singularly mild when

we set out on our return. There had been a violent storm of wind and snow the previous night, after which the mercury rose to 16° above zero. We waited until noon before our reindeers could be collected, and then set off, with the kind farewell wishes of the four Norwegian inhabitants of the place. I confess to a feeling of relief when we turned our faces southward, and commenced our return to daylight. We had at last seen the Polar night, the day without a sunrise; we had driven our reindeer under the arches of the aurora borealis; we had learned enough of the Lapps to convince us that further acquaintance would be of little profit; and it now seemed time to attempt an escape from the limbo of Death into which we had ventured. Our faces had already begun to look pale and faded from three weeks of alternate darkness and twilight, but the novelty of our life preserved us from any feeling of depression and prevented any perceptible effect upon our bodily health, such as would assuredly have followed a protracted experience of the Arctic Winter. Every day now would bring us further over the steep northern shoulder of the Earth, and nearer to that great heart of life in the south, where her blood pulsates with eternal warmth. Already there was a perceptible increase of the sun's altitude, and at noonday a thin upper slice of his disc was visible for about half an hour.

By Herr Berger's advice, we engaged as guide to Lippa järvi, a Lapp, who had formerly acted as postman, and professed to be able to find his way in the dark. The wind had blown so violently that it was probable we should have to break our own road for the whole distance. Leaving Kautokeino, we travelled up the valley of a frozen stream.

towards desolate ranges of hills, or rather shelves of the table-land, running north-east and south-west. They were spotted with patches of stunted birch, hardly rising above the snow. Our deer were recruited, and we made very good progress while the twilight lasted. At some Lapp tents, where we stopped to make inquiries about the ice, I was much amused by the appearance of a group of children, who strikingly resembled bear-cubs standing on their hind legs. They were coated with reindeer hide from head to foot, with only a little full-moon of tawny red face visible.

We stopped at Siepe an hour to bait the deer. The single wooden hut was crowded with Lapps, one of whom, apparently the owner, spoke a little Norwegian. He knew who we were, and asked me many questions about America. He was most anxious to know what was our religion, and what course the Government took with regard to different sects. He seemed a little surprised, and not less pleased, to hear that all varieties of belief were tolerated, and that no one sect possessed any peculiar privileges over another. (It is only very recently that dissenters from the Orthodox Church have been allowed to erect houses of worship in Norway.) While we were speaking on these matters, an old woman, kneeling near us, was muttering prayers to herself, wringing her hands, sobbing, and giving other evidences of violent religious excitement. This appeared to be a common occurrence, as none of the Lapps took the slightest notice of it. I have no doubt that much of that hallucination which led to the murders at Kautokeino still exists among the people, kept alive by secret indulgence. Those missionaries have much to answer for who have planted the seeds of spiritual disease among this ignorant and impressible race.

The night was cold and splendidly clear. We were obliged to leave the river on account of rotten ice, and took to the open plains, where our deers sank to their bellies in the loose snow. The leading animals became fractious, and we were obliged to stop every few minutes, until their paroxysms subsided. I could not perceive that the Lapps themselves exercised much more control over them than we, who were new to the business. The domesticated reindeer still retains his wild instincts, and never fails to protest against the necessity of labor. The most docile will fly from the track, plunge, face about and refuse to draw, when you least expect it. They are possessed by an incorrigible stupidity. Their sagacity applies only to their animal wants, and they seem almost totally deficient in memory. They never become attached to men, and the only sign of recognition they show, is sometimes to allow certain persons to catch them more easily than others. In point of speed they are not equal to the horse, and an hour's run generally exhausts them. When one considers their size, however, their strength and power of endurance seem marvellous. Herr Berger informed me that he had driven a reindeer from Alten to Kautokeino, 112 miles, in twenty-six hours, and from the latter place to Muoniovara in thirty. I was also struck by the remarkable adaptation of the animal to its uses. Its hoof resembles that of the camel, being formed for snow, as the latter for sand. It is broad, cloven and flexible, the separate divisions spreading out so as to present a resisting surface when the foot is set down, and falling together when it is lifted. Thus in snow where a horse would founder in the space of a hundred yards, the deer easily works his way, mile after mile, drawing the sliding, canoe-like pulk, burdened with his master's weight, after him.

The Lapps generally treat their animals with the greatest patience and forbearance, but otherwise do not exhibit any particular attachment for them. They are indebted to them for food, clothing, habitation and conveyance, and their very existence may therefore almost be said to depend on that of their herds. It is surprising, however, what a number of deer are requisite for the support of a family. Von Buch says that a Lapp who has a hundred deer is poor, and will be finally driven to descend to the coast, and take to fishing. The does are never made to labour, but are kept in the woods for milking and breeding. Their milk is rich and nourishing, but less agreeable to the taste than that of the cow. The cheese made from it is strong and not particularly palatable. It yields an oil which is the sovereign specific for frozen flesh. The male deer used for draft are always castrated, which operation the old Lapp women perform by slowly chewing the glands between their teeth until they are reduced to a pulp, without wounding the hide.

During this journey I had ample opportunity of familiarising myself with reindeer travel. It is picturesque enough at the outset, but when the novelty of the thing is worn off nothing is left but a continual drain upon one's patience. Nothing can exceed the coolness with which your deer jumps off the track, slackens his tow-rope, turns around and looks you in the face, as much as to say: "What are you going to do about it?" The simplicity and stupidity of his countenance seem to you to be admirably feigned, and unless you are an old hand you are inevitably provoked. This is particularly pleasant on the marshy table-lands of Lapland, where, if he takes a notion to bolt with you, your pulk bounces over the hard tussocks, sheers sideways down the sudden pitches, or swamps itself in beds of loose snow. Harness a frisky sturgeon to a "dug-out," in a rough sea, and you will have some idea of this method of travelling. While I acknowledge the Providential disposition of things which has given the reindeer to the Lapp, I cannot avoid thanking Heaven that I am not a Lapp, and that I shall never travel again with reindeer.

The aberrations of our deer obliged us to take a very sinuous course. Sometimes we headed north, and sometimes south, and the way seemed so long that I mistrusted the quality of our guide; but at last a light shone ahead. It was the hut of Eitajärvi. A lot of pulks lay in front of it, and the old Finn stood already with a fir torch, waiting to light us in. On arriving, Anton was greeted by his sister Caroline, who had come thus far from Muoniovara, on her way to visit some relatives at Altengaard. She was in company with some Finns, who had left Lippajärvi the day previous, but losing their way in the storm, had wandered about for twenty-four hours, exposed to its full violence Think of an American girl of eighteen sitting in an open pulk, with the thermometer at zero, a furious wind and blinding snow beating upon her, and neither rest nor food for a day! There are few who would survive twelve hours, yet Caroline was as fresh, lively, and cheerful as ever, and immediately set about cooking our supper. We found a fire in the cold guest's room, the place swept and cleaned, and a good bed of deer-skins in one corner. The temperature had sunk to 12° below zero, and the wind blew through wide cracks in the floor, but between the fire and the reciprocal warmth of our bodies we secured a comfortable sleep—a thing of the first consequence in such a climate.

Our deer started well in the morning, and the Lapp guide knew his way perfectly. The wind had blown so strongly that the track was cleared rather than filled, and we slipped up the long slopes at a rapid rate. I recognised the narrow valley where we first struck the northern streams, and the snowy plain beyond, where our first Lapp guide lost his way. By this time it was beginning to grow lighter, showing us the dreary wastes of table-land which we had before crossed in the fog. North of us was a plain of unbroken snow, extending to a level line on the horizon, where it met the dark violet sky. Were the colour changed, it would have perfectly represented the sandy plateaux of the Nubian Desert, in so many particulars does the extreme North imitate the extreme South. But the sun, which never deserts the desert, had not yet returned to these solitudes. Far, far away, on the edge of the sky, a dull red glimmer showed where he moved. Not the table-land of Pamir, in Thibet, the cradle of the Oxus and the Indus, but this lower Lapland terrace, is entitled to the designation of the " Roof of the World." We were on the summit, creeping along her mountain rafters, and looking southward, off her shelving eaves, to catch a glimpse of the light playing on her majestic front. Here, for once, we seemed to look down on the horizon, and I thought of Europe and the Tropics as lying below. Our journey northward had been an ascent, but now the world's steep sloped downward before us into sunshine and warmer air. In ascending the Andes or the Himalayas, you pass through all climates and belts of vegetation between the Equator and the Pole, and so a journey due north, beyond the circle of the sun, simply reverses the phenomenon, and impresses one like the ascent of a mountain on the grandest possible scale.

In two hours from the time we left Eitajärvi we reached the Lapp encampment. The herds of deer had been driven in from the woods, and were clustered among the birch bushes around the tents. We had some difficulty in getting our own deer past them, until the Lapps came to our assistance. We made no halt, but pushed on, through deeper snows than before, over the desolate plain. As far as Palajärvi we ran with our gunwales below the snow-level, while the foremost pulks were frequently swamped under the white waves that broke over them. We passed through a picturesque gorge between two hills about 500 feet high, and beyond it came upon wide lakes covered deep with snow, under which there was a tolerable track, which the leading deer was able to find with his feet. Beyond these lakes there was a ridge, which we had no sooner crossed than a dismally grand prospect opened before us. We overlooked a valley-basin, marked with belts of stunted birch, and stretching away for several miles to the foot of a bleak snowy mountain, which I at once recognised as Lippavara. After rounding its western point and turning southward again, we were rejoiced with the sight of some fir trees, from which the snow had been shaken, brightening even with their gloomy green the white monotony of the Lapland wilderness. It was like a sudden gleam of sunshine.

We reached Lippajärva at twelve, having made twenty-eight miles of hard travel in five hours. Here we stopped two hours to cook a meal and change our deer, and then pushed on to reach Palajoki the same night. We drove through the birch woods, no longer glorious as before, for the snow had been shaken off, and there was no sunset light to transfigure them. Still on, ploughing through deep seas in the gathering darkness, over marshy plains, all with a slant southward, draining into the Muonio, until we reached the birchen ridge of Suontajärvi, with its beautiful firs rising here and there, silent and immovable. Even the trees have no voices in the North, let the wind blow as it will. There is nothing to be heard but the sharp whistle of the dry snow—the same dreary music which accompanies the African simoom. The night was very dark, and we began to grow exceedingly tired of sitting flat in our pulks. I looked sharp for the Palajock Elv, the high fir-fringed banks of which I remembered, for they denoted our approach to the Muonio; but it was long, long before we descended from the marshes upon the winding road of snow-covered ice. In vain I shifted my aching legs and worked my benumbed hands, looking out ahead for the embouchure of the river. Braisted and I encouraged each other, whenever we were near enough to hear, by the reminder that we had only one more day with reindeer. After a long time spent in this way, the high banks flattened, level snows and woods succeeded, and we sailed into the port of Palajoki.

The old Finnish lady curtsied very deeply as she recognised us, and hastened to cook our coffee and reindeer, and to make us a good bed with sheets. On our former visit the old lady and her sons had watched us undress and get into bed, but on this occasion three buxom daughters, of ages ranging from sixteen to twenty-two, appeared about the time for retiring, and stationed themselves in a row near the door, where they watched us with silent curiosity. As we had shown no hesitation in the first case, we determined to be equally courageous now, and commenced removing our garments with great deliberation, allowing them every opportunity of inspecting their fashion and the manner of wearing them. The work thus proceeded in mutual silence until we were nearly ready for repose, when Braisted, by pulling off a stocking and displaying a muscular calf, suddenly alarmed the youngest, who darted to the door and rushed out. The second caught the panic, and followed, and the third and oldest was therefore obliged to do likewise, though with evident reluctance. I was greatly amused at such an unsophisticated display of curiosity. The perfect composure of the girls, and the steadiness with which they watched us, showed that they were quite unconscious of having committed any impropriety.

The morning was clear and cold. Our deer had strayed so far into the woods that we did not get under way before the forenoon twilight commenced. We expected to find a broken road down the Muonio, but a heavy snow had fallen the day previous, and the track was completely filled. Long Isaac found so much difficulty in taking the lead, his deer constantly bolting from the path, that Anton finally relieved him, and by standing upright in the pulk and thumping the deer's flanks, succeeded in keeping up the animal's spirits and forcing a way. It was slow work, however, and the sun, rolling his whole disc above the horizon, announced midday before we reached Kyrkessuando. As we drove up to the little inn, we were boisterously welcomed by Häl, Herr Forström's brown wolf-dog, who had strayed thus far from home. Our deer were beginning to give out, and we were very anxious to reach Muoniovara in time for dinner, so we only waited long enough to give the animals a feed of moss and procure some hot milk for ourselves.

The snow-storm, which had moved over a narrow belt of country, had not extended below this place, and the road was consequently well broken. We urged our deer into a fast trot, and slid down the icy floor of the Muonio, past hills whose snows flashed scarlet and rose-orange in the long splendour of sunset. Hunger and the fatigue which our journey was producing at last, made us extremely sensitive to the cold, though it was not more than 20° below zero. My blood became so chilled, that I was apprehensive the extremities would freeze, and the most vigorous motion of the muscles barely sufficed to keep at bay the numbness which attacked them. At dusk we drove through Upper Muonioniska, and our impatience kept the reindeers so well in motion that before five o'clock (although long after dark,) we were climbing the well-known slope to Herr Forström's house at Muoniovara. Here we found the merchant, not yet departed to the Lapp fair at Karessuando, and Mr. Wolley, who welcomed us with the cordiality of an old friend. Our snug room at the carpenter's was already warmed and set in order, and after our reindeer drive of 250 miles through the wildest parts of Lapland, we felt a home-like sense of happiness and comfort in smoking our pipes before the familiar iron stove.

The trip to Kautokeino embraced about all I saw of Lapp life during the winter journey. The romance of the tribe, as I have already said, has totally departed with their conversion, while their habits of life scarcely improved in the least, are sufficiently repulsive to prevent any closer experience than I have had, unless the gain were greater. Mr. Wolley, who had been three years in Lapland, also informed me that the superstitious and picturesque traditions of the people have almost wholly disappeared, and the coarse mysticism and rant which they have engrafted upon their imperfect Christianity does not differ materially from the same excrescence in more civilized races. They have not even (the better for them, it is true) any characteristic and picturesque vices—but have become, certainly to their own great advantage, a pious, fanatical, moral, ignorant and commonplace people. I have described them exactly as I found them, and as they have been described to me by those who knew them well. The readers of "Afraja" may be a little disappointed with the picture, as I confess I have been (in an artistic sense, only) with the reality; but the Lapps have lost many vices with their poetic *diablerie*, and nobody has a right to complain.

It is a pity that many traits which are really characteristic and interesting in a people cannot be mentioned on account of that morbid prudery so prevalent in our day, which insults the unconscious innocence of nature. Oh, that one could imitate the honest unreserve of the old travellers—the conscientiousness which insisted on telling not only the truth, but the whole truth! This is scarcely possible, now; but at the same time I have not been willing to emasculate my accounts of the tribes of men to the extent perhaps required by our ultra-conventionalism, and must insist, now and then, on being allowed a little Flemish fidelity to nature. In the description of races, as in the biography of individuals, the most important half of life is generally omitted.

CHAPTER XIII.

ABOUT THE FINNS.

WE remained but another day in Muoniovara, after our return from Kautokeino, and this was devoted to preparations for the return journey to Haparanda. My first intention had been to make an excursion across the country to the iron mountains of Gellivara, thence to Quickjock, at the foot of the Northern Alp, Sulitelma, "Queen of Snows," and so southward through the heart of Swedish Lappmark; but I found that such a journey would be attended with much difficulty and delay. In the first place, there were no broken roads at this season, except on the routes of inland trade; much of the intermediate country is a wilderness, where one must camp many nights in the snow; food was very scarce, the Lapps having hardly enough for their own necessities, and the delays at every place where guides and reindeer must be changed, would have prolonged the journey far beyond the time which I had allotted to the North. I began to doubt, also, whether one would be sufficiently repaid for the great fatigue and danger which such a trip would have involved. There is no sensation of which one wearies sooner than disgust; and, much as I enjoy a degree of barbarism in milder climates, I suspected that a long companionship with Lapps in a polar winter would be a little too much for me. So I turned my face toward Stockholm, heartily glad that I had made the journey, yet not dissatisfied that I was looking forward to its termination.

Before setting out on our return, I shall devote a few pages to the Finns. For the principal facts concerning them, I am mostly indebted to Mr. Wolley, whose acquaintance with the language, and residence of three years in Lapland, have made him perfectly familiar with the race. As I have already remarked, they are a more picturesque people than the Swedes, with stronger lights and shades of character, more ardent temperaments, and a more deeply-rooted national feeling. They seem to be rather clannish and exclusive, in fact, disliking both Swedes and Russians, and rarely intermarrying with them. The sharply-defined boundaries of language and race, at the head of the Bothnian Gulf, are a striking evidence of this. Like their distant relatives, the Hungarian Magyars, they retain many distinct traces of their remote Asiatic origin. It is partly owing to this fact, and partly to that curious approach of extremes which we observe in nature no less than in humanity, that all suggestive traits of resemblance in these regions point to the Orient rather than to Europe.

I have already described the physical characteristics of the Finns, and have nothing to add, except that I found the same type everywhere, even among the mixed-blooded Quäns of Kautokeino—high cheek-bones, square, strong jaws, full yet firm lips, low, broad foreheads, dark eyes and hair, and a deeper, warmer red on the cheeks than on those of the rosy

Swedes. The average height is, perhaps, not quite equal to that of the latter race, but in physical vigor I can see no inferiority, and there are among them many men of splendid stature, strength, and proportion. Von Buch ascribes the marked difference of stature between the Finns and the Lapps, both living under precisely the same influences of climate, to the more cleanly habits of the former and their constant use of the vapor-bath; but I have always found that blood and descent, even where the variation from the primitive stock is but slight, are more potent than climate or custom. The Finns have been so long christianised and civilised (according to the European idea of civilisation), that whatever peculiar characteristic they retain must be looked for mainly in those habits which illustrate their mental and moral natures. In their domestic life, they correspond in most particulars to the Swedes of the same class.

They are passionate, and therefore prone to excesses—imaginative, and therefore, owing to their scanty education, superstitious. Thus the religious element, especially the fantastic aberrations thereof engendered by Lestadius and other missionaries, while it has tended greatly to repress the vice, has in the same proportion increased the weakness. Drunkenness, formerly so prevalent as to be the curse of Lapland, is now exceedingly rare, and so are the crimes for which it is responsible. The most flagrant case which has occurred in the neighborhood of Muoniovara for some years past, was that of a woman who attempted to poison her father-in-law by mixing the scrapings of lucifer matches with his coffee, in order to get rid of the burden of supporting him.

Although the evidence was very convincing, the matter was hushed up, in order to avoid a scandal upon the Church, the woman being a steadfast member. In regard to drunkenness, I have heard it stated that, while it was formerly no unusual thing for a Finn to be frozen to death in this condition, the same catastrophe never befell a Lapp, owing to his mechanical habit of keeping his arms and feet in motion—a habit which he preserves even while utterly stupefied and unconscious.

A singular spiritual epidemic ran through Polar Finland three or four years ago, cotemporary with the religious excitement in Norwegian Lapland, and partly occasioned by the same reckless men. It consisted of sobbings, strong nervous convulsions, and occasional attacks of that state of semi-consciousness called trance, the subjects of which were looked upon as having been possessed by the Spirit, and transported to the other world, where visions like those of John on Patmos, were revealed to them. The missionaries, instead of repressing this unhealthy delusion, rather encouraged it, and even went so far as to publish as supernatural revelations, the senseless ravings of these poor deluded people. The epidemic spread until there was scarcely a family some member of which was not affected by it, and even yet it has not wholly subsided. The fit would come upon the infected persons at any time, no matter where they were, or how employed. It usually commenced with a convulsive catching of the breath, which increased in violence, accompanied by sobbing, and sometimes by cries or groans, until the victim was either exhausted or fell into a trance, which lasted some hours. The persons who were affected were always treated with the greatest respect during the attack; no one ventured to smile, no matter how absurd a form the visitation might take. The principle of abstinence from strong drinks was promulgated about the same time, and much of the temperance of the Finns and Lapps is undoubtedly owing the impression made upon their natures by these phenomena.

The same epidemic has often prevailed in the United States, England and Germany. The barking and dancing mania which visited Kentucky thirty or forty years ago, and the performances of the "Holy Rollers," were even more ludicrous and unnatural. Such appearances are a puzzle alike to the physiologist and the philosopher; their frequency shows that they are based on some weak spot in human nature; and in proportion as we pity the victims we have a right to condemn those who sow the seeds of the pestilence. True religion is never spasmodic; it is calm as the existence of God. I know of nothing more shocking than such attempts to substitute rockets and blue lights for Heaven's eternal sunshine.

So far as regards their moral character, the Finns have as little cause for reproach as any other people. We found them as universally honest and honourable in their dealings as the Northern Swedes, who are not surpassed in the world in this respect. Yet their countenances express more cunning and reserve, and the virtue may be partly a negative one, resulting from that indolence which characterises the frigid and the torrid zone. Thus, also, notwithstanding physical signs which denote more ardent animal passions than their neighbors, they are equally chaste, and have as high a standard of sexual purity. Illegitimate births are quite rare, and are looked upon as a lasting shame and disgrace to both parties. The practice of "bundling" which, until recently, was very common among Finnish lovers, very seldom led to such results, and their marriage speedily removed the dishonour. Their manners, socially, in this respect, are curiously contradictory. Thus, while both sexes freely mingle in the bath, in a state of nature, while the women unhesitatingly scrub, rub and dry their husbands, brothers or male friends, while the salutation for both sexes is an embrace with the right arm, a kiss is considered grossly immodest and improper. A Finnish woman expressed the greatest astonishment and horror, at hearing from Mr. Wolley that it was a very common thing in England for a husband and wife to kiss each other. "If my husband were to attempt such a thing," said she, "I would beat him about the ears so that he would feel it for a week." Yet in conversation they are very plain and unreserved, though by no means gross. They acknowledge that such things as generation, gestation and parturition exist, and it may be that this very absence of mystery tends to keep chaste so excitable and imaginative a race.

Notwithstanding their superstition, their love of poetry, and the wild, rich, musical character of their language, there is a singular absence of legendary lore in this part of Finland. Perhaps this is owing to the fact that their ancestors have emigrated hither, principally within the last two centuries, from the early home of the race—Tavastland, the shores of the Pajana Lake, and the Gulf of Finland. It is a difficult matter to preserve family traditions among them, or even any extended genealogical record, from the circumstance that a Finn takes his name, not only from his father's surname, but from his residence. Thus, Isaki takes the name of "Anderinpoika" from his father Anderi, and adds "Niemi," the local name of his habitation. His son Nils will be called Nils Isakipoika, with the addition of the name of his residence, wherever that may be; and his family name will be changed as often as his house. There may be a dozen different names in the course of one generation, and the list soon becomes too complicated and confused for an uneducated memory. It is no wonder, therefore, that the Finn knows very little except about what happened during his own life, or, at best, his father's. I never heard the Kalewala spoken of, and doubt very much whether it is known to the natives of this region. The only songs we heard, north of Haparanda, were hymns—devout, but dismal. There must be ballads and household songs yet alive, but the recent spiritual fever has silenced them for the time.

I was at first a little surprised to find the natives of the North so slow, indolent and improvident. We have an idea that a cold climate is bracing and stimulating—*ergo*, the further north you go, the more active and energetic you will find the people. But the touch of ice is like that of fire. The tropics relax, the pole benumbs, and the practical result is the same in both cases. In the long, long winter, when there are but four hours of twilight to twenty of darkness—when the cows are housed, the wood cut, the hay gathered, the barley bran and fir bark stowed away for bread, and the summer's catch of fish salted—what can a man do when his load of wood or hay is hauled home, but eat, gossip and sleep? To bed at nine, and out of it at eight in the morning, smoking and dozing between the slow performance of his few daily duties, he becomes at last as listless and dull as a hibernating bear. In the summer he has perpetual daylight, and need not hurry. Besides, why should he give himself special trouble to produce an unusually large crop of flax or barley, when a single night may make his labours utterly profitless? Even in midsummer the blighting frost may fall: nature seems to take a cruel pleasure in thwarting him: he is fortunate only through chance; and thus a sort of Arab fatalism and acquiescence in whatever happens, takes possession of him. His improvidence is also to be ascribed to the same cause. Such fearful famine and suffering as existed in Finland and Lapland during the winter of 1856-7 might no doubt have been partially prevented, but no human power could have wholly forestalled it.

The polar zone was never designed for the abode of man. In the pre-Adamite times, when England was covered with palm-forests, and elephants ranged through Siberia, things may have been widely different, and the human race then (if there was any) may have planted vineyards on these frozen hills and lived in bamboo huts. But since the geological *émeutes* and revolutions, and the establishment of the terrestrial *régime*, I cannot for the life of me see whatever induced beings endowed with human reason, to transplant themselves hither and here take root, while such vast spaces lie waste and useless in more genial climes. A man may be pardoned for remaining where the providences of birth and education have thrown him, but I cannot excuse the first colonists for inflicting such a home upon centuries of descendants. Compare even their physical life—the pure animal satisfaction in existence, for that is not a trifling matter after all—with that of the Nubians, or the Malays, or the Polynesians! It is the difference between a poor hare, hunted and worried year after year by hounds and visions of hounds and the familiar, confiding wren, happiest of creatures, because secure of protection everywhere. Oh that the circle of the ecliptic would coincide with that of the equator! That the sun would shine from pole to pole for evermore, and all lands be habitable and hospitable, and the Saharan sands (according to Fourier) be converted into bowers of the Hesperides, and the bitter salt of the ocean brine (*vide* the same author) become delicious champagne punch, wherein it would be pleasure to drown! But I am afraid that mankind is not yet fit for such a millennium.

Meanwhile it is truly comforting to find that even here, where men live under such discouraging circumstances that one would charitably forgive them the possession of many vices, they are, according to their light, fully as true, and honest, and pure, as the inhabitants of the most favoured countries in the world. Love for each other, trust in each other, faith in God, are all vital among them; and their shortcomings are so few and so easily accounted for, that one must respect them and feel that his faith in man is not lessened in knowing them. You who spend your lives at home can never know how much good there is in the world. In rude unrefined races, evil naturally rises to the surface, and one can discern the character of the stream beneath its scum. It is only in the highest civilization where the outside is goodly to the eye, too often concealing an interior foul to the core.

But I have no time to moralise on these matters. My duty is that of a chronicler; and if I perform that conscientiously, the lessons which my observations suggest will need no pointing out. I cannot close this chapter, however, without confessing my obligations to Mr. Wolley, whose thorough knowledge of the Lapps and Finns enabled me to test the truth of my own impressions, and to mature opinions which I should otherwise, from my own short experience, have hesitated in stating. Mr. Wolley, with that pluck and persistence of English character which Emerson so much admires, had made himself master of all that Lapland can furnish to the traveller, but intended remaining another year for scientific purposes. If he gives to the world—as I hope and trust he will—the result of this long and patient inquiry and investigation, we shall have at last a standard authority for this little-known corner of Europe. We were also indebted to Mr. Wolley for much personal kindness, which I take pleasure in acknowledging in the only way he cannot prevent.

CHAPTER XIV.

EXPERIENCES OF ARCTIC WEATHER.

WE bade a final adieu to Muoniovara on the afternoon of the 24th of January, leaving Mr. Wolley to wait for June and the birds in that dismal seclusion. Instead of resuming *skjuts*, we engaged horses as far as Kengis from Herr Forström and a neighbouring Finn, with a couple of shock-headed natives as postillions. Our sleds were mounted upon two rough Finnish sledges, the only advantage of which was to make harder work for the horses—but the people would have it so. The sun was down, but a long, long twilight succeeded, with some faint show of a zodiacal light. There was a tolerable track on the river, but our Finns walked their horses the whole way, and we were nearly seven hours in making Parkajoki. The air was very sharp; my nose, feet and hands kept me busily employed, and I began to fear that I was becoming unusually sensitive to cold, for the thermometer indicated but 15° below zero when we started. At Parkajoki, however, my doubts were removed and my sensations explained, on finding that the temperature had fallen to 44° below.

We slept warmly and well on our old bed of reindeer skins

in one corner of the milk-room. When Braisted, who rose first, opened the door, a thick white mist burst in and rolled heavily along the floor. I went out, attired only in my shirt and drawers, to have a look at the weather. I found the air very still and keen, though not painfully cold—but I was still full of the warmth of sleep. The mercury, however, had sunk into the very bulb of the thermometer, and was frozen so solid that I held it in the full glare of the fire for about a minute and a half before it thawed sufficiently to mount. The temperature was probably 50° below zero, if not more—greater than any we had yet experienced. But it was six o'clock, and we must travel. Fortifying ourselves with coffee and a little meat, and relying for defence in case of extremity on a bottle of powerful rum with which we had supplied ourselves, we muffled up with more than usual care, and started for Kihlangi.

We devoted ourselves entirely to keeping warm, and during the ride of six hours suffered very little except from the gradual diminution of our bodily temperature. It was a dreary journey, following the course of the Muonio between black, snow-laden forests. The sun rose to a height of seven or eight degrees at meridian; when we came over the same road, on our way north, he only showed half his disc. At Kihlangi the people recognised us, and were as well disposed as their stupidity would allow. The old woman cooked part of our reindeer joint, which, with half a dozen cups of strong coffee, brought back a comfortable warmth to our extremities. There were still twenty-four miles to be traversed; the horses were already exhausted, and the temperature only rose to—42° at mid-day, after

8*

which it fell again. We had a terrible journey. Step by step the horses slowly pulled us through the snow, every hour seeming lengthened to a day, as we worked our benumbed fingers and toes until the muscles were almost powerless, and yet it was dangerous to cease. Gradually the blood grew colder in the main channels; insidious chills succeeded, followed by a drowsy torpor, like that which is produced by a heavy dose of opium, until we were fain to have recourse to the rum, a horrid, vitriolic beverage, which burned our throats and stomachs like melted lead, yet gave us a temporary relief.

We almost despaired of reaching Jokijalka, on finding, about ten o'clock at night, that our postillions had taken us to the village of Kolare, and stopped before a large log house, where they seemed to think we would spend the night. Everybody had gone to bed, we knew not where we were, and had set our hearts upon the comfortable guest's room at Jokijalki. It was impossible to make the fellows understand me, but they saw that we were angry, and after a short consultation passed on. We again entered the snowy woods, which were dimly lighted up by an aurora behind us—a strange, mysterious, ghastly illumination, like the phosphorescent glow of a putrefying world. We were desperately cold, our very blood freezing in our veins, and our limbs numb and torpid. To keep entirely awake was impossible. We talked incessantly, making random answers, as continual fleeting dreams crossed the current of our consciousness. A heavy thump on the back was pardoned by him who received it, and a punch between the eyes would have been thankfully accepted had it been necessary.

At last, at last, Kolare church on the river bank came in sight; we crossed to the Russian side, and drove into the yard of the inn. It was nearly midnight, 47° below zero and we had been for seventeen hours exposed to such a temperature. Everybody had long been asleep. Locks and bolts are unknown, however, so we rushed into the family room, lit fir splinters, and inspected the faces of the sleeping group until we found the landlord, who arose and kindled a fresh fire in the milk-room. They made us coffee and a small bed, saying that the guest's room was too cold, which indeed it was, being little less than the outside temperature. On opening the door in the morning, the cold air rushed in as thick and white as steam. We had a little meat cooked, but could not eat enough, at such an early hour, to supply much fuel. As for taking anything with us for refreshment on the road, it was out of the question. One of our Finns turned back to Muoniovara with the laziest horse, and we got another from our Russian landlord. But it was a long, long journey to the next station (twenty miles), and the continuance of the extreme cold began to tell upon us. This part of the road was very heavy, as on the journey up—seemingly a belt of exposed country where the snow drifts more than elsewhere.

At Kexisvara we found two of the three pleasant women, who cooked our last fragment of reindeer meat, and sent off for horses to Kardis. We here parted with our other Finn, very glad to get rid of his horse, and take a fresh start. We had no difficulty now in making our way with the people, as they all recognised us and remembered our overpayments; besides which, I had enlarged my Finnish vocabulary at Muoniovara. Our horses were better, our sledges lighter and we were not long in reaching the iron-works at Kengis, which we passed at dusk. I should willingly have called upon the hospitable *bruk-patron*, but we were in too great a hurry to get out of the frigid zone. We were warmed by our meal, and sang lustily as we slid down the Torneå, finding its dreary, sparsely-settled banks cheerful and smiling by contrast with the frightful solitudes we had left. After some hours the postillion stopped before a house on the Swedish bank to hay his horses. We went up and found a single inhabitant; a man who was splitting fir for torches, but the conversation was limited to alternate puffs from our pipes. There was a fine aurora behind us—a low arch of white fire, with streamers radiating outward, shifting and dancing along its curve.

It was nearly ten o'clock before we reached Kardis, half unconscious from the cold. Our horse ran into the wrong place, and we lost sight of the baggage-sled, our only guide in the darkness. We could no longer trust the animal's instinct, but had to depend on our own, which is perhaps truer: at least, I have often found in myself traces of that blind, unreasoning faculty which guides the bee and the bird, and have never been deceived in trusting to it. We found the inn, and carried a cloud of frozen vapor into the kitchen with us, as we opened the door. The graceful wreaths of ice-smoke rolled before our feet, as before those of ascending saints in the old pictures, but ourselves, hair from head to foot, except two pairs of eyes, which looked out through icy loop-holes, resembled the reverse of saints. I told the landlord in Finnish that we wanted to sleep—"*mia tarvi nuku* à." He pointed to a bed in the corner, out of which rose a sick girl, of about seventeen, very pale, and evidently suffering. They placed some benches near the fire, removed the bedding, and disposed her as comfortably as the place permitted. We got some hot milk and hard bread, threw some reindeer skins on the vacant truck, and lay down, but not to sleep much. The room was so close and warm, and the dozen persons in it so alternately snoring and restless, that our rest was continually disturbed. We, therefore, rose early and aroused the lazy natives.

The cold was still at 47° below zero. The roads were so much better, however, that we descended again to our own runners, and our lively horses trotted rapidly down the Torneå. The signs of settlement and comparative civilisation which now increased with every mile were really cheering. Part of our way lay through the Swedish woods and over the intervening morasses, where the firs were hung with weepers of black-green moss, and stood solid and silent in their mantles of snow, lighted with a magnificent golden flush at sunrise. The morning was icy-clear and dazzling. There was not the least warmth in the sun's rays, but it was pleasant to see him with a white face once more. We could still stare at him without winking, but the reflection from the jewelled snow pained our eyes. The cold was so keen that we were obliged to keep our faces buried between our caps and boas, leaving only the smallest possible vacancy for the eyes. This was exceedingly disagreeable, on account of the moisture from the breath, which kept the squirrel tails constantly wet and sticky. Nevertheless, the cold penetrated through the little aperture; my eyes and forehead were like marble, the eyeballs like lumps of ice, sending a sharp pang of cold backward into the brain. I realised distinctly how a statue must feel.

Beyond Pello, where we stopped to "fire up," our road lay mostly on the Russian side. While crossing the Torneå at sunset, we met a drove of seventy or eighty reindeer, in charge of a dozen Lapps, who were bringing a cargo from Haparanda. We were obliged to turn off the road and wait until they had passed. The landlord at Juoxengi, who was quite drunk, hailed us with a shout and a laugh, and began talking about Kautokeino. We had some difficulty in getting rid of his conversation, and his importunities for us to stay all night. This was the place where they tried to make us leave, on the way up. I replied to the landlord's torrent of Finnish with some choice specimens of Kentucky oratory, which seemed to make but little impression on him. He gave us excellent horses, however, and we sped away again, by the light of another brilliant auroral arch.

Our long exposure to the extreme cold, coupled as it was with lack of rest and nourishment, now began to tell upon us. Our temperature fell so low that we again had recourse to the rum, which alone, I verily believe, prevented us from freezing bodily. One is locked in the iron embrace of the polar air, until the very life seems to be squeezed out of him. I huddled myself in my poesk, worked my fingers and toes, buried my nose in the damp, frozen fur, and laboured like a Hercules to keep myself awake and alive—but almost in vain. Braisted and I kept watch over each other, or attempted it, for about the only consciousness either of us had was that of the peril of falling asleep. We talked of anything and everything, sang, thumped each other, but the very next minute would catch ourselves falling over the side of the sled. A thousand dreams worried my brain and mixed themselves with my talk; and the absurdities thus created helped to arouse me. Speaking of seeing some wolves in the woods of California, I gravely continued: "I took out my sword, sharpened it on the grindstone and dared him to come on," when a punch in the ribs stopped me. Another time, while talking of hippopotami in the White Nile, I said: "If you want any skins, you must go to the Hudson's Bay Company. They have a depôt of them on Vancouver's Island." Braisted gave me much trouble, by assuring me in the most natural wide-awake voice that he was not in the least sleepy, when the reins had dropped from his hands and his head rocked on his shoulder. I could never be certain whether he was asleep or awake. Our only plan was not to let the conversation flag a minute.

At Torakankorwa we changed horses without delay, and hurried on to Matarengi. On turning out of the road to avoid a hay-sled, we were whirled completely over. There was no fun in this, at such a time. I fell head foremost into deep snow, getting a lump in my right eye, which completely blinded me for a time. My forehead, eyebrows, and the bridge of my nose were insufferably painful. On reaching Matarengi I found my nose frozen through, and considerably swollen. The people were in bed, but we went into the kitchen, where a dozen or more were stowed about, and called for the landlord. Three young girls, who were in bed in one corner, rose and dressed themselves in our presence without the least hesitation, boiled some milk, and gave us bread and butter. We had a single small bed, which kept us warm by obliging us to lie close. Sometime in the night, two Swedes arrived, who blustered about and made so much noise, that Braisted finally silenced them by threats of personal violence, delivered in very good English.

In the morning the mercury froze, after showing 49° below zero. The cold was by this time rather alarming, especially after our experiences of the previous day. The air was hazy with the fine, frozen atoms of moisture, a raw wind blew from the north, the sky was like steel which has been breathed upon—in short, the cold was visible to the naked eye. We warmed our gloves and boots, and swathed our heads so completely that not a feature was to be seen. I had a little loophole between my cap and boa, but it was soon filled up with frost from my breath, and helped to keep in the warmth. The road was hard and smooth as marble. We had good horses, and leaving Avasaxa and the polar circle behind us, we sped down the solid bed of the Torneå to Niemis. On the second stage we began to freeze for want of food. The air was really terrible; nobody ventured out of doors who could stay in the house. The smoke was white and dense, like steam; the wind was a blast from the Norseman's hell, and the touch of it on your face almost made you scream. Nothing can be more severe—flaying, branding with a hot iron, cutting with a dull knife, &c., may be something like it, but no worse.

The sun rose through the frozen air a little after nine and mounted quite high at noon. At Päckilä we procured some hot milk and smoked reindeer, tolerable horses and a stout boy of fourteen to drive our baggage-sled. Every on we met had a face either frozen, or about to freeze. Such a succession of countenances, fiery red, purple, blue, black almost, with white frost spots, and surrounded with rings of icy hair and fur, I never saw before. We thanked God again and again that our faces were turned southward, and that the deadly wind was blowing on our backs. When we reached Korpykilä, our boy's face, though solid and greasy as a bag of lard, was badly frozen. His nose was quite white and swollen, as if blistered by fire, and there were frozen blotches on both cheeks. The landlord rubbed the parts instantly with rum, and performed the same operation on our noses.

On this day, for the first time in more than a month, we saw daylight, and I cannot describe how cheering was the effect of those pure, white, brilliant rays, in spite of the iron landscape they illumined. It was no longer the setting light of the level Arctic sun; not the twilight gleams of shifting colour, beautiful, but dim; not the faded, mock daylight which sometimes glimmered for a half-hour at noon; but the true white, full, golden day, which we had almost forgotten. So nearly, indeed, that I did not for some time suspect the cause of the unusual whiteness and brightness. Its effect upon the trees was superb. The twigs of the birch and the needles of the fir were coated with crystal, and sparkled like jets of jewels spouted up from the immaculate snow. The clumps of birches can be compared to nothing but frozen fountains—frozen in full action, with their showery sheaves of spray arrested before they fell. It was a wonderful, a fairy world we beheld—too beautiful to be lifeless, but every face we met reminded us the more that this was the chill beauty of Death—of dead Nature. Death was in the sparkling air, in the jewelled trees, in the spotless snow Take off your mitten, and his hand will grasp yours like a vice; uncover your mouth, and your frozen lips will soon acknowledge his kiss.

Even while I looked the same icy chills were running through my blood, precursors of that drowsy torpor which I was so anxious to avoid. But no; it *would come*, and I dozed until both hands became so stiff that it was barely possible to restore their powers of motion and feeling. It was not quite dark when we reached Kuckulä, the last station, but thence to Haparanda our horses were old and lazy, and our postillion was a little boy, whose weak voice had no effect. Braisted kept his hands warm in jerking and urging, but I sat and froze. Village after village was passed, but we looked in vain for the lights of Torneå. We were thoroughly exhausted with our five days' battle against the dreadful cold, when at last a row of lights gleamed across the river, and we drove up to the inn. The landlord met us with just the same words as on the first visit, and, strange enough, put us into the same room, where the same old Norrland merchant was again quartered in the same stage of tipsiness. The kind Fredrika did not recognise us in our Lapp dresses, until I had unrobed, when she cried out in joyful surprise, "Why, you were here before!"

We had been so completely chilled that it was a long time before any perceptible warmth returned. But a generous meal, with a bottle of what was called "*gammal scherry*" (though the Devil and his servants, the manufacturers of chemical wines, only knew what it was), started the flagging circulation. We then went to bed, tingling and stinging in every nerve from the departing cold. Every one complained of the severity of the weather, which, we were told, had not been equalled for many years past. But such a bed, and such a rest as I had! Lying between clean sheets, with my feet buried in soft fur, I wallowed in a flood of downy, delicious sensations until sunrise. In the morning we ventured to wash our faces and brush our teeth for the first time in five days, put on clean shirts, and felt once more like responsible beings. The natives never wash when the weather is so cold, and cautioned us against it. The wind had fallen but the mercury again froze at 47° below zero. Nevertheless, we went out after breakfast to call upon Dr. Wretholm, and walk over the Torneå.

The old Doctor was overjoyed to see us again. "Ah !" said he, "it is a good fortune that you have got back alive. When the weather was so cold, I thought of you, travelling over the Norwegian *fjeller*, and thought you must certainly be frozen to death." His wife was no less cordial in her welcome. They brought us ale and Swedish punch, with reindeer cheese for our frozen noses, and insisted on having their horse put into the sled to take us over to Torneå and bring us back to dinner. The doctor's boy drove us, facing the wind with our faces exposed, at —42°, but one night's rest and good food enabled us to bear it without inconvenience. Torneå is a plain Swedish town, more compactly built than Haparanda, yet scarcely larger. The old church is rather picturesque, and there were some tolerable houses, which appeared to be government buildings, but the only things particularly Russian which we noticed were a Cossack sentry, whose purple face showed that he was nearly frozen, and a guide-post with "150 versts to Uleaborg" upon it. On returning to the Doctor's we found a meal ready, with a capital salad of frozen salmon, *bouillon*, ale, and coffee. The family were reading the Swedish translation of "Dred" in the *Aftonblad*, and were interested in hearing some account of Mrs. Beecher Stowe. We had a most agreeable and interesting visit to these kind, simple-hearted people.

I made a sunset sketch of Torneå. I proposed also to draw Fredrika, but she at once refused, in great alarm. "Not for anything in the world," said she, "would I have it done!" What superstitious fears possessed her I could not discover. We made arrangements to start for Kalix the next day, on our way to Stockholm. The extreme temperature still continued. The air was hazy with the frozen moisture—the smoke froze in solid masses—the snow was brittle and hard as metal—iron stuck like glue—in short, none of the signs of an Arctic winter were wanting. Nevertheless, we trusted to the day's rest and fatter fare on the road for strength to continue the battle.

CHAPTER XV.

INCIDENTS OF THE RETURN JOURNEY.

We left Haparanda on the 30th of January. After six days of true Arctic weather—severer than any registered by De Haven's expedition, during a winter in the polar ice— the temperature rose suddenly to 26° below zero. We were happy and jolly at getting fairly started for Stockholm at last, and having such mild (!) weather to travel in. The difference in our sensations was remarkable. We could boldly bare our faces and look about us; our feet kept warm and glowing, and we felt no more the hazardous chill and torpor of the preceding days. On the second stage the winter road crossed an arm of the Bothnian Gulf. The path was well marked out with fir-trees—a pretty avenue, four or five miles in length, over the broad, white plain. On the way we saw an eruption of the ice, which had been violently thrown up by the confined air. Masses three feet thick and solid as granite were burst asunder and piled atop of each other.

We travelled too fast this day for the proper enjoyment of the wonderful scenery on the road. I thought I had exhausted my admiration of these winter forests—but no, miracles will never cease. Such fountains, candelabra, Gothic pinnacles, tufts of plumes, colossal sprays of coral, and the embodiments of the fairy pencillings of frost on window panes, wrought in crystal and silver, are beyond the power of pen or pencil. It was a wilderness of beauty; we knew not where to look, nor which forms to choose, in the dazzling confusion. Silent and all unmoved by the wind they stood, sharp and brittle as of virgin ore—not trees of earth, but the glorified forests of All-Father Odin's paradise, the celestial city of Asgaard. No living forms of vegetation are so lovely. Tropical palms, the tree-ferns of Penang, the lotus of Indian rivers, the feathery bamboo, the arrowy areca —what are they beside these marvellous growths of winter, these shining sprays of pearl, ivory and opal, gleaming in the soft orange light of the Arctic sun?

At Sångis we met a handsome young fellow with a moustache, who proved to be the *Länsman* of Kalix. I was surprised to find that he knew all about us. He wondered at our coming here north, when we might stay at home thought once would be enough for us, and had himself been no further than Stockholm. I recognised our approach to Nåsby by the barrels set in the snow—an ingenious plan of marking the road in places where the snow drifts, as the wind creates a whirl or eddy around them. We were glad to see Nåsby and its two-story inn once more. The pleasant little hand-maiden smiled all over her face when she saw us again. Nåsby is a crack place: the horses were ready at once, and fine creatures they were, taking us up the Kalix to Månsbyn, eight miles in one hour. The road was hard as a rock and smooth as a table, from much ploughing and rolling.

The next day was dark and lowering, threatening snow, with a raw wind from the north-west, and an average temperature of 15° below zero. We turned the north-western corner of the Bothnian Gulf in the afternoon, and pushed on to Old Luleå by supper-time. At Persö, on the journey north, I had forgotten my cigar-case, an old, familiar friend of some years' standing, and was overjoyed to find that the servant-girl had carefully preserved it, thinking I might return some day. We drove through the streets of empty stables and past the massive church of Old Luleå, to the inn, where we had before met the surly landlord. There he was again, and the house was full, as the first time. However we obtained the promise of a bed in the large room, and meanwhile walked up and down to keep ourselves warm. The guests' rooms were filled with gentlemen of the neighborhood, smoking and carousing. After an hour had passed, a tall, handsome, strong fellow came out of the rooms, and informed us that as we were strangers he would give up the room to us and seek lodgings elsewhere. He had drunk just enough to be mellow and happy, and insisted on delaying his own supper to let us eat first. Who should come along at this juncture but the young fellow we had seen in company with Brother Horton at Månsbyn, who hailed us with: "Thank you for the last time!" With him was a very gentlemanly man who spoke English. They were both accompanied by ladies, and were returning from the ball of Piteå. The guests all treated us with great courtesy and respect, and the landlord retired and showed his surly face no more. Our first friend informed me that he had been born and brought up in the neighborhood, but could not recollect such a severe winter.

As we descended upon the Luleå River in the morning we met ten sleighs coming from the ball. The horses were all in requisition at the various stations, but an extra supply had been provided, and we were not detained anywhere. The Norrland sleds are so long that a man may place his baggage in the front part and lie down at full length behind it. A high back shields the traveller from the wind, and upon a step in the rear stands the driver, with a pair of rein as long as a main-top-bowline, in order to reach the horse, who is at the opposite end of a very long pair of shafts. In these sleds one may travel with much comfort, and less danger of overturning, though not so great speed as in the short, light, open frames we bought in Sundsvall. The latter are seldom seen so far north, and were a frequent object of curiosity to the peasants at the stations. There is also a sled with a body something like a Hansom cab, entirely closed, with a window in front, but they are heavy, easily overturned, and only fit for luxurious travellers.

We approached Piteå at sunset. The view over the broad embouchure of the river, studded with islands, was quite picturesque, and the town itself, scattered along the shore and over the slopes of the hills made a fair appearance. It reminded me somewhat of a small New-England country town, with its square frame houses and an occasional garden. Here I was rejoiced by the sight of a cherry-tree, the most northern fruit-tree which I saw. On our way up, we thought Piteå, at night and in a snow-storm, next door to the North Pole. Now, coming from the north, seeing its snowy hills and house-roofs rosy with the glow of sunset, it was warm and southern by contrast. The four principal towns of

West and North Bothnia are thus characterised in an old verse of Swedish doggerel: Umeå, *the fine*; Piteå, *the needle-making*; Luleå, *the lazy*; and in Torneå, *everybody gets drunk*.

We took some refreshment, pushed on and reached Abyn between nine and ten o'clock, having travelled seventy miles since morning. The sleighing was superb. How I longed for a dashing American cutter, with a span of fast horses, a dozen strings of bells and an ebony driver! Such a turn-out would rather astonish the northern solitudes, and the slow, quaint northern population. The next day we had a temperature of 2° above zero, with snow falling, but succeeded in reaching Skellefteå for breakfast. For the last two or three miles we travelled along a hill-side overlooking a broad, beautiful valley, cleared and divided into cultivated fields, and thickly sprinkled with villages and farm-houses. Skellefteå itself made an imposing appearance, as the lofty dome of its Grecian church came in sight around the shoulder of the hill. We took the wrong road, and in turning about split one of our shafts, but Braisted served it with some spare rope, using the hatchet-handle as a marlingspike, so that it held stoutly all the rest of the way to Stockholm.

We went on to Burea that night, and the next day to Djekneboda, sixty miles farther. The temperature fluctuated about the region of zero, with a heavy sky and light snow-falls. As we proceeded southward the forests became larger, and the trees began to show a dark green foliage where the wind had blown away the snow, which was refreshing to see, after the black or dark indigo hue they wear farther north. On the 4th of February, at noon, we passed through Umeå, and congratulated ourselves on getting below the southern limit of the Lapland climate. There is nothing to say about these towns; they are mere villages with less than a thousand inhabitants each, and no peculiar interest, either local or historical, attaching to any of them. We have slept in Luleå, and Piteå, and dined in Umeå,—and further my journal saith not.

The 5th, however, was a day to be noticed. We started from Angersjö, with a violent snow-storm blowing in our teeth—thermometer at zero. Our road entered the hilly country of Norrland, where we found green forests, beautiful little dells, pleasant valleys, and ash and beech intermingled with the monotonous but graceful purple birch. We were overwhelmed with gusts of fine snow shaken from the trees as we passed. Blinding white clouds swept the road, and once again we heard the howl of the wind among boughs that were free to toss. At Afwa, which we reached at one o'clock, we found a pale, weak, sickly young Swede, with faded moustaches, who had decided to remain there until next day. This circumstance induced us to go on, but after we had waited half an hour and were preparing to start, the weather being now ten times worse than before, he announced his resolution to start also. He had drunk four large glasses of milk and two cups of coffee during the half hour.

We went ahead, breaking through drifts of loose snow which overtopped our sleds, and lashed by the furious wind, which drove full in our faces. There were two or three plows at work, but we had no benefit from them, so long as we were not directly in their wake. Up and down went our way, over dark hills and through valleys wild with the storm, and ending in chaos as they opened toward the Bothnian Gulf. Hour after hour passed by, the storm still increased, and the snow beat in our eyes so that we were completely blinded. It was impossible to keep them open, and yet the moment we shut them the lashes began to freeze together. I had a heavy weight of ice on my lids, and long icicles depending from every corner of my beard. Yet our frozen noses appeared to be much improved by the exposure, and began to give promise of healing without leaving a red blotch as a lasting record of what they had endured. We finally gave up all attempts to see or to guide the horse, but plunged along at random through the chaos, until the postillion piloted our baggage-sled into the inn-yard of Onska, and our horse followed it. The Swede was close upon our heels, but I engaged a separate room, so that we were freed from the depressing influence of his company. He may have been the best fellow in the world, so far as his heart was concerned, but was too weak in the knees to be an agreeable associate. There was no more stiffness of fibre in him than in a wet towel, and I would as soon wear a damp shirt as live in the same room with such a man. After all, it is not strange that one prefers nerve and energy, even when they are dashed with a flavour of vice, to the negative virtues of a character too weak and insipid to be tempted.

Our inn, in this little Norrland village, was about as comfortable and as elegant as three-fourths of the hotels in Stockholm. The rooms were well furnished; none of the usual appliances were wanting; the attendance was all that could be desired ; the fare good and abundant, and the charges less than half of what would be demanded in the capital. Yet Stockholm, small as it is, claims to be for Sweden what Paris is to France, and its inhabitants look with an eye of compassion on those of the provinces. Norrland, in spite of its long winter, has a bracing, healthy climate, and had it not been for letters from home, facilities for studying Swedish, occasional recreation and the other attractions of a capital, I should have preferred waiting in some of those wild valleys for the spring to open. The people, notwithstanding their seclusion from the world, have a brighter and more intelligent look than the peasants of Uppland, and were there a liberal system of common school education in Sweden, the raw material here might be worked up into products alike honourable and useful to the country.

The Norrlanders seem to me to possess an indolent, almost phlegmatic temperament, and yet there are few who do not show a latent capacity for exertion. The latter trait, perhaps, is the true core and substance of their nature; the former is an overgrowth resulting from habits and circumstances. Like the peasants, or rather small farmers, further north, they are exposed to the risk of seeing their summer's labours rendered fruitless by a single night of frost. Such a catastrophe, which no amount of industry and foresight can prevent, recurring frequently (perhaps once in three years on an average), makes them indifferent, if not reckless; while that patience and cheerfulness which is an integral part of the Scandinavian as of the Saxon character, renders them contented and unrepining under such repeated disappointments. There is the stuff here for a noble people, although nature and a long course of neglect and misrule have done their best to destroy it.

The Norrlanders live simply, perhaps frugally, but there seems to be little real destitution among them. We saw sometimes in front of a church, a representation of a beggar with his hat in his hand, under which was an iron box, with an appeal to travellers to drop something in for the poor of the parish; but of actual beggars we found none. The houses, although small, are warm and substantial, mostly with double windows, and a little vestibule in front of the door, to create an intermediate temperature between the outer and inner air. The beds, even in many of the inns, are in the family room, but during the day are either converted into sofas or narrow frames which occupy but little space. At night, the bedstead is drawn out to the required breadth, single or double, as may be desired. The family room is always covered with a strong home-made rag carpet, the walls generally hung with colored prints and lithographs, illustrating religion or royalty, and as many greenhouse plants as the owner can afford to decorate the windows. I have seen, even beyond Umeå, some fine specimens of cactus, pelargonium, calla, and other exotics. It is singular that, with the universal passion of the Swedes for flowers and for music, they have produced no distinguished painters or composers—but, indeed, a Linnæus.

We spent the evening cosily in the stately inn's best room, with its white curtains, polished floor, and beds of sumptuous linen. The great clipper-plows were out early in the morning, to cut a path through the drifts of the storm, but it was nearly noon before the road was sufficiently cleared to enable us to travel. The temperature, by contrast with what we had so recently endured, seemed almost tropical—actually 25° above zero, with a soft, southern breeze, and patches of brilliant blue sky between the parting clouds. Our deliverance from the Arctic cold was complete.

CHAPTER XVI.

CONCLUSION OF THE ARCTIC TRIP.

On leaving Onska, we experienced considerable delay on account of the storm. The roads were drifted to such an extent that even the ploughs could not be passed through in many places, and the peasants were obliged to work with their broad wooden spades. The sky, however, was wholly clear and of a pure daylight blue, such as we had not seen for two months. The sun rode high in the firmament, like a strong healthy sun again, with some warmth in his beams as they struck our faces, and the air was all mildness and balm. It was heavenly, after our Arctic life. The country, too, boldly undulating, with fir-forested hills, green and warm in the sunshine, and wild, picturesque valleys sunk between, shining in their covering of snow, charmed us completely. Again we saw the soft blue of the distant ranges as they melted away behind each other, suggesting space, and light, and warmth. Give me daylight and sunshine, after all! Our Arctic trip seems like a long, long night full of splendid dreams, but yet night and not day.

On the road, we bought a quantity of the linen handkerchiefs of the country, at prices varying from twenty-five to forty cents a piece, according to the size and quality. The bedding, in all the inns, was of home-made linen, and I do not recollect an instance where it was not brought out, fresh and sweet from the press, for us. In this, as in all other household arrangements, the people are very tidy and cleanly though a little deficient as regards their own persons. Their clothing, however, is of a healthy substantial character, and the women consult comfort rather than ornament. Many of them wear cloth pantaloons under their petticoats, which, therefore, they are able to gather under their arms in wading through snow-drifts. I did not see a low-necked dress or a thin shoe north of Stockholm.

> "The damsel who trips at daybreak
> Is shod like a mountaineer."

Yet a sensible man would sooner take such a damsel to wife than any delicate Cinderella of the ball-room. I protest I lose all patience when I think of the habits of our American women, especially our country girls. If ever the Saxon race does deteriorate on our side of the Atlantic, as some ethnologists anticipate, it will be wholly their fault.

We stopped for the night at Hörnäs, and had a charming ride the next day among the hills and along the inlets of the Gulf. The same bold, picturesque scenery, which had appeared so dark and forbidding to us on our way north, now, under the spring-like sky, cheered and inspired us. At the station of Docksta, we found the peasant girls scrubbing the outer steps, barefooted. At night, we occupied our old quarters at Weda, on the Angermann river. The next morning the temperature was 25° above zero, and at noon rose to 39°. It was delightful to travel once more with cap-lappets turned up, fur collar turned down, face and neck free, and hands bare. On our second stage we had an overgrown, insolent boy for postillion, who persisted in driving slow, and refused to let us pass him. He finally became impertinent, whereupon Braisted ran forward and turned his horse out of the road, so that I could drive past. The boy then seized my horse by the head; B. pitched him into a snow-bank, and we took the lead. We had not gone far before we took the road to Hernösand, through mistake, and afterwards kept it through spite, thus adding about seven miles to our day's journey. A stretch of magnificent dark-green forests brought us to a narrow strait which separates the island of Hernösand from the main land. The ice was already softening, and the upper layer repeatedly broke through under us.

Hernösand is a pretty town, of about 2000 inhabitants, with a considerable commerce. It is also the capital of the most northern bishopric of Sweden. The church, on an eminence above the town, is, next to that of Skelefteå, the finest we saw in the north. We took a walk while breakfast was preparing, and in the space of twenty minutes saw all there was to be seen. By leaving the regular road, however, we had incurred a delay of two hours, which did not add to our amiability. Therefore, when the postillion, furiously angry now as well as insolent, came in to threaten us with legal prosecution in case we did not pay him heavy damages for what he called an assault, I cut the discussion short by driving him out of the room, and that was the last we saw of him. We reached Fjäl as the moon rose,—a globe of silver fire in a perfect violet sky. Two merry boys, who sang and shouted the whole way, drove us like the wind around the bay to Wifsta. The moonlight was as bright as the Arctic noonday, and the snowy landscape flashed and glittered under its resplendent shower. From the last hill we saw Sundsvall, which lay beneath us, with its wintry roofs, like a city of ivory and crystal, shining for us with the fairy promise of a warm supper and a good bed.

On the 9th, we drove along the shores of the magnificent bay of Sundsvall. Six vessels lay frozen in, at a considerable distance from the town. Near the southern extremity of the bay, we passed the village of Svartvik, which, the postillion informed us, is all owned by one person, who carries on ship-building. The appearance of the place justified his statements. The labourers' houses were mostly new, all built on precisely the same model, and with an unusual air of comfort and neatness. In the centre of the village stood a handsome white church, with a clock tower, and near it the parsonage and school-house. At the foot of the slope were the yards, where several vessels were on the stocks, and a number of sturdy workmen busy at their several tasks. There was an air of "associated labour" and the "model lodging-house" about the whole place, which was truly refreshing to behold, except a touch of barren utilitarianism in the cutting away of the graceful firs left from the forest and thus depriving the houses of all shade and ornament. We met many wood-teams, hauling knees and spars, and were sorely troubled to get out of their way. Beyond the bay, the hills of Norrland ceased, sinking into those broad monotonous undulations which extend nearly all the way to

Stockholm. Gardens with thriving fruit-trees now began to be more frequent, giving evidence of a climate where man has a right to live. I doubt whether it was ever meant that the human race should settle in any zone so frigid that fruit cannot ripen.

Thenceforth we had the roughest roads which were ever made upon a foundation of snow. The increase in travel and in the temperature of the air, and most of all, the short, loosely-attached sleds used to support the ship-timber, had worn them into a succession of holes, channels, and troughs, in and out of which we thumped from morning till night. On going down hill, the violent shocks frequently threw our runners completely into the air, and the wrench was so great that it was a miracle how the sled escaped fracture. All the joints, it is true, began to work apart, and the ash shafts bent in the most ticklish way; but the rough little conveyance which had already done us such hard service held out gallantly to the end. We reached Mo Myskie on the second night after leaving Sundsvall, and I was greeted with "*Salaam aleikoom, ya Sidi!*" from the jolly old Tripolitan landlord. There was an unusual amount of travel northward on the following day, and we were detained at every station, so that it was nearly midnight before we reached the extortionate inn at Gefle. The morning dawned with a snow-storm, but we were within 120 miles of Stockholm, and drove in the teeth of it to Elfkarleby. The renowned cascades of the Dal were by no means what I expected, but it was at least a satisfaction to see living water, after the silent rivers and fettered rapids of the North.

The snow was now getting rapidly thinner. So scant

was it on the exposed Upsala plain that we fully expected being obliged to leave our sleds on the way. Even before reaching Upsala, our postillions chose the less-travelled field-roads whenever they led in the same direction, and beyond that town we were charged additional post-money for the circuits we were obliged to make to keep our runners on the snow. On the evening of the 13th we reached Rotebro, only fourteen miles from Stockholm, and the next morning, in splendid sunshine, drove past Haga park and palace, into the North-Gate, down the long Drottninggatan and up to Kahn's Hotel, where we presented our sleds to the *valet-de-place*, pulled off our heavy boots, threw aside our furs for the remainder of the winter, and sat down to read the pile of letters and papers which Herr Kahn brought us. It was precisely two months since our departure in December, and in that time we had performed a journey of 2200 miles, 250 of which were by reindeer, and nearly 500 inside of the Arctic Circle. Our frozen noses had peeled off, and the new skin showed no signs of the damage they had sustained—so that we had come out of the fight not only without a scar, but with a marked increase of robust vitality.

I must confess, however, that, interesting as was the journey, and happily as we endured its exposures, I should not wish to make it again. It is well to see the North, even *after* the South; but, as there is no one who visits the tropics without longing ever after to return again, so, I imagine, there is no one who, having once seen a winter inside the Arctic Circle, would ever wish to see another. In spite of the warm, gorgeous, and ever-changing play of colour hovering over the path of the unseen sun, in spite of the dazzling auroral dances and the magical transfiguration of the forests, the absence of true daylight and of all signs of warmth and life exercises at last a depressing influence on the spirits. The snow, so beautiful while the sunrise-setting illumination lasts, wears a ghastly monotony at all other times, and the air, so exhilarating, even at the lowest temperature, becomes an enemy to be kept out, when you know its terrible power to benumb and destroy. To the native of a warmer zone, this presence of an unseen destructive force in nature weighs like a nightmare upon the mind. The inhabitants of the North also seem to undergo a species of hibernation, as well as the animals. Nearly half their time is passed in sleep; they are silent in comparison with the natives of the other parts of the world; there is little exuberant gaiety and cheerfulness, but patience, indifference, apathy almost. Aspects of nature which appear to be hostile to man, often develop and bring into play his best energies, but there are others which depress and paralyse his powers. I am convinced that the extreme North, like the Tropics, is unfavourable to the best mental and physical condition of the human race. The proper zone of man lies between 30° and 55° North.

To one who has not an unusual capacity to enjoy the experiences of varied travel, I should not recommend such a journey. With me, the realization of a long-cherished desire, the sense of novelty, the opportunity for contrasting extremes, and the interest with which the people inspired me, far outweighed all inconveniences and privations. In fact, I was not fully aware of the gloom and cold in which I had lived until we returned far enough southward to enjoy eight hours of sunshine, and a temperature above the freezing point. It was a second birth into a living world. Although we had experienced little positive suffering from the intense cold, except on the return from Muoniovara to Haparanda, our bodies had already accommodated themselves to a low temperature, and the sudden transition to 30° above zero came upon us like the warmth of June. My friend, Dr. Kane, once described to me the comfort he felt when the mercury rose to 7° below zero, making it pleasant to be on deck. The circumstance was then incomprehensible to me, but is now quite plain. I can also the better realise the terrible sufferings of himself and his men, exposed to a storm in a temperature of—47°, when the same degree of cold, with a very light wind, turned my own blood to ice.

Most of our physical sensations are relative, and the mere enumeration of so many degrees of heat or cold gives no idea of their effect upon the system. I should have frozen at home in a temperature which I found very comfortable in Lapland, with my solid diet of meat and butter, and my garments of reindeer. The following is a correct scale of the physical effect of cold, calculated for the latitude of 65° to 70° North:

15° *above zero*—Unpleasantly warm.

Zero—Mild and agreeable.

10° *below zero*—Pleasantly fresh and bracing

20° *below zero*—Sharp, but not severely cold. Keep your fingers and toes in motion, and rub your nose occasionally.

30° *below zero*—Very cold; take particular care of your nose and extremities: eat the fattest food, and plenty of it

40° *below*—Intensely cold; keep awake at all hazards, muffle up to the eyes, and test your circulation frequently, that it may not stop somewhere before you know it.

50° *below*—A struggle for life.

* We kept a record of the temperature from the time we left Sundsvall (Dec. 21) until our return to Stockholm. As a matter of interest, I subjoin it, changing the degrees from Reaumur to Fahrenheit. We tested the thermometer repeatedly on the way, and found it very generally reliable, although in extremely low temperature it showed from one to two degrees more than a spirit thermometer. The observations were taken at from 9 to 8 A. M., 12 to 2 P. M., and 7 to 11 P. M, whenever it was possible.

		Morning.	*Noon.*	*Evening.*
December 21		+ 6	..	zero.
" 22		+ 6	..	— 3
" 23		—22	—29	—22
" 24		— 6	—22	—22
" 25		—35	—38	mer. frozen.
" 26		—30	—24	—31
" 27 (storm)		—18	—18	—18
" 28 (storm)		zero.	zero.	zero.
" 29		— 6	—13	—13
" 30		— 6	—13	—22
" 31 (storm)		— 3	+ 9	+ 9
January	1, 1857	+ 3	+ 3	+ 3
"	2	— 6	— 6	— 6
"	3	—30	—22	—22
"	4	—18	..	—22
"	5	—31	—30	—33
"	6	—20	— 4	zero.
"	7	+ 4	+18	+25
"	8	+18	..	—11
"	9	—28	—44	—44
"	10 (storm)	— 5	..	— 2
"	11 (storm)	— 2	zero.	— 5

		Morning.	Noon.	Evening.
January	12, 1857 (storm)	− 5	− 4	− 4
"	13 (storm)	+ 5	+ 5	+ 5
"	14	− 6	−13	− 6
"	15	− 8	−13	−33
"	16	− 9	−10	−11
"	17 (fog)	zero.	zero.	zero.
"	18	−10	−18	−23
"	19 (storm)	− 3	− 3	− 9
"	20	+20	..	+ 6
"	21	− 4	zero.	zero.
"	22	+ 2	− 6	−13
"	23	−13	− 3	−13
"	24	−15	−22	−44
"	25 mer. froz.	−50?	−42	mer. frozen
"	26	−45	−35	−39
"	27	frozen −47?	−45	−35
"	28	frozen −49?	−47	−44
"	29	−47?	−43	−43
"	30	−27	−11	−35
"	31	−17	−16	− 7
February	1	zero.	− 9	−13
"	2	+ 2	+ 6	zero.
"	3	zero.	zero.	zero.
"	4	− 9	zero.	− 3
"	5 (storm)	+ 3	+ 3	+ 3
"	6	+25	+25	+18
"	7	+14	+18	+25
"	8	+25	+39	+22
"	9	+ 5	+22	+16
"	10	+25	+37	+37
"	11	+34	+34	+32
"	12	+32	+37	+23
"	13	+16	+30	+21
"	14	+25	+30	+25

CHAPTER XVII.

LIFE IN STOCKHOLM.

The Swedes are proud of Stockholm, and justly so. No European capital, except Constantinople, can boast such picturesque beauty of position, and none whatever affords so great a range of shifting yet ever lovely aspects. Travellers are fond of calling it, in the imitative nomenclature of commonplace, the "Venice of the North"—but it is no Venice. It is not that swan of the Adriatic, singing her death-song in the purple sunset, but a northern eaglet, nested on the islands and rocky shores of the pale green Mälar lake. The *Stad*, or city proper, occupies three islands, which lie in the mouth of the narrow strait, by which the waters of the lake, after having come a hundred miles from the westward, and washed in their course the shores of thirteen hundred islands, pour themselves into the outer archipelago which is claimed by the Baltic Sea. On the largest of these islands, according to tradition, Agne, King of Sweden, was strangled with his own golden chain, by the Finnish princess Skiolfa, whom he had taken prisoner. This was sixteen hundred years ago, and a thousand years later, Bir ger Jarl, on the same spot, built the stronghold which was the seed out of which Stockholm has grown.

This island, and the adjoining *Riddarholm*, or Island of the Knights, contain all the ancient historic landmarks of the city, and nearly all of its most remarkable buildings. The towers of the Storkyrka and the Riddarholm's Church lift themselves high into the air; the dark red mass of the *Riddarhus*, or House of Nobles, and the white turrets and quadrangles of the penitentiary are conspicuous among the old white, tile-roofed blocks of houses; while, rising above the whole, the most prominent object in every view of Stockholm, is the *Slot*, or Royal Palace. This is one of the noblest royal residences in Europe. Standing on an immense basement terrace of granite, its grand quadrangle of between three and four hundred feet square, with wings (resembling, in general design, the Pitti Palace at Florence), is elevated quite above the rest of the city, which it crowns as with a mural diadem. The chaste and simple majesty of this edifice, and its admirable proportions, are a perpetual gratification to the eye, which is always drawn to it, as a central point, and thereby prevented from dwelling on whatever inharmonious or unsightly features there may be in the general view.

Splendid bridges of granite connect the island with the northern and southern suburbs, each of which is much greater n extent than the city proper. The palace fronts directly upon the *Norrbro*, or Northern Bridge, the great thoroughfare of Stockholm, which leads to the Square of Gustavus Adolphus, flanked on either side by the palace of the Crown Prince and the Opera House. The northern suburb is the fashionable quarter, containing all the newest streets and the handsomest private residences. The ground rises gradually from the water, and as very little attention is paid to grading, the streets follow the undulations of the low hills over which they spread, rising to the windmills on the outer heights and sinking into the hollows between. The southern suburb, however, is a single long hill, up the steep side of which the houses climb, row after row, until they reach the Church of St. Catherine, which crowns the very summit. In front of the city (that is eastward, and toward the Baltic), lie two other islands, connected by bridges with the northern suburb. Still beyond is the Djurgård, or Deer-Park, a singularly picturesque island, nearly the whole of which is occupied by a public park, and the summer villas of the wealthy Stockholmers. Its natural advantages are superior to those of any other park in Europe. Even in April, when there was scarcely a sign of spring, its cliffs of grey rock, its rolling lawns of brown grass, and its venerable oaks, with their iron trunks and gnarled, contorted boughs, with blue glimpses of ice-free water on all sides, attracted hundreds of visitors daily.

The streets of Stockholm are, with but two or three exceptions, narrow and badly paved. The municipal regulations in regard to them appear to be sadly deficient. They are quite as filthy as those of New-York, and the American reader will therefore have some idea of their horrid condition. A few *trottoirs* have been recently introduced, but even in the Drottning-gatan, the principal street, they are barely wide enough for two persons to walk abreast. The pavements are rough, slipperry, and dangerous both to man and beast. I have no doubt that the great number of cripples in Stockholm is owing to this cause. On the other hand, the houses are models of solidity and stability. They are all of stone, or brick stuccoed over, with staircases of stone or iron, wood being prohibited by law, and roofs of copper, slate or tiles. In fact, the Swedes have singularly luxurious ideas concerning roofs, spending much more money upon them, proportionately, than on the house itself. You even see wooden shanties with copper roofs, got up regardless of expense. The houses are well lighted (which is quite necessary in the dark streets), and supplied with double windows against the cold. The air-tight Russian stove is universal. It has the advantage of keeping up sufficient warmth with a very small supply of fuel, but at the expense of ventilation. I find nothing yet equal to the old-fashioned fire-place in this respect, though I must confess I prefer the Russian stove to our hot-air furnaces. Carpets are very common in Sweden, and thus the dwellings have an air of warmth and comfort which is not found in Germany and other parts of the Continent. The arrangements for sleeping and washing are tolerable, though scanty, as compared with England, but the cleanliness of Swedish houses makes amends for many deficiencies.

The manner of living in Stockholm, nevertheless, is not very agreeable to the stranger. There is no hotel, except Kahn's, where one can obtain both beds and meals. The practice is to hire rooms, generally with the privilege of having your coffee in the morning, and to get your meals at a restaurant, of which there are many, tolerably cheap and not particularly good. Even Davison's, the best and most fashionable, has but an ordinary *cuisine*. Rooms are quite dear—particularly during our sojourn, when the Diet was in session and the city crowded with country visitors—and the inclusive expenses of living were equal to Berlin and greater than in Paris. I found that it cost just about as much to be stationary here, as to travel with post-horses in the Northern provinces. The Swedes generally have a cup of coffee on getting out of bed, or before, a substantial breakfast at nine, dinner at three, and tea in the evening. The wealthier families dine an hour or two later, but the crowds at the restaurants indicate the prevailing time. Dinner, and frequently breakfast, is prefaced with a *smörgås* (butter-goose), consisting of anchovies, pickled herrings, cheese and brandy. Soup which is generally sweet, comes in the middle and sometimes at the end of dinner, and the universal dessert is preserved fruit covered with whipped cream. I have had occasion to notice the fondness of the Swedes for sugar, which some persons seem to apply to almost every dish, except fish and oysters. I have often seen them season crab soup with powdered sugar. A favorite dish is raw salmon, buried in the earth until it is quite sodden—a great delicacy, they say, but I have not yet been hungry enough to eat it. Meat, which is abundant, is rarely properly cooked, and game, of which Sweden has a great variety, is injured by being swamped in sauces. He must be very fastidious, however, who cannot live passably well in Stockholm, especially if he has frequent invitations to dine with private families, many of whom have very excellent cooks.

My Swedish friends all said, "You should see Stockholm

in summer! You have passed the worst part of the whole year among us, and you leave just when our fine days begin." I needed no assurance, however, of the summer charm of the place. In those long, golden evenings, which give place to an unfading twilight, when the birch is a network of silver and green, and the meadows are sown with the bright wild flowers of the North, those labyrinths of land and water must be truly enchanting. But were the glories of the Northern Summer increased tenfold, I could not make my home where such a price must be paid for them. From the time of our arrival, in February, until towards the close of April, the weather was of that kind which aggravates one to the loss of all patience. We had dull, raw, cloudy skies, a penetrating, unnerving, and depressing atmosphere, mud under foot, alternating with slushy snow,—in short, everything that is disagreeable in winter, without its brisk and bracing qualities. I found this season much more difficult to endure than all the cold of Lapland, and in spite of pleasant society and the charms of rest after a fatiguing journey, our sojourn in Stockholm was for a time sufficiently tedious.

At first, we lived a rather secluded life in our rooms in the Beridarebansgatan, in the northern suburb, devoting ourselves principally to gymnastics and the study of the Swedish language,—both of which can be prosecuted to more advantage in Stockholm than anywhere else. For, among the distinguished men of Sweden may be reckoned Ling, the inventor of what may be termed anatomical gymnastics. His system not only aims at reducing to a science the muscular development of the body, but, by means of both active and passive movements, at reaching the seat of disease and stimulating the various organs to healthy action. In the former of these objects, Ling has certainly succeeded; there is no other system of muscular training that will bear comparison with his; and if he has to some extent failed in the latter, it is because, with the enthusiasm of a man possessed by a new discovery, he claimed too much. His successor, Prof. Branting, possesses equal enthusiasm, and his faith in gymnastics, as a panacea for all human infirmities, is most unbounded. The institution under his charge is supported by Government, and, in addition to the officers of the army and navy, who are obliged to make a complete gymnastic course, is largely attended by invalids of all ages and classes.

Neither of us required the system as a medical application. I wished to increase the girth of my chest, somewhat diminished by a sedentary life, and Braisted needed a safety-valve for his surplus strength. However, the professor, by dint of much questioning, ascertained that one of us was sometimes afflicted with cold feet, and the other with head-aches, and thereupon clapped us both upon the sick list. On entering the hall, on the first morning of our attendance, a piece of paper containing the movements prescribed for our individual cases, was stuck in our bosoms. On inspecting the lists, we found we had ten movements apiece, and no two of them alike. What they were we could only dimly guess from such cabalistic terms as "*Stødgångst*," "*Krhalfligg*," "*Simhång*," or "*Høgstrgrsitt*." The hall, about eighty feet in length by thirty in height, was furnished with the usual appliances for gymnastic exercises. Some fifty or sixty patients were present, part of whom were walking up and down the middle passage with an air of great solemnity, while the others, gathered in various little groups on either side, appeared to be undergoing uncouth forms of torture There was no voluntary exercise, if I except an old gentleman in a black velvet coat, who repeatedly suspended himself by the hands, head downwards, and who died of apoplexy not long afterwards; every one was being exercised upon. Here, a lathy young man, bent sideways over a spar, was struggling, with a very red face, to right himself, while a stout teacher held him down; there, a corpulent gentleman, in the hands of five robust assistants, was having his body violently revolved upon the base of his hip joints, as if they were trying to unscrew him from his legs; and yonder again, an individual, suspended by his arms from a cross-bar, had his feet held up and his legs stretched apart by another, while a third pounded vigorously with closed fists upon his seat of honour. Now and then a prolonged yell, accompanied with all sorts of burlesque variations, issued from the throats of the assembly. The object of this was at first not clear to me, but I afterwards discovered that the full use of the lungs was considered by Ling a very important part of the exercises. Altogether, it was a peculiar scene, and not without a marked grotesque character.

On exhibiting my *matsedel*, or "bill of fare," to the first teacher who happened to be disengaged, I received my first movement, which consisted in being held with my back against a post, while I turned my body from side to side against strong resistance, employing the muscles of the chest only. I was then told to walk for five minutes before taking the second movement. It is unnecessary to recapitulate the various contortions I was made to perform; suffice it to say, that I felt very sore after them, which Professor Branting considered a promising sign, and that, at the end of a month, I was taken off the sick list and put among the *friskas*, or healthy patients, to whom more and severer movements, in part active, are allotted. This department was under the special charge of Baron Vegesach, an admirable teacher, and withal a master of fencing with the bayonet, a branch of defensive art which the Swedes have the honour of originating. The drill of the young officers in bayonet exercise was one of the finest things of the kind I ever saw. I prospered so well under the Baron's tuition, that at the end of the second month I was able to climb a smooth mast, to run up ropes with my hands, and to perform various other previous impossibilities, while my chest had increased an inch and a half in circumference, the addition being solid muscle.

During the time of my attendance I could not help but notice the effect of the discipline upon the other patients, especially the children. The weak and listless gradually straightened themselves; the pale and sallow took colour and lively expression; the crippled and paralytic recovered the use of their limbs; in short, all, with the exception of two or three hypochondriacs, exhibited a very marked improvement. The cheerfulness and geniality which pervaded the company, and of which Professor Branting himself was the best example, no doubt assisted the cure. All, both teachers and pupils, met on a platform of the most absolute equality, and willingly took turns in lending a hand wherever it was needed. I have had my feet held up by a foreign ambassador, while a pair of Swedish counts applied the proper degree of resistance to the muscles of my arms and shoulders. The result of my observation and experience was, that Ling's system of physical education is undoubtedly the best in the world, and that, as a remedial agent in all cases of congenital weakness or deformity, as well as in those diseases which arise from a deranged circulation, its value can scarcely be over-estimated. It may even afford indirect assistance in more serious organic diseases, but I do not believe that it is of much service in those cases where chemical agencies are generally employed. Professor Branting, however, asserts that it is a specific for all diseases whatsoever, including consumption, malignant fevers, and venereal affections. One thing at least is certain—that in an age when physical training is most needed and most neglected, this system deserves to be introduced into every civilised country, as an indispensable branch in the education of youth.

I found the Swedish language as easy to read as it is difficult to speak correctly. The simplicity of its structure, which differs but slightly from English, accounts for the former quality, while the peculiar use of the definite article as a terminal syllable, attached to the noun, is a great impediment to fluent speaking. The passive form of the verb also requires much practice before it becomes familiar, and the mode of address in conversation is awkward and inconvenient beyond measure. The word *you*, or its correspondent, is never used, except in speaking to inferiors; wherever it occurs in other languages, the title of the person addressed must be repeated; as, for example: "How is the Herr Justizrad? I called at the Herr Justizrâd's house this morning, but the Herr Justizrâd was not at home." Some of the more progressive Swedes are endeavouring to do away with this absurdity, by substituting the second person plural, *ni*, which is already used in literature, but even they only dare to use it in their own private circle. The Swedes, especially in Stockholm, speak with a peculiar drawl and singing accent, exactly similar to that which is often heard in Scotland. It is very inferior to the natural, musical rhythm of Spanish, to which, in its vocalisation, Swedish has a great resemblance. Except Finnish, which is music itself, it is the most melodious of northern languages, and the mellow flow of its poetry is often scarcely surpassed by the Italian. The infinitive verb always ends in *a*, and the language is full of soft, gliding iambics, which give a peculiar grace to its poetry.

It is rather singular that the Swedish prose, in point of finish and elegance, is far behind the Swedish poetry. One cause of this may be, that it is scarcely more than fifty years since the prose writers of the country began to use their native language. The works of Linnæus, Swedenborg, and other authors of the past century must now be translated into Swedish. Besides, there are two prose dialects—a conversational and a declamatory, the latter being much more artificial and involved than the former. All public addresses, as well as prose documents of a weighty or serious character, must be spoken or written in this pompous and antiquated style, owing to which, naturally, the country is almost destitute of orators. But the poets,—especially men of the sparkling fancy of Bellman, or the rich lyrical inspiration of Tegnér, are not to be fettered by such conventionalities; and they have given the verse of Sweden an ease, and grace, and elegance, which one vainly seeks in its prose. In Stockholm, the French taste, so visible in the manners of the people, has also affected the language, and a number of French words and forms of expression, which have filtered through society, from the higher to the lower classes, are now in general use. The spelling, however, is made to conform to Swedish pronunciation, and one is amused at finding on placards such words as "*trottoar*," "*salong*," and "*paviljong*."

No country is richer in song-literature than Sweden. The popular songs and ballads of the different provinces, wedded to airs as original and characteristic as the words, number many hundreds. There are few Swedes who cannot sing, and I doubt whether any country in Europe would be able to furnish so many fine voices. Yet the taste for what is foreign and unaccustomed rules, and the minstrels of the cafes and the Djurgård are almost without exception German. Latterly, two or three bands of native singers have been formed, who give concerts devoted entirely to the country melodies of Sweden ; and I believe they have been tolerably successful.

In these studies, relieved occasionally by rambles over the hills, whenever there was an hour's sunshine, and by occasional evenings with Swedish, English, and American friends, we passed the months of March and April, waiting for the tardy spring. Of the shifting and picturesque views which

Stockholm presents to the stranger's eye, from whatever point he beholds her, we never wearied; but we began at last to tire of our ice-olation, and to look forward to the reopening of the Gotha Canal, as a means of escape. Day after day it was a new satisfaction to behold the majestic palace crowning the island-city and looking far and wide over the frozen lakes; the tall, slender spire of the Riddarholm, soaring above the ashes of Charles XII. and Gustavus Adolphus, was always a welcome sight; but we had seen enough of the hideous statues which ornament the public squares, (Charles XII. not among them, and the imbecile Charles XIII. occupying the best place); we grew tired of the monotonous perambulators on the Forrbro, and the tameness and sameness of Stockholm life in winter; and therefore hailed the lengthening days which heralded our deliverance.

As to the sights of the capital, are they not described in the guide-books? The champion of the Reformation lies in his chapel, under a cloud of his captured banners: opposite to him, the magnificent madman of the North, with hundreds of Polish and Russian ensigns rustling above his heads. In the royal armory you see the sword and the bloody shirt of the one, the bullet-pierced hat and cloak of the other, still coated with the mud of the trench at Fredrickshall. There are robes and weapons of the other Carls and Gustavs, but the splendour of Swedish history is embodied in these two names, and in that of Gustavus Vasa, who lies entombed in the old cathedral at Upsala. When I had grasped their swords, and the sabre of Czar Peter, captured at Narva, I felt that there were no other relics in Sweden which could make my heart throb a beat the faster.

CHAPTER XVIII.

MANNERS AND MORALS OF STOCKHOLM.

As a people, the Swedes are very hospitable, and particularly sc toward foreigners. There is perhaps no country in Europe where travellers are treated with so much kindness and allowed so many social privileges. This is fortunate, as the conventionalities of the country are more rigid than the laws of the Medes and Persians. Nothing excites greater scandal than an infraction of the numberless little formalities with which the descendants of the honest, spontaneous, impulsive old Scandinavians have, somehow or other, allowed themselves to be fettered, and were not all possible allowance made for the stranger, he would have but a dismal time of it. Notwithstanding these habits have become a second nature, they are still a false nature, and give a painfully stiff and constrained air to society. The Swedes pride themselves on being the politest people in Europe. Voltaire called them the "Frenchmen of the North," and they are greatly flattered by the epithet. But how much better, to call themselves *Swedes ?*—to preserve the fine, manly characteristics of their ancient stock, rather than imitate a people so alien to them in blood, in character, and in antecedents.

Those meaningless social courtesies which sit well enough upon the gay, volatile, mercurial Frenchman, seem absurd affectations when practiced by the tall, grave, sedate Scandinavian. The intelligent Swedes feel this, but they are powerless to make headway against the influence of a court which was wholly French, even before Bernadotte's time. "We are a race of apes," said one of them to me bitterly. Gustavus III. was thoroughly French in his tastes, but the ruin of Swedish nationality in Stockholm was already commenced when he ascended the throne.

Stockholm manners, at present, are a curious mixture of English and French, the latter element, of course, being predominant. In costume, the gentlemen are English, with exaggeration. Nowhere are to be seen such enormously tall and stiff black chimney-pots (misnamed *hats*), nowhere such straight-cut overcoats, descending to the very heels. You might stick all the men you see into pasteboard cards, like a row of pins, so precisely are they clothed upon the same model. But when you meet one of these grim, funereal figures, he pulls off his hat with a politeness which is more than French; he keeps it off, perhaps, while he is speaking; you shake hands and accept his invitation to enter his house. After you are within, he greets you a second time with the same ceremonies, as if you had then first met; he says, "*Tak for sist!*" (equivalent to; "thank you for the pleasure of your company the last time we met!") and, after your visit is over, you part with equal formality. At dinner the guests stand gravely around the table with clasped hands, before sitting down. This is repeated on rising, after which they bow to each other and shake hands with the host and hostess.

Formerly they used to say "I thank you for the meal," a custom still retained in Denmark and Norway. Not long ago the guests were obliged to make a subsequent visit of ceremony to thank the host for his entertainment, and he was obliged to invite them all to a second dinner, in consequence thereof; so that giving one dinner always involved giving two. Fortunately the obligation was cancelled by the second, or the visits and dinners might have gone on alternately, *ad infinitum.*

At dinners and evening parties, white gloves and white cravats are invariably worn, and generally white vests. The same custom is observed at funerals, even the drivers of the hearse and carriages being furnished with resplendent white gloves for the occasion. I have a horror of white cravats, and took advantage of the traveller's privilege to wear a black one. I never could understand why, in England, where the boundaries of caste are so distinctly marked, a gentleman's full dress should be his servant's livery. The chimney-pots are no protection to the head in raw or very cold weather, and it required no little courage in me to appear in fur or felt. "I wish I could wear such a comfortable hat," said a Swede to me; "but I *dare not*; you are a traveller, and it is permitted; but a Swede would lose his position in society, if he were to do so." Another gentleman informed me that his own sisters refused to appear in the streets with him, because he wore a cap. A former English Consul greatly shocked the people by carrying home his own marketing. A few gentlemen have independence enough to set aside, in their own houses, some of the more disagreeable features of this conventionalism, and the success of two or three, who held weekly soirees through the winter, on a more free and unrestrained plan, may in the end restore somewhat of naturalness and spontaneity to the society of Stockholm.

The continual taking off of your hat to everybody you know, is a great annoyance to many strangers. A lift of the hat, as in Germany, is not snfficient. You must remove it entirely, and hold it in the air a second or two before you replace it. King Oscar once said to an acquaintance of mine, who was commiserating him for being obliged to keep his hat off, the whole length of the Drottning-gatan, in a violent snow-storm: "You are quite right; it was exceedingly disagreeable, and I could not help wishing that instead of being king of Sweden, I were king of Thibet, where, according to Huc, the polite salutation is simply to stick out your tongue." The consideration extended to foreigners is, I am told, quite withdrawn after they become residents; so that, as an Englishman informed me, Stockholm is much more pleasant the first year than the second. The principle, on the whole, is about the same as governs English, and most American society, only in Sweden its tyranny is more severely felt, on account of the French imitations which have been engrafted upon it.

I do not wish to be understood as saying a word in censure of that genial courtesy which is characteristic of the Swedes, not less of the *bonder*, or country farmers, than of the nobility. They are by nature a courteous people, and if, throughout the country, something of the primness and formality of ancient manners has been preserved, it the rather serves to give a quaint and picturesque grace to society. The affectation of French manners applies prin-

10*

cipally to the capital, which, both in manners and morals, can by no means be taken as a standard for the whole country. The Swedes are neither licentious, nor extravagantly over-mannered: the Stockholmers are both. During the whole of our journey to Lapland, we were invariably treated with a courtesy which bordered on kindness, and had abundant opportunities of noticing the general amenity which exists in the intercourse even of the poorest classes. The only really rude people we saw, were travelling traders, especially those from the capital, who thought to add to their importance by a little swaggering.

I recollect hearing of but a single instance in which the usual world-wide rules of hospitality were grossly violated. This occurred to an English traveller, who spent some time in the interior of the country. While taking tea one evening with a prominent family of the province, he happened to make use of his thumb and fore-finger in helping himself to a lump of sugar. The mistress of the house immediately sent out the servant, who reappeared after a short time with another sugar-bowl, filled with fresh lumps. Noticing this, the traveller, in order to ascertain whether his harmless deviation from Swedish customs had really contaminated the whole sugar-bowl, sweetened his second cup in the same manner. The result was precisely the same: the servant was again sent out, and again returned with a fresh supply. The traveller, thereupon, coolly walked to the stove, opened the door, and threw in his cup, saucer, and tea-spoon, affecting to take it for granted that they never could be used again.

Speaking of King Oscar reminds me that I should not

fail to say a word about this liberal and enlightened monarch. There is probably no king in Europe at present, who possesses such extensive acquirements, or is animated by a more genuine desire for the good of his kingdom. The slow progress which Sweden has made in introducing needful reforms is owing to the conservative spirit of the nobility and the priesthood, who possess half the legislative power. I do not believe there is a greater enemy to progress than an established church. Oscar is deservedly popular throughout Sweden, and I wish I could believe that his successor will exhibit equal intelligence and liberality. During my stay I saw all the members of the Royal Family frequently, and once had an informal self-presentation to the whole of them. I was descending the stairway of Kahn's Hotel one afternoon, when a tall, black-bearded, Frenchy gentleman coming up, brushed so close to me in the narrow passage that he received the full benefit of a cloud of smoke which I was ejaculating. It was the Crown Prince, as a servant whispered to me, but as my cigar was genuine Havana, and he is said to be a connoisseur of the article, there was no harm done. As I reached the street door a dragoon dashed up, preceding the carriages containing the Royal Family, who were coming to view Professor Enslen's panoramas. First, the Crown Princess, with her children; she bowed gracefully in answer to my greeting. The Princess Eugenia, a lady of twenty-seven, or thereabouts, with a thoroughly cheerful and amiable face, came next and nodded, smiling. With her was the Queen, a daughter of Eugene Beauharnais, a handsome woman for her years, with the dark hair and eyes of her grandmother, Josephine. King

Oscar followed, at the head of a company of officers and nobles, among whom was his second son, Prince Oscar, the handsomest young man in Stockholm. He wore his Admiral's uniform, and made me a naval salute as he passed. The King is about medium height, with a symmetrical head, a bold, finely-cut nose, keen, intelligent eyes, and a heavy grey moustache. There was something gallant, dashing, and manly in his air, despite his fifty-seven years. He gave me the impression of an honest, energetic and thoroughly accomplished man; and this is the character he bears throughout Sweden, except with a small class, who charge him with being insincere, and too much under the influence of the Queen, against whom, however, they can find no charge, except that of her Catholicism.

I was sorry to notice, not only in Stockholm, but more or less throughout Sweden, a spirit of detraction in regard to everything Swedish. Whenever I mentioned with admiration the name of a distinguished Swede, I was almost always sure to hear, in return, some disparaging remark, or a story to his disadvantage. Yet, singularly enough, the Swedes are rather sensitive to foreign criticism, seeming to reserve for themselves the privilege of being censorious. No amount of renown, nor even the sanctity which death gives to genius, can prevent a certain class of them from exhibiting the vices and weaknesses of their countrymen. Much the severest things which I heard said about Sweden, were said by Swedes themselves, and I was frequently obliged to rely upon my own contrary impressions, to protect me from the chance of being persuaded to paint things worse than they really are.

Just before leaving Stockholm I made application, through the Hon. Mr. Schroeder, our Minister Resident, and Baron Lagerheim, for the privilege of an interview with the king. A few days previously, however, he had been attacked with that illness which has obliged him to withdraw from the labours of government, and was advised by his physicians to receive no one. He sent me a very kind message, with an invitation to renew my request as soon as his health should be restored. Gentlemen who had opportunities of knowing the fact, assured me that his health broke down under an accumulation of labour and anxiety, in his endeavours to bring the question of religious liberty before the Diet—a measure in which he had to contend with the united influence of the clergy, the House of Peasants, whom the clergy rule to a great extent, and a portion of the House of Nobles. It is not often that a king is in advance of the general sentiment of his people, and in losing the services of Oscar, I fear that Sweden has lost her best man. The Crown Prince, now Prince Regent, is said to be amiably weak in his character, rather reactionary in his views, and very ambitious of military glory. At least, that is the average of the various opinions which I heard expressed concerning him.

After speaking of the manners of Stockholm, I must not close this chapter without saying a few words about its morals. It has been called the most licentious city in Europe, and, I have no doubt, with the most perfect justice. Vienna may surpass it in the amount of conjugal infidelity, but certainly not in general incontinence. Very nearly half the registered births are illegitimate, to say nothing of the illegitimate children born *in* wedlock. Of the servant-girls, shop-girls, and seamstresses in the city, it is very safe to say that scarcely ten out of a hundred are chaste, while, as rakish young Swedes have coolly informed me, many girls of respectable parentage, belonging to the middle class, are not much better. The men, of course, are much worse than the women, and even in Paris one sees fewer physical signs of excessive debauchery. Here, the number of broken-down young men and blear-eyed, hoary sinners, is astonishing. I have never been in any place where licentiousness was so open and avowed—and yet, where the slang of a sham morality was so prevalent. There are no houses of prostitution in Stockholm, and the city would be scandalised at the idea of allowing such a thing. A few years ago two were established and the fact was no sooner known than a virtuous mob arose and violently pulled them down! At the restaurants, young blades order their dinners of the female waiters, with an arm around their waists, while the old men place their hands unblushingly upon their bosoms. All the baths in Stockholm are attended by women (generally middle-aged and hideous, I must confess), who perform the usual scrubbing and shampooing with the greatest nonchalance. One does not wonder when he is told of young men who have passed safely through the ordeals of Berlin and Paris, and have come at last to Stockholm to be ruined.*

* The substance of the foregoing paragraph was contained in a letter published in *The New-York Tribune* during my travels in the North, and which was afterwards translated and commented upon by the Swedish papers. The latter charged me with having drawn too dark a picture and I therefore took some pains to test my statements, both by means of

It is but fair to say that the Swedes account for the large proportion of illegitimate births, by stating that many unfortunate females come up from the country to hide their shame in the capital, which is no doubt true. Everything that I have said has been derived from residents of Stockholm, who, proud as they are, and sensitive, cannot conceal this

the Government statistics, and the views of my Swedish friends. I see no reason to change my first impression: had I accepted all that was told me by natives of the capital, I should have made the picture much darker. The question is simply whether there is much difference between the general adoption of illicit connections, or the existence of open prostitution. The latter is almost unknown; the former is almost universal, the supply being kept up by the miserable rates of wages paid to female servants and seamstresses. The former get, on an average, fifty *rigsdaler* ($13) per year, out of which they must clothe themselves: few of the latter can make one rigsdaler a day. These connections are also encouraged by the fact, that marriage legitimates all the children previously born. In fact, during the time of my visit to Stockholm, a measure was proposed in the House of Clergy, securing to bastards the same right of inheritance, as to legitimate children. Such measures, however just they may be so far as the innocent offspring of a guilty connection are concerned, have a direct tendency to impair the sanctity of marriage, and consequently the general standard of morality.

This, the most vital of all the social problems, is strangely neglected. The diseases and excesses which it engenders are far more devastating than those which spring from any other vice, and yet no philanthropist is bold enough to look the question in the face. The virtuous shrink from it, the vicious don't care about it, the godly simply condemn, and the ungodly indulge—and so the world rolls on, and hundreds of thousands go down annually to utter ruin. It is useless to attempt the extirpation of a vice which is inherent in the very nature of man, and the alternative of either utterly ignoring, or of attempting to check and regulate it, is a question of the most vital importance to the whole human race.

glaring depravity. The population of Stockholm, as is proved by statistics, has only been increased during the last fifty years by immigration from the country, the number of deaths among the inhabitants exceeding the births by several hundreds every year. I was once speaking with a Swede about these facts, which he seemed inclined to doubt. "But," said I, "they are derived from your own statistics." "Well," he answered, with a naïve attempt to find some compensating good, "you must at least admit that the Swedish statistics are as exact as any in the world!"

Drunkenness is a leading vice among the Swedes, as we had daily evidence. Six years ago the consumption of brandy throughout the kingdom was *nine gallons* for every man, woman, and child annually; but it has decreased considerably since then, mainly through the manufacture of beer and porter. "*Bajerskt öl*" (Bavarian beer) is now to be had everywhere, and is rapidly becoming the favourite drink of the people. Sweden and the United States will in the end establish the fact that lager beer is more efficacious in preventing intemperance than any amount of prohibitory law. Brandy-drinking is still, nevertheless, one of the greatest curses of Sweden. It is no unusual thing to see boys of twelve or fourteen take their glass of fiery *finkel* before dinner. The celebrated Swedish punch, made of arrack, wine, and sugar, is a universal evening drink, and one of the most insidious ever invented, despite its agreeable flavor. There is a movement in favor of total abstinence, but it seems to have made but little progress, except as it is connected with some of the new religious ideas, which are now preached throughout the country.

I have rarely witnessed a sadder example of ruin, than one evening in a Stockholm café. A tall, distinguished-looking man of about forty, in an advanced state of drunkenness, was seated at a table opposite to us. He looked at me awhile, apparently endeavoring to keep hold of some thought with which his mind was occupied. Rising at last he staggered across the room, stood before me, and repeated the words of Bellman:

> "Så vandra våra stora män'
> Från ljuset ned til skuggan." *

A wild, despairing laugh followed the lines, and he turned away, but came back again and again to repeat them. He was a nobleman of excellent family, a man of great intellectual attainments, who, a few years ago, was considered one of the most promising young men in Sweden. I saw him frequently afterwards, and always in the same condition, but he never accosted me again. The Swedes say the same thing of Bellman himself, and of Tegner, and many others, with how much justice I care not to know, for a man's faults are to be accounted for to God, and not to a gossiping public.

* "Thus our great men wander from the light down into the shades."

CHAPTER XIX.

JOURNEY TO GOTTENBURG AND COPENHAGEN.

I NEVER knew a more sudden transition from winter to summer than we experienced on the journey southward from Stockholm. When we left that city on the evening of the 6th of May, there were no signs of spring except a few early violets and anemones on the sheltered southern banks in Haga Park; the grass was still brown and dead, the trees bare, and the air keen; but the harbour was free from ice and the canal open, and our winter isolation was therefore at an end. A little circulation entered into the languid veins of society; steamers from Germany began to arrive; fresh faces appeared in the streets, and less formal costumes— merchants and bagmen only, it is true, but people of a more dashing and genial air. We were evidently, as the Swedes said, leaving Stockholm just as it began to be pleasant and lively.

The steamer left the Riddarholm pier at midnight, and took her way westward up the Mälar Lake to Södertelje. The boats which ply on the Gotha canal are small, but neat and comfortable. The price of a passage to Gottenburg, a distance of 370 miles, is about $8.50. This, however, does not include meals, which are furnished at a fixed price, amounting to $6 more. The time occupied by the voyage varies from two and a half to four days. In the night we passed through the lock at Södertelje, where St. Olaf, when a heathen Viking, cut a channel for his ships into the long Baltic estuary which here closely approaches the lake, and in the morning found ourselves running down the eastern shore of Sweden, under the shelter of its fringe of jagged rocky islets. Towards noon we left the Baltic, and steamed up the long, narrow Bay of Söderköping, passing, on the way, the magnificent ruins of Stegeborg Castle, the first mediæval relic I had seen in Sweden. Its square massive walls, and tall round tower of grey stone, differed in no respect from those of cotemporary ruins in Germany.

Before reaching Söderköping, we entered the canal, a very complete and substantial work of the kind, about eighty feet in breadth, but much more crooked than would seem to be actually necessary. For this reason the boats make but moderate speed, averaging not more than six or seven miles an hour, exclusive of the detention at the locks. The country is undulating, and neither rich nor populous before reaching the beautiful Roxen Lake, beyond which we entered upon a charming district. Here the canal rises, by eleven successive locks, to the rich uplands separating the Roxen from the Wetter, a gently rolling plain, chequered so far as the eye could reach, with green squares of springing wheat and the dark mould of the newly ploughed barley fields. While the boat was passing the locks, we walked forward to a curious old church, called Vreta Kloster. The building dates from the year 1128, and contains the tombs of three Swedish kings, together with that of the Count Douglas, who fled hither from Scotland in the time of Cromwell. The Douglas estate is in this neighbourhood, and is, I believe, still in the possession of the family. The church must at one time have presented a fine, venerable appearance: but all its dark rich colouring and gilding are now buried under a thick coat of white-wash.

We had already a prophecy of the long summer days of the North, in the perpetual twilight which lingered in the sky, moving around from sunset to sunrise. During the second night we crossed the Wetter Lake, which I did not see; for when I came on deck we were already on the Viken, the most beautiful sheet of water between Stockholm and Gottenburg. Its irregular shores, covered with forests of fir and birch, thrust out long narrow headlands which divide it into deep bays, studded with wild wooded islands. But the scenery was still that of winter, except in the absence of ice and snow. We had not made much southing, but we expected to find the western side of Sweden much warmer than the eastern. The highest part of the canal, more than 300 feet above the sea, was now passed, however, and as we descended the long barren hills towards the Wener Lake I found a few early wild flowers in the woods. In the afternoon we came upon the Wener, the third lake in Europe, being one hundred miles in extent by about fifty in breadth. To the west, it spread away to a level line against the sky; but, as I looked southward, I perceived two opposite promontories, with scattered islands between, dividing the body of water into almost equal portions. The scenery of the Wener has great resemblance to that of the northern portion of Lake

Michigan. Further down on the eastern shore, the hill of Kinnekulle, the highest land in Southern Sweden, rises to the height of nearly a thousand feet above the water, with a graceful and very gradual sweep; but otherwise the scenery s rather tame, and, I suspect, depends for most of its beauty upon the summer foliage.

There were two or three intelligent and agreeable passengers on board, who showed a more than usual knowledge of America and her institutions. The captain, however, as we walked the deck together, betrayed the same general impression which prevails throughout the Continent (Germany in particular), that we are a thoroughly *material* people, having little taste for or appreciation of anything which is not practical and distinctly utilitarian. Nothing can be further from the truth; yet I have the greatest difficulty in making people comprehend that a true feeling for science, art, and literature can co-exist with our great practical genius. There is more intellectual activity in the Free States than in any other part of the world, a more general cultivation, and, taking the collective population, I venture to say, a more enlightened taste. Nowhere are greater sums spent for books and works of art, or for the promotion of scientific objects. Yet this cry of "Materialism" has become the cant and slang of European talk concerning America, and is obtruded so frequently and so offensively that I have sometimes been inclined to doubt whether the good breeding of Continental society has not been too highly rated.

While on the steamer, I heard an interesting story of a Swedish nobleman, who is at present attempting a practical protest against the absurd and fossilised ideas by which his class is governed. The nobility of Sweden are as proud as they are poor, and, as the father's title is inherited by each of his sons, the country is overrun with Counts and Barons who, repudiating any means of support that is not somehow connected with the service of the government, live in a continual state of debt and dilapidation. Count R——, however, has sense enough to know that honest labor is always honourable, and has brought up his eldest son to earn his living by the work of his own hands. For the past three years, the latter has been in the United States, working as a day-labourer on farms and on Western railroads. His experiences, I learn, have not been agreeable, but he is a young man of too much spirit and courage to give up the attempt, and has hitherto refused to listen to the entreaties of his family, that he shall come home and take charge of one of his father's estates. The second son is now a clerk in a mercantile house in Gottenburg, while the Count has given his daughter in marriage to a radical and untitled editor, whose acquaintance I was afterwards so fortunate as to make, and who confirmed the entire truth of the story.

We were to pass the locks at Trollhätta in the middle of the night, but I determined to visit the celebrated falls of the Götha River, even at such a time, and gave orders that we should be called. The stupid boy, however, woke up the wrong passenger, and the last locks were reached before the mistake was discovered. By sunrise we had reached Lilla Edet, on the Götha River, where the buds were swelling on the early trees, and the grass, in sunny places, showed a little sprouting greenness. We shot rapidly down the swift brown stream, between brown, bald, stony hills, whose forests have all been stripped off to feed the hostile camp-fires of past centuries. Bits of bottom land, held in the curves of the river, looked rich and promising, and where the hills fell back a little, there were groves and country-houses—but the scenery, in general, was bleak and unfriendly, until we drew near Gottenburg. Two round, detached forts, built according to Vauban's ideas (which the Swedes say he stole from Sweden, where they were already in practice) announced our approach, and before noon we were alongside the pier. Here, to my great surprise, a Custom-house officer appeared and asked us to open our trunks. "But we came by the canal from Stockholm!" "That makes no difference," he replied; "your luggage must be examined." I then appealed to the captain, who stated that, in consequence of the steamer's being obliged to enter the Baltic waters for two or three hours between Södertelje and Söderköping, the law took it for granted that we might have boarded some foreign vessel during that time and procured contraband goods. In other words, though sailing in a narrow sound, between the Swedish islands and the Swedish coast, we had virtually been in a foreign country! It would scarcely be believed that this sagacious law is of quite recent enactment.

We remained until the next morning in Gottenburg. This is, in every respect, a more energetic and wide-awake place than Stockholm. It has, not the same unrivalled beauty of position, but is more liberally laid out and kept in better order. Although the population is only about 40,000, its commerce is much greater than that of the capital, and so are, proportionately, its wealth and public spirit.

The Magister Hedlund, a very intelligent and accomplished gentleman, to whom I had a letter from Mügge, the novelist, took me up the valley a distance of five or six miles, to a very picturesque village among the hills, which is fast growing into a manufacturing town. Large cotton, woollen, and paper mills bestride a strong stream, which has such a tall that it leaps from one mill-wheel to another for the distance of nearly half a mile. On our return, we visited a number of wells hollowed in the rocky strata of the hills, to which the country people have given the name of "The Giant's Pots." A clergyman of the neighbourhood, even, has written a pamphlet to prove that they were the work of the antediluvian giants, who excavated them for the purpose of mixing dough for their loaves of bread and batter for their puddings. They are simply those holes which a pebble grinds in a softer rock, under the rotary action of a current of water, but on an immense scale, some of them being ten feet in diameter, by fifteen or eighteen in depth. At Herr Hedlund's house, I met a number of gentlemen, whose courtesy and intelligence gave me a very favourable impression of the society of the place.

The next morning, at five o'clock, the steamer Viken, from Christiania, arrived, and we took passage for Copenhagen. After issuing from the *Skärgaard*, or rocky archipelago which protects the approach to Gottenburg from the sea, we made a direct course to Elsinore, down the Swedish coast, but too distant to observe more than its general outline. This part of Sweden, however—the province of Halland—is very rough and stony, and not until after passing the Sound does one see the fertile hills and vales of

Scania. The Cattegat was as smooth as an inland sea, and our voyage could not have been pleasanter. In the afternoon Zealand rose blue from the wave, and the increase in the number of small sailing craft denoted our approach to the Sound. The opposite shores drew nearer to each other, and finally the spires of Helsingborg, on the Swedish shore, and the square mass of Kronborg Castle, under the guns of which the Sound dues have been so long demanded, appeared in sight. In spite of its bare, wintry aspect, the panorama was charming. The picturesque Gothic buttresses and gables of Kronborg rose above the zigzag of its turfed outworks; beyond were the houses and gardens of Helsingör (Elsinore)—while on the glassy breast of the Sound a fleet of merchant vessels lay at anchor, and beyond, the fields and towns of Sweden gleamed in the light of the setting sun. Yet here, again, I must find fault with Campbell, splendid lyrist as he is. We should have been sailing

"By thy *wild and stormy steep*,
Elsinore !"

only that the level shore, with its fair gardens and groves, wouldn't admit the possibility of such a thing. The music of the line remains the same, but you must not read it on the spot.

There was a beautiful American clipper at anchor off the Castle. "There," said a Danish passenger to me, "is one of the ships which have taken from us the sovereignty of the Sound." "I am very glad of it," I replied; "and I can only wonder why the maritime nations of Europe have so long submitted to such an imposition." "I am glad, also," said he, "that the question has at last been settled, and our privilege given up—and I believe we are all, even the Government itself, entirely satisfied with the arrangement." I heard the same opinion afterwards expressed in Copenhagen, and felt gratified, as an American, to hear the result attributed to the initiative taken by our Government; but I also remembered the Camden and Amboy Railroad Company, and could not help wishing that the same principle might be applied at home. We have a Denmark, lying between New-York and Philadelphia, and I have often paid *sund* dues for crossing her territory.

At dusk, we landed under the battlements of Copenhagen. "Are you travellers or merchants?" asked the Custom-house officers. "Travellers," we replied. "Then," was the answer, "there is no necessity for examining your trunks," and we were politely ushered out at the opposite door, and drove without further hindrance to a hotel. A gentleman from Stockholm had said to me: "When you get to Copenhagen you will find yourself in Europe:" and I was at once struck with the truth of his remark. Although Copenhagen is by no means a commercial city—scarcely more so than Stockholm—its streets are gay, brilliant and bustling, and have an air of life and joyousness which contrasts strikingly with the gravity of the latter capital. From without, it makes very little impression, being built on a low, level ground, and surrounded by high earthen fortifications, but its interior is full of quaint and attractive points. There is already a strong admixture of the German element in the population, softening by its warmth and frankness the Scandinavian reserve. In their fondness for out-door recreation, the Danes quite equal the Viennese, and their Summer-garden of Tivoli is one of the largest and liveliest in all Europe. In costume, there is such a thing as individuality; in manners, somewhat of independence. The Danish nature appears to be more pliant and flexible than the Swedish, but I cannot judge whether the charge of inconstancy and dissimulation, which I have heard brought against it, is just. With regard to morals, Copenhagen is said to be an improvement upon Stockholm.

During our short stay of three days, we saw the principal sights of the place. The first, and one of the pleasantest to me, was the park of Rosenborg Palace, with its fresh, green turf, starred with dandelions, and its grand avenues of chestnuts and lindens, just starting into leaf. On the 11th of May, we found spring at last, after six months of uninterrupted winter. I don't much enjoy going the round of a new city, attended by a valet-de-place, and performing the programme laid down by a guide-book, nor is it an agreeable task to describe such things in catalogue style; so I shall merely say that the most interesting things in Copenhagen are the Museum of Northern Antiquities, the Historical Collections in Rosenborg Palace, Thorwaldsen's Museum, and the Church of our Lady, containing the great sculptor's statues of Christ and the Apostles. We have seen very good casts of the latter in New-York, but one must visit the Museum erected by the Danish people, which is also Thorwaldsen's mausoleum, to learn the number, variety and beauty of his works. Here are the casts of between three and four hundred statues, busts and bas reliefs, with a number in marble. No artist has ever had so noble a monument.

On the day after my arrival, I sent a note to Hans Christian Andersen, reminding him of the greeting which he had once sent me through a mutual friend, and asking him to appoint an hour for me to call upon him. The same afternoon, as I was sitting in my room, the door quietly opened, and a tall, loosely-jointed figure entered. He wore a neat evening dress of black, with a white cravat; his head was thrown back, and his plain, irregular features wore an expression of the greatest cheerfulness and kindly humour. I recognised him at once, and forgetting that we had never met —so much did he seem like an old, familiar acquaintance— cried out "Andersen!" and jumped up to greet him. "Ah," said he stretching out both his hands, "here you are! Now I should have been vexed if you had gone through Copenhagen and I had not known it." He sat down, and I had a delightful hour's chat with him. One sees the man so plainly in his works, that his readers may almost be said to know him personally. He is thoroughly simple and natural, and those who call him egotistical forget that his egotism is only a naïve and unthinking sincerity, like that of a child. In fact, he is the youngest man for his years that I ever knew. "When I was sixteen," said he, "I used to think to myself, 'when I am twenty-four, then will I be old indeed'—but now I am fifty-two, and I have just the same feeling of youth as at twenty." He was greatly delighted when Braisted, who was in the room with me, spoke of having read his "Improvisatore" in the Sandwich Islands. "Why, is it possible?"

he exclaimed: "when I hear of my books going so far around the earth, I sometimes wonder if it can be really true that I have written them." He explained to me the plot of his new novel, "To Be, or Not To Be," and ended by presenting me with the illustrated edition of his stories. "Now, don't forget me," said he, with a delightful entreaty in his voice, as he rose to leave, "for we shall meet again. Were it not for sea-sickness, I should see you in America; and who knows but I may come, in spite of it?" God bless you, Andersen! I said, in my thoughts. It is so cheering to meet a man whose very weaknesses are made attractive through the perfect candour of his nature!

Goldschmidt, the author of "The Jew," whose acquaintance I made, is himself a Jew, and a man of great earnestness and enthusiasm. He is the editor of the "North and South," a monthly periodical, and had just completed, as he informed me, a second romance, which was soon to be published. Like most of the authors and editors in Northern Europe, he is well acquainted with American literature.

Professor Rafn, the distinguished archæologist of Northern lore, is still as active as ever, notwithstanding he is well advanced in years. After going up an innumerable number of steps, I found him at the very top of a high old building in the *Kronprinzensgade*, in a study crammed with old Norsk and Icelandic volumes. He is a slender old man, with a thin face, and high, narrow head, clear grey eyes, and a hale red on his cheeks. The dust of antiquity does not lie very heavily on his grey locks; his enthusiasm for his studies is of that fresh and lively character which mellows the whole nature of the man. I admired and enjoyed it, when, after being fairly started on his favourite topic, he opened one of his own splendid folios, and read me some ringing stanzas of Icelandic poetry. He spoke much of Mr. Marsh, our former minister to Turkey, whose proficiency in the northern languages he considered very remarkable.

CHAPTER XX.

RETURN TO THE NORTH.—CHRISTIANIA.

I WAS obliged to visit both Germany and England, before returning to spend the summer in Norway. As neither of those countries comes within the scope of the present work, I shall spare the reader a recapitulation of my travels for six weeks after leaving Copenhagen. Midsummer's Day was ten days past before I was ready to resume the journey, and there was no time to be lost, if I wished to see the midnight sun from the cliffs of the North Cape. I therefore took the most direct route from London, by the way of Hull, whence a steamer was to sail on the 3rd of July for Christiania.

We chose one of the steamers of the English line, to our subsequent regret, as the Norwegian vessels are preferable, in most respects. I went on board on Friday evening, and on asking for my berth, was taken into a small state-room containing ten. "Oh, there's only *seven* gentleman goin' in here, this time," said the steward, noticing my look of dismay, "and then you can sleep on a sofa in the saloon, if you like it better." On referring to the steamer's framed certificate, I found that she was 250 tons' burden, and constructed to carry 171 cabin and 230 deck passengers! The state-room for ten passengers had a single wash-basin, but I believe we had as many as four small towels, which was a source of congratulation. " What a jolly nice boat it is!" I heard one of the English passengers exclaim. The steward, who stood up for the dignity of the vessel, said : " Oh, you'll find it very pleasant; we 'ave only twenty passengers and we once 'ad heighty-four."

In the morning we were upon the North Sea, rolling with a short, nauseating motion, under a dismal, rainy sky. " It always rains when you leave Hull," said the mate, " and it always rains when you come back to it." I divided my time between sea-sickness and Charles Reade's novel of "Never too Late to Mend," a cheery companion under such circumstances. The purposed rowdyism of the man's style shows a little too plainly, but his language is so racy and muscular, his characters so fairly and sharply drawn, that one must not be censorious. Towards evening I remembered that it was the Fourth, and so procured a specific for sea-sickness, with which Braisted and I, sitting alone on the main hatch, in the rain, privately remembered our Fatherland. There was on board an American sea-captain, of Norwegian birth, as I afterwards found, who would gladly have joined us. The other passengers were three Norwegians, three fossil Englishmen, two snobbish do., and some jolly, good-natured, free-and-easy youths, bound to Norway, with dogs, guns, rods, fishing tackle, and oil-cloth overalls.

We had a fair wind and smooth sea, but the most favourable circumstances could not get more than eight knots an hour out of our steamer. After forty-eight hours, however, the coast of Norway came in sight—a fringe of scattered rocks, behind which rose bleak hills, enveloped in mist and rain. Our captain, who had been running on this route some years, did not know where we were, and was for putting to sea again, but one of the Norwegian passengers offered his services as pilot and soon brought us to the fjord of Christiansand. We first passed through a *Skärgaard*—archipelago, or "garden of rocks," as it is picturesquely termed in Norsk—and then between hills of dark-red rock, covered by a sprinkling of fir-trees, to a sheltered and tranquil harbour, upon which lay the little town. By this time the rain came down, not in drops, but in separate threads or streams, as if the nozzle of an immense watering-pot had been held over us. After three months of drouth, which had burned up the soil and entirely ruined the hay-crops, it was now raining for the first time in Southern Norway. The young Englishmen bravely put on their water-proofs and set out to visit the town in the midst of the deluge; but as it contains no sight of special interest, I made up my mind that, like Constantinople, it was more attractive from without than within, and remained on board. An amphitheatre of rugged hills surrounds the place, broken only by a charming little valley, which stretches off to the westward.

The fishermen brought us some fresh mackerel for our breakfast. They are not more than half the size of ours, and of a brighter green along the back; their flavour, however, is delicious. With these mackerels, four salmons, a custom-house officer, and a Norwegian parson, we set off at noon for Christiania. The coast was visible, but at a considerable distance, all day. Fleeting gleams of sunshine

11*

sometimes showed the broken inland ranges of mountains with jagged saw-tooth peaks shooting up here and there. When night came there was no darkness, but a strong golden gleam, whereby one could read until after ten o'clock. We reached the mouth of Christiania Fjord a little after midnight, and most of the passengers arose to view the scenery. After passing the branch which leads to Drammen, the fjord contracts so as to resemble a river or one of our island-studded New England lakes. The alternation of bare rocky islets, red-ribbed cliffs, fir-woods, grey-green birchen groves, tracts of farm land, and red-frame cottages, rendered this part of the voyage delightful, although, as the morning advanced, we saw everything through a gauzy veil of rain. Finally, the watering-pot was turned on again, obliging even oil-cloths to beat a retreat to the cabin, and so continued until we reached Christiania.

After a mild custom-house visitation, not a word being said about passports, we stepped ashore in republican Norway, and were piloted by a fellow-passenger to the Victoria Hotel, where an old friend awaited me. He who had walked with me in the colonnades of Karnak, among the sands of Kôm-Ombos, and under the palms of Philæ, was there to resume our old companionship on the bleak fjelds of Norway and on the shores of the Arctic Sea. We at once set about preparing for the journey. First, to the banker's who supplied me with a sufficient quantity of small money for the post-stations on the road to Drontheim ; then to a seller of *carrioles* of whom we procured three, at $36 apiece, to be resold to him for $24, at the expiration of two months; and then to supply ourselves with maps, posting-book, hammer, nails rope, gimlets, and other necessary helps in case of a breakdown. The carriole (*carry-all*, *lucus a non lucendo*, because it only carries one) is the national Norwegian vehicle, and deserves special mention. It resembles a reindeer-pulk, mounted on a pair of wheels, with long, flat, flexible ash shafts, and no springs. The seat, much like the stern of a canoe, and rather narrow for a traveller of large basis, slopes down into a trough for the feet, with a dashboard in front. Your single valise is strapped on a flat board behind, upon which your postillion sits. The whole machine resembles an American sulky in appearance, except that it is springless, and nearly the whole weight is forward of the axle. We also purchased simple and strong harness, which easily accommodates itself to any horse.

Christiania furnishes a remarkable example of the progress which Norway has made since its union with Sweden and the adoption of a free Constitution. In its signs of growth and improvement, the city reminds one of an American town. Its population has risen to 40,000, and though inferior to Gottenburg in its commerce, it is only surpassed by Stockholm in size. The old log houses of which it once was built have almost entirely disappeared; the streets are broad, tolerably paved, and have—what Stockholm cannot yet boast of—decent side-walks. From the little nucleus o the old town, near the water, branch off handsome new streets, where you often come suddenly from stately three-story blocks upon the rough rock and meadow land. The broad *Carl-Johansgade*, leading directly to the imposing white front of the Royal Palace, upon an eminence in the rear of the city, is worthy of any European capital. On the old market square a very handsome market hall of brick, in semi-Byzantine style, has recently been erected, and the only apparent point in which Christiania has not kept up with the times, is the want of piers for her shipping. A railroad, about forty miles in length, is already in operation as far as Eidsvold, at the foot of the long Miösen Lake, on which steamers ply to Lillehammer, at its head, affording an outlet for the produce of the fertile Guldbrandsdal and the adjacent country. The Norwegian Constitution is in almost all respects as free as that of any American state, and it is cheering to see what material well-being and solid progress have followed its adoption.

The environs of Christiania are remarkably beautiful. From the quiet basin of the fjord, which vanishes between blue, interlocking islands to the southward, the land rises gradually on all sides, speckled with smiling country-seats and farm-houses, which trench less and less on the dark evergreen forests as they recede, until the latter keep their old dominion and sweep in unbroken lines to the summits of the mountains on either hand. The ancient citadel of Aggershus, perched upon a rock, commands the approach to the city, fine old linden trees rising above its white walls and tiled roofs; beyond, over the trees of the palace park, in which stand the new Museum and University, towers the long palace-front, behind which commences a range of villas and gardens, stretching westward around a deep bight of the fjord, until they reach the new palace of Oscar-hall, on a peninsula facing the city. As we floated over the glassy water, in a skiff, on the afternoon following our arrival, watching the scattered sun-gleams move across the lovely panorama, we found it difficult to believe that we were in the latitude of Greenland. The dark, rich green of the foliage, the balmy odours which filled the air, the deep blue of the distant hills and islands, and the soft, warm colors of the houses, all belonged to the south. Only the air, fresh without being cold, elastic, and exciting, not a delicious opiate, was wholly northern, and when I took a swim under the castle walls, I found that the water was northern too. It was the height of summer, and the showers of roses in the gardens, the strawberries and cherries in the market, show that the summer's best gifts are still enjoyed here.

The English were off the next day with their dogs, guns, fishing tackle, waterproofs, clay pipes, and native language, except one, who became home-sick and went back in the next steamer. We also prepared to set out for Ringerike, the ancient dominion of King Ring, on our way to the Dovre-fjeld and Drontheim.

CHAPTER XXI.

INCIDENTS OF CARRIOLE TRAVEL.

It is rather singular that whenever you are about to start upon a new journey, you almost always fall in with some one who has just made it, and who overwhelms you with all sorts of warning and advice. This has happened to me so frequently that I have long ago ceased to regard any such communications, unless the individual from whom they come inspires me with more than usual confidence. While inspecting our carrioles at the hotel in Christiania, I was accosted by a Hamburg merchant, who had just arrived from Drontheim, by way of the Dovre Fjeld and the Miösen Lake. " Ah," said he, " those things won't last long. That oil-cloth covering for your luggage will be torn to pieces in a few days by the postillions climbing upon it. Then they hold on to your seat and rip the cloth lining with their long nails; besides, the rope reins wear the leather off your dash board, and you will be lucky if your wheels and axles don't snap on the rough roads." Now, here was a man who had travelled much in Norway, spoke the language perfectly, and might be supposed to know something; but his face betrayed the croaker, and I knew, moreover, that of all fretfully luxurious men, merchants—and especially North-German merchants—are the worst, so I let him talk and kept my own private opinion unchanged.

At dinner he renewed the warnings. "You will have great delay in getting horses at the stations. The only way is to be rough and swaggering, and threaten the people—and even that won't always answer." Most likely, I thought. —"Of course you have a supply of provisions with you?" he continued. "No," said I, "I always adopt the diet of the country in which I travel."—"But you can't do it here!" he exclaimed in horror, "you can't do it here! They have no wine, nor no white bread, nor no fresh meat; and they don't know how to cook anything!" "I am perfectly aware of that," I answered; "but as long as I am not obliged to come down to bread made of fir-bark and barley-straw, as last winter in Lapland, I shall not complain."—"You possess the courage of a hero if you can do such a thing; but you will not start now, in this rain?" We answered by bidding him a polite adieu, for the post-horses had come, and our carrioles were at the door. As if to reward our resolution, the rain, which had been falling heavily all the morning, ceased at that moment, and the grey blanket of heaven broke and rolled up into loose masses of cloud.

I mounted into the canoe-shaped seat, drew the leathern apron over my legs, and we set out, in single file, through the streets of Christiania. The carriole, as I have already said, has usually no springs (ours had none at least), except those which it makes in bounding over the stones. We had not gone a hundred yards before I was ready to cry out—"Lord, have mercy upon me!" Such a shattering of the joints, such a vibration of the vertebræ, such a churning of the viscera, I had not felt since travelling by banghy-cart in India. Breathing went on by fits and starts, between the jolts; my teeth struck together so that I put away my pipe, lest I should bite off the stem, and the pleasant sensation of having been pounded in every limb crept on apace. Once off the paving-stones, it was a little better; beyond the hard turnpike which followed, better still; and on the gravel and sand of the first broad hill, we found the travel easy enough to allay our fears. The two *skydsbonder*, or postillions, who accompanied us, sat upon our portmanteaus, and were continually jumping off to lighten the ascent of the hills. The descents were achieved at full trotting speed, the horses leaning back, supporting themselves against the weight of the carrioles, and throwing out their feet very firmly, so as to avoid the danger of slipping. Thus, no matter how steep the hill, they took it with perfect assurance and boldness, never making a stumble. There was just sufficient risk left, however, to make these flying descents pleasant and exhilarating.

Our road led westward, over high hills and across deep valleys, down which we had occasional glimpses of the blue fjord and its rocky islands. The grass and grain were a rich, dark green, sweeping into a velvety blue in the distance, and against this deep ground, the bright red of the houses showed with strong effect—a contrast which was sublued and harmonised by the still darker masses of the evergreen forests, covering the mountain ranges. At the end of twelve or thirteen miles we reached the first post-station, at the foot of the mountains which bound the inland prospect from Christiania on the west. As it was not a *"fast"* station, we were subject to the possibility of waiting two or three hours for horses, but fortunately were accosted on the road by one of the farmers who supply the *skyds*, and changed at his house. The Norwegian *skyds* differs from the Swedish *skjuts* in having horses ready only at the fast stations, which are comparatively few, while at all others you must wait from one to three hours, according to the distance from which the horses must be brought. In Sweden there are always from two to four horses ready, and you are only obliged to wait after these are exhausted. There, also, the regulations are better, and likewise more strictly enforced. It is, at best, an awkward mode of travelling— very pleasant, when everything goes rightly, but very annoying when otherwise.

We now commenced climbing the mountain by a series of terribly steep ascents, every opening in the woods disclosing a wider and grander view backward over the lovely Christiania Fjord and the intermediate valleys. Beyond the crest we came upon a wild mountain plateau, a thousand feet above the sea, and entirely covered with forests of spruce and fir. It was a black and dismal region, under the lowering sky: not a house or a grain field to be seen, and thus we drove for more than two hours, to the solitary inn of Krogkleven, where we stopped for the night in order to visit the celebrated King's View in the morning. We got a tolerable supper and good beds, sent off a messenger to the station of Sundvolden, at the foot of the mountain, to order horses for us, and set out soon after sunrise, piloted by the landlord's son, Olaf. Half an hour's walk through the forest brought us to a pile of rocks on the crest of the mountain, which fell away abruptly to the westward. At our feet lay the Tyri Fjord, with its deeply indented shores and its irregular, scattered islands, shining blue and bright in the morning sun, while away beyond it stretched a great semicircle of rolling hills covered with green farms, dotted with red farm-houses, and here and there a white church glimmering like a spangle on the breast of the landscape. Behind this soft, warm, beautiful region, rose dark, wooded hills, with lofty mountain-ridges above them, until, far and faint, under and among the clouds, streaks of snow betrayed some peaks of the Nore Fjeld, sixty or seventy miles distant. This is one of the most famous views in Norway, and has been compared to that from the Righi, but without sufficient reason. The sudden change, however, from the gloomy wilderness through which you first pass to the sunlit picture of the enchanting lake, and green, inhabited hills and valleys, may well excuse the raptures of travellers. Ringerike, the realm of King Ring, is a lovely land, not only as seen from this eagle's nest, but when you have descended upon its level. I believe the monarch's real name was Halfdan the Black. So beloved was he in life that after death his body was divided into four portions, so that each province might possess some part of him. Yet the noblest fame is transitory, and nobody now knows exactly where any one of his quarters was buried.

A terrible descent, through a chasm between perpendicular cliffs some hundreds of feet in height, leads from Krogkleven to the level of the Tyri Fjord. There is no attempt here, nor indeed upon the most of the Norwegian roads we travelled, to mitigate, by well-arranged curves, the steepness of the hills. Straight down you go, no matter of how breakneck a character the declivity may be. There are no drags to the carrioles and country carts, and were not the native horses the toughest and surest-footed little animals in the world, this sort of travel would be trying to the nerves.

Our ride along the banks of the Tyri Fjord, in the clear morning sunshine, was charming. The scenery was strikingly like that on the lake of Zug, in Switzerland, and we missed the only green turf, which this year's rainless spring had left brown and withered. In all Sweden we had seen no such landscapes, not even in Norrland. There, however, the *people* carried off the palm. We found no farm-houses here so stately and clean as the Swedish, no such symmetrical forms and frank, friendly faces. The Norwegians are big enough, and strong enough, to be sure, but their carriage is awkward, and their faces not only plain but ugly. The countrywomen we saw were remarkable in this latter respect, but nothing could exceed their development of waist, bosom and arms. Here is the stuff of which Vikings were made, I thought, but there has been no refining or ennobling since those times. These are the rough primitive formations of the human race—the bare granite and gneiss, from which sprouts no luxuriant foliage, but at best a few simple and hardy flowers. I found much less difficulty in communicating with the Norwegians than I anticipated. The language is so similar to the Swedish that I used the latter, with a few alterations, and easily made myself understood. The Norwegian dialect, I imagine, stands in about the same relation to pure Danish as the Scotch does to the English

To my ear, it is less musical and sonorous than the Swedish though it is often accented in the same peculiar sing-song way.

Leaving the Tyri Fjord, we entered a rolling, well-cultivated country, with some pleasant meadow scenery. The crops did not appear to be thriving remarkably, probably on account of the dry weather. The hay crop, which the farmers were just cutting, was very scanty; rye and winter barley were coming into head, but the ears were thin and light, while spring barley and oats were not more than six inches in height. There were many fields of potatoes, however, which gave a better promise. So far as one could judge from looking over the fields, Norwegian husbandry is yet in a very imperfect state, and I suspect that the resources of the soil are not half developed. The whole country was radient with flowers, and some fields were literally mosaics of blue, purple, pink, yellow, and crimson bloom. Clumps of wild roses fringed the road, and the air was delicious with a thousand odours. Nature was throbbing with the fullness of her short midsummer life, with that sudden and splendid rebound from the long trance of winter which she nowhere makes except in the extreme north.

At Klåkken, which is called a *lilsigelse* station, where horses must be specially engaged, we were obliged to wait two hours and a half, while they were sent for from a distance of four miles. The utter coolness and indifference of the people to our desire to get on faster was quite natural, and all the better for them, no doubt, but it was provoking to us. We whiled away a part of the time with breakfast, which was composed mainly of boiled eggs and an immense dish of wild strawberries, of very small size but exquisitely fragrant flavour. The next station brought us to Vasbunden, at the head of the beautiful Randsfjord, which was luckily a fast station, and the fresh horses were forthcoming in two minutes. Our road all the afternoon lay along the eastern bank of the Fjord, coursing up and down the hills through a succession of the loveliest landscape pictures. This part of Norway will bear a comparison with the softer parts of Switzerland, such as the lakes of Zurich and Thun. The hilly shores of the Fjord were covered with scattered farms, the villages being merely churches with half a dozen houses clustered about them.

At sunset we left the lake and climbed a long wooded mountain to a height of more than two thousand feet. It was a weary pull until we reached the summit, but we rolled swiftly down the other side to the inn of Teterud, our destination, which we reached about 10 P.M. It was quite light enough to read, yet every one was in bed, and the place seemed deserted, until we remembered what latitude we were in. Finally, the landlord appeared, followed by a girl, whom, on account of her size and blubber, Braisted compared to a cow-whale. She had been turned out of her bed to make room for us, and we two instantly rolled into the warm hollow she had left, my Nilotic friend occupying a separate bed in another corner. The guests' room was an immense apartment; eight sets of quadrilles might have been danced in it at one time. The walls were hung with extraordinary pictures of the Six Days of Creation, in which the Almighty was represented as an old man dressed in a long gown, with a peculiarly good-humoured leer, suggesting a wink, on his face. I have frequently seen the same series of pictures in the Swedish inns. In the morning I was aroused by Braisted exclaiming, "There she blows!" and the whale came up to the surface with a huge pot of coffee, some sugar candy, excellent cream, and musty biscuit.

It was raining when we started, and I put on a light coat, purchased in London, and recommended in the advertisement as being "light in texture, gentlemanly in appearance, and impervious to wet," with strong doubts of its power to resist a Norwegian rain. Fortunately, it was not put to a severe test; we had passing showers only, heavy, though short. The country, between the Randsfjord and the Miösen Lake was open and rolling, everywhere under cultivation, and apparently rich and prosperous. Our road was admirable, and we rolled along at the rate of one Norsk mile (seven miles) an hour, through a land in full blossom, and an atmosphere of vernal odors. At the end of the second station we struck the main road from Christiania to Drontheim. In the station-house I found translations of the works of Dickens and Captain Chamier on the table. The landlord was the most polite and attentive Norwegian we had seen; but he made us pay for it, charging one and a half marks apiece for a breakfast of boiled eggs and cheese.

Starting again in a heavy shower, we crossed the crest of a hill, and saw all at once the splendid Miösen Lake spread out before us, the lofty Island of Helge, covered with farms and forests, lying in the centre of the picture. Our road went northward along the side of the vast, sweeping slope of farm-land which bounds the lake on the west. Its rough and muddy condition showed how little land-travel there is at present, since the establishment of a daily line of steamers on the lake. At the station of Gjövik, a glass furnace, situated in a wooded little dell on the shore, I found a young Norwegian who spoke tolerable English, and who seemed astounded at our not taking the steamer in preference to our carrioles. He hardly thought it possible that we could be going all the way to Lillehammer, at the head of the lake, by the land road. When we set out, our postillion took a way leading up the hills in the rear of the place. Knowing that our course was along the shore, we asked him if we were on the road to Sveen, the next station. "Oh, yes; it's all right," said he, "this is a new road." It was, in truth, a superb highway; broad and perfectly macadamised, and leading along the brink of a deep rocky chasm, down which thundered a powerful stream. From the top of this glen we struck inland, keeping more and more to the westward. Again we asked the postillion, and again received the same answer. Finally, when we had travelled six or seven miles, and the lake had wholly disappeared, I stopped and demanded where Sveen was. "Sveen is not on this road," he answered; "we are going to Mustad!" "But," I exclaimed, "we are bound for Sveen and Lillehammer!" "Oh," said he, with infuriating coolness, "*you can go there afterwards!*" You may judge that the carrioles were whirled around in a hurry, and that the only answer to the fellow's remonstrances was a shaking by the neck which frightened him into silence.

We drove back to Gjövik in a drenching shower, which failed to cool our anger. On reaching the station I at once made a complaint against the postillion, and the landlord called a man who spoke good English, to settle the matter. The latter brought me a bill of $2 for going to Mustad and back. Knowing that the horses belonged to farmers, who were not to blame in the least, we had agreed to pay for their use; but I remonstrated against paying the full price when we had not gone the whole distance, and had not intended to go at all. "Why, then, did you order horses for Mustad?" he asked. "I did no such thing!" I exclaimed, in amazement. "You did!" he persisted, and an investigation ensued, which resulted in the discovery that the Norwegian who had advised us to go by steamer, had gratuitously taken upon himself to tell the landlord to send us to the Randsfjord, and had given the postillion similar directions! The latter, imagining, perhaps, that we didn't actually know our own plans, had followed his instructions. I must say that I never before received such an astonishing mark of kindness. The ill-concealed satisfaction of the people at our mishap made it all the more exasperating. The end of it was that two or three marks were taken off the account, which we then paid, and in an hour afterwards shipped ourselves and carrioles on board a steamer for Lillehammer. The Norwegian who had caused all this trouble came along just before we embarked, and heard the story with the most sublime indifference, proffering not a word of apology, regret, or explanation. Judging from this specimen, the King of Sweden and Norway has good reason to style himself King of the Goths and Vandals.

I was glad, nevertheless, that we had an opportunity of seeing the Miösen, from the deck of a steamer. Moving over the glassy pale-green water, midway between its shores we had a far better exhibition of its beauties than from the land-road. It is a superb piece of water, sixty miles in length by from two to five in breadth, with mountain shores of picturesque and ever-varying outline. The lower slopes are farm land, dotted with the large *gaards*, or mansions of the farmers, many of which have a truly stately air; beyond them are forests of fir, spruce, and larch, while in the glens between, winding groves of birch, alder, and ash come down to fringe the banks of the lake. Wandering gleams of sunshine, falling through the broken clouds, touched here and there the shadowed slopes and threw belts of light upon the water—and these illuminated spots finely relieved the otherwise sombre depth of colour. Our boat was slow, and we had between two and three hours of unsurpassed scenery before reaching our destination. An immense raft of timber, gathered from the loose logs which are floated down the Lougen Elv, lay at the head of the lake, which contracts into the famous Guldbrandsdal. On the brow of a steep hill on the right lay the little town of Lillehammer, where we were ere long quartered in a very comfortable hotel.

12

CHAPTER XXII.

GULDBRANDSDAL AND THE DOVRE FJELD.

WE left Lillehammer on a heavenly Sabbath morning. There was scarcely a cloud in the sky, the air was warm and balmy, and the verdure of the valley, freshened by the previous day's rain, sparkled and glittered in the sun. The Miösen Lake lay blue and still to the south, and the bald tops of the mountains which inclose Guldbrandsdal stood sharp and clear, and almost shadowless, in the flood of light which streamed up the valley. Of Lillehammer, I can only say that it is a common-place town of about a thousand inhabitants. It had a cathedral and bishop some six hundred years ago, no traces of either of which now remain. We drove out of it upon a splendid new road, leading up the eastern bank of the river, and just high enough on the mountain side to give the loveliest views either way. Our horses were fast and spirited, and the motion of our carrioles over the firmly macadamised road was just sufficient to keep the blood in nimble circulation. Rigid Sabbatarians may be shocked at our travelling on that day; but there were few hearts in all the churches of Christendom whose hymns of praise were more sincere and devout than ours. The

Lougen roared an anthem for us from his rocky bed; the mountain streams, flashing down their hollow channels, seemed hastening to join it; the mountains themselves stood silent, with uncovered heads; and over all the pale-blue northern heaven looked lovingly and gladly down— a smile of God upon the grateful earth. There is no Sabbath worship better than the simple enjoyment of such a day.

Toward the close of the stage, our road descended to the banks of the Lougen, which here falls in a violent rapid— almost a cataract—over a barrier of rocks. Masses of water, broken or wrenched from the body of the river, are hurled intermittently high into the air, scattering as they fall, with fragments of rainbows dancing over them. In this scene I at once recognised the wild landscape by the pencil of Dahl, the Norwegian painter, which had made such an impression upon me in Copenhagen. In Guldbrandsdal, we found at once what we had missed in the scenery of Ringerike—swift, foaming streams. Here they leapt from every rift of the upper crags, brightening the gloom of the fir-woods which clothed the mountain-sides, like silver braiding upon a funeral garment. This valley is the pride of Norway, nearly as much for its richness as for its beauty and grandeur. The houses were larger an' more substantial, the fields blooming, with frequent orchards of fruit-trees, and the farmers, in their Sunday attire showed in their faces a little more intelligence than the people we had seen on our way thither. Their countenances had a plain, homely stamp; and of all the large-limbed, strong-backed forms I saw, not one could be called graceful, or even symmetrical. Something awkward and uncouth stamps the country people of Norway. Honest and simple-minded they are said to be, and probably are; but of native refinement of feeling they can have little, unless all outward signs of character are false.

We changed horses at Moshûûs, and drove up a level splendid road to Holmen, along the river-bank. The highway, thus far, is entirely new, and does great credit to Norwegian enterprise. There is not a better road in all Europe; and when it shall be carried through to Drontheim, the terrors which this trip has for timid travellers will entirely disappear. It is a pity that the *skyds* system should not be improved in equal ratio, instead of becoming even more inconvenient than at present. Holmen, hitherto a fast station, is now no longer so; and the same retrograde change is going on at other places along the road. The waiting at the *tilsigelse* stations is the great drawback to travelling by *skyds* in Norway. You must either wait two hours or pay fast prices, which the people are not legally entitled to ask. Travellers may write complaints in the space allotted in the post-books for such things, but with very little result, if one may judge from the perfect indifference which the station-masters exhibit when you threaten to do so. I was more than once tauntingly asked whether I would not write a complaint. In Sweden, I found but one instance of inattention at the stations, during two months' travel, and expected, from the boasted honesty of the Norwegians, to meet with an equally fortunate experience. Travellers, however, and especially English, are fast teaching the people the usual arts of imposition. Oh, you hard-shelled, unplastic, insulated Englishmen! You introduce towels and fresh water and tea, and beef-steak, wherever you go, it is true; but you teach high prices, and swindling, and insolence likewise!

A short distance beyond Holmen, the new road terminated, and we took the old track over steep spurs of the mountain, rising merely to descend and rise again. The Lougen River here forms a broad, tranquil lake, a mile in width, in which the opposite mountains were splendidly reflected. The water is pale, milky-green colour, which, under certain effects of light, has a wonderful aerial transparency. As we approached Lösnäs, after this long and tedious stage, I was startled by the appearance of a steamer on the river. It is utterly impossible for any to ascend the rapids below Moshûûs; and she must therefore have been built there. We could discover no necessity for such an undertaking in the thin scattered population and their slow, indifferent habits Her sudden apparition in such a place was like that of an omnibus in the desert.

The magnificent vista of the valley was for a time closed by the snowy peaks of the Rundan Fjeld; but as the direction of the river changed they disappeared, the valley contracted, and its black walls, two thousand feet high, almost overhung us. Below, however, were still fresh meadows, twinkling birchen groves and comfortable farm-houses. Out of a gorge on our right, plunged a cataract from a height of eighty or ninety feet, and a little further on, high up the mountain, a gush of braided silver foam burst out of the dark woods, covered with gleaming drapery the face of a huge perpendicular crag, and disappeared in the woods again. My friend drew up his horse in wonder and rapture. "I know all Switzerland and the Tyrol," he exclaimed, "but I have never seen a cataract so wonderfully framed in the setting of a forest." In the evening, as we approached our destination, two streams on the opposite side of the valley, fell from a height of more than a thousand feet, in a series of linked plunges, resembling burnished chains hanging dangling from the tremendous parapet of rock. On the meadow before us, commanding a full view of this wild and glorious scene, stood a stately *gaard*, entirely deserted, its barns, out-houses and gardens utterly empty and desolate. Its aspect saddened the whole landscape.

We stopped at the station of Lillehaave, which had only been established the day before, and we were probably the first travellers who had sojourned there. Consequently the people were unspoiled, and it was quite refreshing to be courteously received, furnished with a trout supper and excellent beds, and to pay therefor an honest price. The morning was lowering, and we had rain part of the day; but, thanks to our waterproofs and carriole aprons, we kept comfortably dry. During this day's journey of fifty miles, we had very grand scenery, the mountains gradually increasing in height and abruptness as we ascended the Guldbrandsdal, with still more imposing cataracts " blowing their trumpets from the steeps." At Viik, I found a complaint in the post-book, written by an Englishman who had come with us from Hull, stating that the landlord had made him pay five dollars for beating his dog off his own. The complaint was written in English, of course, and therefore useless so far as the authorities were concerned. The landlord whom I expected, from this account, to find a surly, swindling fellow, accosted us civilly, and invited us into his house to see some old weapons, principally battle-axes. There was a cross-bow, a battered, antique sword, and a buff coat, which may have been stripped from one of Sinclair's men in the pass of Kringelen. The logs of his house, or part of them, are said to have been taken from the dwelling in which the saint-king Olaf—the apostle of Christianity in the North,—was born. They are of the red Norwegian pine, which has a great durability; and the legend may be true, although this would make them eight hundred and fifty years old.

Colonel Sinclair was buried in the churchyard at Viik, and about fifteen miles further we passed the defile of Kringelen, where his band was cut to pieces. He landed in Romdal's Fjord, on the western coast, with 900 men intending to force his way across the mountains to relieve Stockholm, which was then (1612) besieged by the Danes. Some three hundred of the peasants collected at Kringelen, gathered together rocks and trunks of trees on the brow of the cliff, and, at a concerted signal, rolled the mass down upon the Scotch, the greater part of whom were crushed to death or hurled into the river. Of the whole force only two escaped. A wooden tablet on the spot says, as near as I could make it out, that there was never such an example of courage and valour known in the world, and calls upon the people to admire this glorious deed of their fathers. "Courage and valour;" cried Braisted, indignantly; "it was a cowardly butchery! If they had so much courage, why did they allow 900 Scotchmen to get into the very heart of the country before they tried to stop them?" Well, war is full of meanness and cowardice. If it were only fair fighting on an open field, there would be less of it.

Beyond Laurgaard, Guldbrandsdal contracts to a narrow gorge, down which the Lougen roars in perpetual foam. This pass is called the Rusten; and the road here is excessively steep and difficult. The forests disappear; only hardy firs and the red pine cling to the ledges of the rocks; and mountains, black, grim, and with snow-streaked summits, tower grandly on all sides. A broad cataract, a hundred feet high, leaped down a chasm on our left, so near to the road that its sprays swept over us, and then shot under a bridge to join the seething flood in the frightful gulf beneath. I was reminded of the Valley of the Reuss, on the road to St. Gothard, like which, the pass of the Rusten leads to a cold and bleak upper valley. Here we noticed the blight of late frost on the barley fields, and were for the first time assailed by beggars. Black storm-clouds hung over the gorge, adding to the savage wildness of its scenery; but the sun came out as we drove up the Valley of Dovre, with its long stretch of grain-fields on the sunny sweep of the hillside, sheltered by the lofty Dovre Fjeld behind them. We stopped for the night at the inn of Toftemoen, long before sunset, although it was eight o'clock, and slept in a half-daylight until morning.

The sun was riding high in the heavens when we left, and dark lowering clouds slowly rolled their masses across the mountain-tops. The Lougen was now an inconsiderable stream, and the superb Guldbrandsdal narrowed to a bare, bleak dell, like those in the high Alps. The grain-fields had a chilled, struggling appearance; the forests forsook the mountain-sides and throve only in sheltered spots at their bases; the houses were mere log cabins, many of which were slipping off their foundation-posts and tottering to their final fall; and the people, poorer than ever, came out of their huts to beg openly and shamelessly as we passed. Over the head of the valley, which here turns westward to the low water-shed dividing it from the famous Romsdal, rose two or three snow-streaked peaks of the Hurunger Fjeld; and the drifts filling the ravines of the mountains on our left descended lower and lower into the valley.

At Dombaas, a lonely station at the foot of the Dovre Fjeld, we turned northward into the heart of the mountains. My postillion, a boy of fifteen, surprised me by speaking very good English. He had learned it in the school at Drontheim. Sometimes, he said, they had a schoolmaster in the house, and sometimes one at Jerkin, twenty miles distant. Our road ascended gradually through half-cut woods of red pine, for two or three miles, after which it entered a long valley, or rather basin, belonging to the table land of the Dovre Fjeld. Stunted heath and dwarfed juniper-bushes mixed with a grey, foxy shrub-willow, covered the soil, and the pale yellow of the reindeer moss stained the rocks. Higher greyer and blacker ridges hemmed in the lifeless landscape; and above them, to the north and west, broad snow-fields shone luminous under the heavy folds of the clouds. We passed an old woman with bare legs and arms, returning from a *söter*, or summer chálet of the shepherds. She was a powerful but purely animal specimen of humanity,—"beef to the heel," as Braisted said. At last a cluster of log huts, with a patch of green pasture-ground

12*

about them, broke the monotony of the scene. It was Fogstuen, or next station, where we were obliged to wait half an hour until the horses had been caught and brought in. The place had a poverty stricken air; and the slovenly woman who acted as landlady seemed disappointed that we did not buy some horridly coarse and ugly woolen gloves of her own manufacture.

Our road now ran for fourteen miles along the plateau of the Dovre, more than 3000 feet above the level of the sea. This is not a plain or table land, but an undulating region, with hills, valleys, and lakes of its own; and more desolate landscapes one can scarcely find elsewhere. Everything is grey, naked, and barren, not on a scale grand enough to be imposing, nor with any picturesqueness of form to relieve its sterility. One can understand the silence and sternness of the Norwegians, when he has travelled this road. But I would not wish my worst enemy to spend more than one summer as a solitary herdsman on these hills. Let any disciple of Zimmerman try the effect of such a solitude. The statistics of insanity in Norway exhibit some of its effects, and that which is most common is most destructive. There never was a greater humbug than the praise of solitude: it is the fruitful mother of all evil, and no man covets it who has not something bad or morbid in his nature.

By noon the central ridge or comb of the Dovre Fjeld rose before us, with the six-hundred-year old station of Jerkin in a warm nook on its southern side. This is renowned as the best post-station in Norway, and is a favourite resort of English travellers and sportsmen, who come hither to climb the peak of Snæhätten, and to stalk reindeer. I did not find the place particularly inviting. The two women who had charge of it for the time were unusually silent and morose, but our dinner was cheap and well gotten up, albeit the trout were not the freshest. We admired the wonderful paintings of the landlord, which although noticed by Murray, give little promise for Norwegian art in these high latitudes. His cows, dogs, and men are all snow-white, and rejoice in an original anatomy.

The horses on this part of the road were excellent, the road admirable, and our transit was therefore thoroughly agreeable. The ascent of the dividing ridge, after leaving Jerkin, is steep and toilsome for half a mile, but with this exception the passage of the Dovre Fjeld is remarkably easy. The highest point which the road crossed is about 4600 feet above the sea, or a little higher than the Brenner Pass in the Tyrol. But there grain grows and orchards bear fruit, while here, under the parallel of 62°, nearly all vegetation ceases, and even the omnivorous northern sheep can find no pasturage. Before and behind you lie wastes of naked grey mountains, relieved only by the snow-patches on their summits. I have seen as desolate tracts of wilderness in the south made beautiful by the lovely hues which they took from the air; but Nature has no such tender fancies in the north. She is a realist of the most unpitying stamp, and gives atmospheric influences which make that which is dark and bleak still darker and bleaker. Black clouds hung low on the horizon, and dull grey sheets of rain swept now and then across the nearer heights. Snæhätten, to the westward, was partly veiled, but we could trace his blunt mound of alternate black rock and snow nearly to the apex. The peak is about 7700 feet above the sea, and was until recently considered the highest in Norway, but the Skagtolstind has been ascertained to be 160 feet higher, and Snæhätten is dethroned.

The river Driv came out of a glen on our left, and entered a deep gorge in front, down which our road lay, following the rapid descent of the foaming stream. At the station of Kongsvold, we had descended to 3000 feet again, yet no trees appeared. Beyond this, the road for ten miles has been with great labour hewn out of the solid rock, at the bottom of a frightful defile, like some of those among the Alps. Formerly, it climbed high up on the mountain-side, running on the brink of almost perpendicular cliffs, and the *Vaarsti*, as it is called, was then reckoned one of the most difficult and dangerous roads in the country. Now it is one of the safest and most delightful. We went down the pass on a sharp trot, almost too fast to enjoy the wild scenery as it deserved. The Driv fell through the cleft in a succession of rapids, while smaller streams leaped to meet him in links of silver cataract down a thousand feet of cliff. Birch and fir now clothed the little terraces and spare corners of soil, and the huge masses of rock, hanging over our heads, were tinted with black, warm brown, and russet orange, in such a manner as to produce the most charming effects of colour. Over the cornices of the mountain-walls, hovering at least two thousand feet above, gleamed here and there the scattered snowy *jötuns* of the highest fjeld.

The pass gradually opened into a narrow valley, where we found a little cultivation again. Here was the post of Drivstuen, kept by a merry old lady. Our next stage descended through increasing habitation and culture to the inn of Rise, where we stopped for the night, having the Dovre Fjeld fairly behind us. The morning looked wild and threatening, but the clouds gradually hauled off to the eastward, leaving us the promise of a fine day. Our road led over hills covered with forests of fir and pine, whence we looked into a broad valley clothed with the same dark garment of forest, to which the dazzling white snows of the fjeld in the background made a striking contrast. We here left the waters of the Driv and struck upon those of the Orkla, which flow into Drontheim Fjord. At Stuen, we got a fair breakfast of eggs, milk, cheese, bread and butter. Eggs are plentiful everywhere, yet, singularly enough, we were nearly a fortnight in Norway before we either saw or heard a single fowl. Where they were kept we could not discover, and why they did not crow was a still greater mystery. Norway is really the land of silence. For an inhabited country, it is the quietest I have ever seen. No wonder that anger and mirth, when they once break through the hard ice of Norwegian life, are so furious and uncontrollable. These inconsistent extremes may always be reconciled, when we understand how nicely the moral nature of man is balanced.

Our road was over a high, undulating tract for two stages, commanding wide views of a wild wooded region, which is said to abound with game. The range of snowy peaks behind us still filled the sky, appearing so near at hand as to deceive the eye in regard to their height. At last, we came upon the brink of a steep descent, overlooking the deep glen of the Orkla, a singularly picturesque valley, issuing from between the bases of the mountains, and winding away to the northward. Down the frightful slant our horses plunged, and in three minutes we were at the bottom, with flower-sown meadows on either hand, and the wooded sides of the glen sweeping up to a waving and fringed outline against the sky. After crossing the stream, we had an ascent as abrupt, on the other side; but half-way up stood the station of Bjærkager, where we left our panting horses. The fas stations were now at an end, but by paying fast prices we got horses with less delay. In the evening, a man travelling on foot offered to carry *förbud* notices for us to the remaining stations, if we would pay for his horse. We accepted; I wrote the orders in my best Norsk, and on the following day we found the horses in readiness everywhere.

The next stage was an inspiring trot through a park-like country, clothed with the freshest turf and studded with clumps of fir, birch, and ash. The air was soft and warm, and filled with balmy scents from the flowering grasses, and the millions of blossoms spangling the ground. In one place, I saw half an acre of the purest violet hue, where the pansy of our gardens grew so thickly that only its blossoms were visible. The silver green of the birch twinkled in the sun, and its jets of delicate foliage started up everywhere with exquisite effect amid the dark masses of the fir. There was little cultivation as yet, but these trees formed natural orchards, which suggested a design in their planting and redeemed the otherwise savage character of the scenery. We dipped at last into a hollow, down which flowed one of the tributaries of the Gûûl Elv, the course of which we thence followed to Drontheim.

One of the stations was a lonely *gaard*, standing apart from the road, on a high hill. As we drove up, a horrid old hag came out to receive us. "Can I get three horses soon?" I asked. "No," she answered with a chuckle. "How soon?" "In a few hours," was her indifferent reply, but the promise of paying fast rates got them in less than one. My friend wanted a glass of wine, but the old woman said she had nothing but milk. We were sitting on the steps with our pipes, shortly afterwards, when she said: "Why don't you go into the house?" "It smells too strongly of paint," I answered. "But you had better go in," said she, and shuffled off. When we entered, behold! there were three glasses of very good Marsala on the table. "How do you sell your milk?" I asked her. "That kind is three skillings a dram," she answered. The secret probably was that she had no license to sell wine. I was reminded of an incident which occurred to me in Maine, during the prevalence of the prohibitory law. I was staying at an hotel in a certain town, and jestingly asked the landlord: "Where is the Maine Law? I should like to see it." "Why," said he, "I have it here in the house;" and he unlocked a back room and astonished me with the sight of a private bar, studded with full decanters.

The men folks were all away at work, and our postillion was a strapping girl of eighteen, who rode behind Braisted. She was gotten up on an immense scale, but nature had expended so much vigour on her body that none was left for her brain. She was a consummate representation of health and stupidity. At the station where we stopped for the night I could not help admiring the solid bulk of the landlady's sister. Although not over twenty four she must have weighed full two hundred. Her waist was of remarkable thickness, and her bust might be made into three average American ones. I can now understand why Mügge calls his heroine Ilda "the strong maiden."

A drive of thirty-five miles down the picturesque valley of the Gûûl brought us to Drontheim the next day—the eighth after leaving Christiania.

CHAPTER XXIII.

DRONTHEIM.—VOYAGE UP THE COAST OF NORWAY.

OUR first view of Drontheim (or *Trondhjem*, as it should properly be written) was from the top of the hill behind the town, at the termination of six miles of execrable road, and perhaps the relief springing from that circumstance heightened the agreeable impression which the scene made upon our minds. Below us, at the bottom of a crescent-shaped bay, lay Drontheim—a mass of dark red, yellow, and brown buildings, with the grey cathedral in the rear. The rich, well cultivated valley of the Nid stretched behind it, on our right, past the Lierfoss, whose column of foam was visible three miles away, until the hills, rising more high and bleak behind each other, completely enclosed it. The rock-fortress of Munkholm, in front of the city, broke the smooth surface of the fjord, whose further shores, dim with passing showers, swept away to the north-east, hiding the termination of this great sea-arm, which is some fifty miles distant. The panorama was certainly on a grand scale, and presented very diversified and picturesque features; but I can by no means agree with Dr. Clarke, who compares it to the Bay of Naples. Not only the rich colours of the Mediterranean are wanting, but those harmonic sweeps and curves of the Italian shores and hills have nothing in common with these rude, ragged, weather beaten, defiant forms.

Descending the hill between rows of neat country-houses, we passed a diminutive fortification, and entered the city. The streets are remarkably wide and roughly paved, crossing each other at right angles, with a Philadelphian regularity. The houses are all two stories high, and raised upon ample foundations, so that the doors are approached by flights of steps—probably on account of the deep snows during the winter. They are almost exclusively of wood, solid logs covered with neat clap-boards, but a recent law forbids the erection of any more wooden houses, and in the course of time, the town, like Christiania, will lose all that is peculiar and characteristic in its architecture. A cleaner place can scarcely be found, and I also noticed, what is quite rare in the North, large square fountains or wells, at the intersection of all the principal streets. The impression which Drontheim makes upon the stranger is therefore a cheerful and genial one. Small and unpretending though it be, it is full of pictures; the dark blue fjord closes the vista of half its streets; hills of grey rock, draped with the greenest turf, overlook it on either side, and the beautiful valley of the Nid, one of the loveliest nooks of Norway, lies in its rear.

We drove to the Hotel de Belle-Vue, one of the two little caravanserais of which the town boasts, and were fortunate in securing the two vacant rooms. The hotel business in Norway is far behind that of any other country, except in regard to charges, where it is far in advance. Considering what one gets for his money, this is the most expensive country in the world for foreigners. Except where the rates are fixed by law, as in posting, the natives pay much less; and here is an instance of double-dealing which does not harmonise with the renowned honesty of the Norwegians. At the Belle-Vue, we were furnished with three very meagre meals a day, at the rate of two dollars and a half. The attendance was performed by two boys of fourteen or fifteen, whose services, as may be supposed, were quite inadequate to the wants of near twenty persons. The whole business of the establishment devolved on these two fellows, the landlady, though good-humoured and corpulent, as was meet, knowing nothing about the business, and, on the whole, it was a wonder that matters were not worse. It is singular that in a pastoral country like Norway one gets nothing but rancid butter, and generally sour cream, where both should be of the finest quality. Nature is sparing of her gifts, to be sure; but what she does furnish is of the best, as it comes from her hand. Of course, one does not look for much culinary skill, and is therefore not disappointed, but the dairy is the primitive domestic art of all races, and it is rather surprising to find it in so backward a state.

My friend, who received no letters, and had no transatlantic interests to claim his time, as I had, applied himself to seeing the place, which he accomplished, with praiseworthy industry, in one day. He walked out to the falls of the Nid, three miles up the valley, and was charmed with them. He then entered the venerable cathedral, where he had the satisfaction of seeing a Protestant clergyman perform high mass in a scarlet surplice, with a gold cross on his back

The State Church of Norway, which, like that of Sweden, is Lutheran of a very antiquated type, not only preserves this ritual, but also the form of confession (in a general way, I believe, and without reference to particular sins) and of absolution. Of course, it is violently dogmatic and illiberal, and there is little vital religious activity in the whole country. Until within a very few years, no other sects were tolerated, and even yet there is simply freedom of conscience, but not equal political rights, for those of other denominations. This concession has perhaps saved the church from becoming a venerable fossil, yet one still finds persons who regret that it should have been made, not knowing that all truth, to retain its temper, must be whetted against an opposing blade. According to the new constitution of Norway, the king must be crowned in the cathedral of Drontheim. Bernadotte received the proper consecration, but Oscar, though King of Norway, has not yet seen fit to accept it. I once heard a Norwegian exclaim, with a sort of jealous satisfaction: "Oscar calls himself King of Norway, but he is a king without a crown!" I cannot see, however, that this fact lessens his authority as sovereign, in the least.

There is a weekly line of steamers, established by the Storthing (Legislative Assembly), to Hammerfest and around the North Cape. The "Nordkap," the largest and best of these boats, was to leave Drontheim on Saturday evening, the 18th of July, and we lost no time in securing berths, as another week would have made it too late for the perpetual sunshine of the northern summer. Here again, one is introduced to a knowledge of customs and regulations unknown elsewhere. The ticket merely secures you a place on board the steamer, but neither a berth nor provisions. The latter you obtain from a restaurateur on board, according to fixed rates; the former depends on the will of the captain, who can stow you where he chooses. On the "Nordkap" the state-rooms were already occupied, and there remained a single small saloon containing eight berths. Here we did very well so long as there were only English and American occupants, who at once voted to have the skylight kept open; but after two Norwegians were added to our company, we lived in a state of perpetual warfare, the latter sharing the national dread of fresh air; and yet one of them was a professor from the University of Christiania, and the other a physician, who had charge of the hospital in Bergen! With this exception, we had every reason to be satisfied with the vessel. She was very stanch and steady-going, with a spacious airy saloon on deck; no captain could have been more kind and gentlemanly, and there was quite as much harmony among the passengers as could reasonably have been expected. Our party consisted of five Americans, three English, two Germans, and one Frenchman (M. Gay, Membre de l'Academie), besides a variety of Norwegians from all parts of the country.

Leaving our carrioles and part of our baggage behind us, we rowed out to the steamer in a heavy shower. The sun was struggling with dark grey rain-clouds all the evening, and just as we hove anchor, threw a splendid triumphal iris across the bay, completely spanning the town, which, with the sheltering hills, glimmered in the rosy mist floating within the bow. Enclosed by such a dazzling frame the picture of Drontheim shone with a magical lustre, like a vision of Asgaard, beckoning to us from the tempestuous seas. But we were bound for the north, the barriers of Niflhem, the land of fog and sleet, and we disregarded the celestial token, though a second perfect rainbow overarched the first, and the two threw their curves over hill and fortress and the bosom of the rainy fjord, until they almost touched our vessel on either side. In spite of the rain, we remained on deck until a late hour, enjoying the bold scenery of the outer fjord—here, precipitous woody shores, gashed with sudden ravines; there, jet-black rocky peaks, resembling the porphyry hills of the African deserts; and now and then, encircling the sheltered coves, soft green fields glowing with misty light, and the purple outlines of snow-streaked mountains in the distance.

The morning was still dark and rainy. We were at first running between mountain-islands of bare rock and the iron coast of the mainland, after which came a stretch of open sea for two hours, and at noon we reached Björö, near the mouth of the Namsen Fjord. Here there was half a dozen red houses on a bright green slope, with a windmill out of gear crowning the rocky hill in the rear. The sky gradually cleared as we entered the Namsen Fjord, which charmed us with the wildness and nakedness of its shores, studded with little nooks and corners of tillage, which sparkled like oases of tropical greenness, in such a rough setting. Precipices of dark-red rock, streaked with foamy lines of water from the snows melting upon their crests, frowned over the narrow channels between the islands, and through their gaps and gorges we caught sight of the loftier ranges inland. Namsos, at the head of the fjord, is a red-roofed town of a few hundred inhabitants, with a pleasant background of barley-fields and birchen groves. The Namsen valley, behind it, is one of the richest in this part of Norway, and is a great resort of English salmon-fishers. There was a vessel of two hundred tons on the stocks, and a few coasting crafts lying at anchor.

We had a beautiful afternoon voyage out another arm of the fjord, and again entered the labyrinth of islands fringing the coast. Already, the days had perceptibly lengthened, and the increased coldness of the air at night indicated our approach to the Arctic Circle. I was surprised at the amount of business done at the little stations where we touched. Few of these contained a dozen houses, yet the quantity of passengers and freight which we discharged and took on board, at each, could only be explained by the fact that these stations are generally outlets for a tolerably large population, hidden in the valleys and fjords behind, which the steamer does not visit. Bleak and desolate as the coast appears, the back country has its fertile districts—its pasture-ground, its corn-land and forests, of which the voyager sees nothing, and thus might be led to form very erroneous conclusions. Before we had been twenty-four hours out from Drontheim, there was a marked change in the appearance of the people we took on board. Not even in the neighborhood of Christiania or in the rich Guldbrandsdal were the inhabitants so well-dressed, so prosperous (judging from outward signs, merely), or so intelligent. They are in every respect more agreeable and promising specimens of humanity than their brothers of Southern Norway, notwithstanding the dark and savage scenery amidst which their lot is cast.

Toward midnight, we approached the rock of Torghätten, rising 1200 feet high, in the shape of a tall-crowned, battered "wide-awake," above the low, rocky isles and reefs which surround it. This rock is famous for a natural tunnel, passing directly through its heart—the path of an arrow which the Giant Horseman (of whom I shall speak presently shot at a disdainful maiden, equally colossal, in the old mythological times, when Odin got drunk nightly in Walhalla. We were all on the look-out for this tunnel, which, according to Murray, is large enough for a ship to go through —if it were not some six hundred feet above the sea-level. We had almost passed the rock and nothing of the kind could be seen; but Capt. Riis, who was on deck, encouraged us to have a little patience, changed the steamer's course, and presently we saw a dark cavern yawning in the face of a precipice on the northern side. It was now midnight, but a sunset light tinged the northern sky, and the Torghätten yet stood in twilight. "Shall we see through it?" was the question; but while we were discussing the chances, a faint star sparkled in the midst of the cavernous gloom. "You see it because you imagine it," cried some; yet, no, it was steadfast, and grew broad and bright, until even the most sceptical recognised the pale midnight sky at the bottom of the gigantic arch.

My friend aroused me at five in the morning to see the Seven Sisters—seven majestic peaks, 4000 feet high, and seated closely side by side, with their feet in the sea. They all wore nightcaps of gray fog, and had a sullen and sleepy air. I imagined they snored, but it was a damp wind driving over the rocks. They were northern beauties, hard-featured and large-boned, and I would not give a graceful southern hill, like Monte Albano or the Paphian Olympus, for the whole of them. So I turned in again, and did not awake until the sun had dried the decks, and the split, twisted and contorted forms of the islands gave promise of those remarkable figures which mark the position of the Arctic Circle. There was already a wonderful change in the scenery. The islands were high and broken, rising like towers and pyramids from the water, and grouped together in the most fantastic confusion. Between their jagged pinnacles, and through their sheer walls of naked rock, we could trace the same formation among the hills of the mainland, while in the rear, white against the sky, stretched the snowy table-land which forms a common summit for all. One is bewildered in the attempt to describe such scenery. There is no central figure, no prevailing character, no sharp contrasts, which may serve as a guide whereby to reach the imagination of the reader. All is confused, disordered, chaotic. One begins to understand the old Norse myth of these stones being thrown by the devil in a vain attempt to prevent the Lord from finishing the world. Grand as they are, singly, you are so puzzled by their numbers and by the fantastic manner in which they seem to dance around you, as the steamer threads the watery labyrinth, that you scarcely appreciate them as they deserve. Take almost any one of these hundreds, and place it inland, anywhere in Europe or America, and it will be visited, sketched and sung to distraction.

At last we saw in the west, far out at sea, the four towers of Threnen, rising perpendicularly many hundred feet from the water. Before us was the *Hestmand*, or Horseman, who bridles his rocky steed with the polar circle. At first, he appeared like a square turret crowning an irregular mass of island-rock, but, as we approached a colossal head rounded itself at the top, and a sweeping cloak fell from the broad shoulder, flowing backward to the horse's flanks. Still, there was no horse; but here again our captain took the steamer considerably out of her course, so that, at a distance of a mile the whole enormous figure, 1500 feet in height, lay clearly before us. A heavy beard fell from the grand, Jupitolian head; the horse, with sharp ears erect and head bent down, seemed to be plunging into the sea, which was already above his belly; the saddle had slipped forward, so that the rider sat upon his shoulders, but with his head proudly lifted, as if conscious of his fate, and taking a last look at the world. Was it not All-Father Odin, on his horse Sleipner, forsaking the new race which had ceased to worship him? The colossi of the Orient—Rameses and Brahma and Boodh —dwindle into insignificance before this sublime natural monument to the lost gods of the North.

At the little fishing-village of Anklakken, near the Horseman, a fair was being held, and a score or more of coasting craft, gay with Norwegian flags, lay at anchor. These *jægts*, as they are called, have a single mast, with a large square sail, precisely like those of the Japanese fishing junks, and their hulls are scarcely less heavy and clumsy. They are the Norwegian boats of a thousand years ago; all attempt to introduce a better form of ship-building having been in vain. But the romantic traveller should not suppose that he beholds the "dragons" of the Vikings, which were a very different craft, and have long since disappeared. The *jægts* are slow, but good seaboats, and as the article haste is not in demand anywhere in Norway, they probably answer every purpose as well as more rational vessels. Those we saw belonged to traders who cruise along the coast during the summer, attending the various fairs, which appear to be the principal recreation of the people. At any rate, they bring some life and activity into these silent solitudes. We had on board the effects of an Englishman who went on shore to see a fair and was left behind by a previous steamer. He had nothing with him but the clothes on his back, and spoke no Norsk: so the captain anxiously looked out for a melancholy, dilapidated individual at every station we touched at—but he looked in vain, for we neither saw nor heard anything of the unfortunate person.

All the afternoon, we had a continuation of the same wonderful scenery—precipices of red rock a thousand feet high, with snowy, turreted summits, and the loveliest green glens between. To the east were vast snow-fields, covering the eternal glaciers of the Alpine range. As we looked up the Salten Fjord, while crossing its mouth, the snows of Sultelma, the highest mountain in Lappmark, 6000 feet above the sea, were visible, about fifty miles distant. Next came the little town of Bödo, where we stopped for the night. It is a cluster of wooden houses, with roofs of green sod, containing about three hundred inhabitants. We found potatoes in the gardens, some currant bushes, and a few hardy vegetables, stunted ash trees and some patches of barley

The sun set a little before eleven o'clock, but left behind him a glory of colours which I have never seen surpassed. The snowy mountains of Lappmark were transmuted into pyramids of scarlet flame, beside which the most gorgeous sunset illuminations of the Alps would have been pale and tame. The sky was a sheet of saffron, amber and rose, reduplicated in the glassy sea, and the peaked island of Landegode in the west, which stood broad against the glow, became a mass of violet hue, topped with cliffs of crimson fire. I sat down on deck and tried to sketch this superb spectacle, in colours which nobody will believe to be real. Before I had finished, the sunset which had lighted one end of Landegode became sunrise at the other, and the fading Alps burned anew with the flames of morning.

CHAPTER XXIV.

THE LOFODEN ISLES.

THE northern summer soon teaches one fashionable habit of life. Like the man whose windows Sidney Smith darkened, and who slept all day because he thought it was night, you keep awake all night because you forget that it is not day. One's perception of time contracts in some mysterious way, and the sun, setting at eleven, seems to be no later than when he set at seven. You think you will enjoy the evening twilight an hour or two before going to bed, and lo! the morning begins to dawn. It seems absurd to turn in and sleep by daylight, but you sleep, nevertheless, until eight or nine o'clock, and get up but little refreshed with your repose. You miss the grateful covering of darkness, the sweet, welcome gloom, which shuts your senses, one after one, like the closing petals of a flower, in the restoring trance of the night. The light comes through your eyelids as you sleep, and a certain nervous life of the body that should sleep too keeps awake and active. I soon began to feel the wear and tear of perpetual daylight, in spite of its novelty and the many advantages which it presents to the traveller.

At Bödo, we were in sight of the Lofoden Islands, which

filled up all the northern and western horizon, rising like blue saw-teeth beyond the broad expanse of the West Fjord, which separates them from the group of the shore islands The next morning, we threaded a perfect labyrinth of rocks, after passing Grotö, and headed across the fjord, for Balstad, on West-Vaagöe, one of the outer isles. This passage is often very rough, especially when the wind blows from the south-west, rolling the heavy swells of the Atlantic into the open mouth of the fjord. We were very much favoured by the weather, having a clear sky, with a light north wind and smooth sea. The long line of jagged peaks, stretching from Værðe in the south west to the giant ridges of Hindöe in the north east, united themselves in the distance with the Alpine chain of the mainland behind us, forming an amphitheatre of sharp, snowy summits, which embraced five-sixths of the entire circle of the horizon, and would have certainly numbered not less than two hundred. Von Buch compares the Lofodens to the jaws of a shark, and most travellers since his time have resuscitated the comparison, but I did not find it so remarkably applicable. There are shark tooth peaks here and there, it is true, but the peculiar conformation of Norway—extensive plateaus, forming the summit-level of the mountains—extends also to these islands, whose only valleys are those which open to the sea, and whose interiors are uninhabitable snowy tracts, mostly above the line of vegetation.

On approaching the islands, we had a fair view of the last outposts of the group—the solid barriers against which the utmost fury of the Atlantic dashes in vain. This side of Værðe lay the large island of Mosköe, between which and a large solitary rock in the middle of the strait dividing them, is the locality of the renowned Maelström—now, alas! almost as mythical as the kraaken or great sea snake of the Norwegian fjords. It is a great pity that the geographical illusions of our boyish days cannot remain. You learn that the noise of Niagara can be heard 120 miles off, and that "some Indians, in their canoes, have ventured down it, with safety." Well, one could give up the Indians without much difficulty; but it is rather discouraging to step out of the Falls Depôt for the first time, within a quarter of a mile of the cataract, and hear no sound except "Cab sir?" "Hotel, sir?" So of the Maelström, denoted on my schoolboy map by a great spiral twist, which suggested to me a tremendous whirl of the ocean currents, aided by the information that "vessels cannot approach nearer than seven miles." In Olney, moreover, there was a picture of a luckless bark, half-way down the vortex. I had been warming my imagination, as we came up the coast, with Campbell's sonorous lines:

> "Round the shores where runic Odin
> Howls his war-song to the gale;
> Round the isles where loud Lofoden
> Whirls to death the roaring whale;"

and, as we looked over the smooth water towards Mosköe felt a renewed desire to make an excursion thither on our return from the north. But, according to Captain Riis, and other modern authorities which I consulted, the Maelström has lost all its terrors and attractions. Under certain conditions of wind and tide, an eddy is formed in the strait it is true, which may be dangerous to small boats—but the place is by no means so much dreaded as the Salten Fjord, where the tide, rushing in, is caught in such a manner as to form a *bore*, as in the Bay of Fundy, and frequently proves destructive to the fishing craft. It is the general opinion that some of the rocks which formerly made the Maelström so terrible have been worn away, or that some submarine convulsion has taken place which has changed the action of the waters; otherwise it is impossible to account for the reputation it once possessed.

It should also be borne in mind that any accident to a boat among these islands is more likely to prove disastrous than elsewhere, since there are probably not a score out of the twenty thousand Lofoden fishermen who pass half their lives on the water, who know how to swim. The water is too cold to make bathing a luxury, and they are not sufficiently prepossessed in favour of cleanliness to make it a duty. Nevertheless, they are bold sailors, in their way, and a tougher, hardier, more athletic class of men it would be difficult to find. Handsome they are not, but quite the reverse, and the most of them have an awkward and uncouth air; but it is refreshing to look at their broad shoulders, their brawny chests, and the massive muscles of their legs and arms. During the whole voyage, I saw but one man who appeared to be diseased. Such men, I suspect, were the Vikings—rough, powerful, ugly, dirty fellows, with a few primitive virtues, and any amount of robust vices. We noticed, however, a marked change for the better in the common people, as we advanced northward. They were altogether better dressed, better mannered, and more independent and intelligent, but with a hard, keen, practical expression of face, such as one finds among the shoremen of New-England. The school system of Norway is still sadly deficient, but there is evidently no lack of natural capacity among these people. Their prevailing vice is intemperance, which here, as in all other parts of the country, is beginning to diminish since restrictions have been placed upon the manufacture and sale of spirituous liquors, simultaneously with the introduction of cheap and excellent fermented drinks. The statistics of their morality also show a better state of things than in the South. There is probably no country population in the world where licentiousness prevails to such an extent as in the districts of Guldbrandsdal and Hedemark.

A voyage of four hours across the West Fjord brought us to the little village of Balstad, at the southern end of West-Vaagöe. The few red, sod-roofed houses were built upon a rocky point, behind which were some patches of bright green pasture, starred with buttercups, overhung by a splendid peak of dark-red rock, two thousand feet in height. It was a fine frontispiece to the Lofoden scenery which now opened before us. Running along the coast of West and East Vaagöe, we had a continual succession of the wildest and grandest pictures—thousand-feet precipices, with turrets and needles of rock piercing the sky, dazzling snow-fields, leaking away in cataracts which filled the ravines with foam, and mazes of bald, sea-worn rocks, which seem to have been thrown down from the scarred peaks in some terrible convulsion of nature. Here and there were hollows, affording stony pasturage for a few sheep and cows,

13*

and little wooden fisher-huts stood on the shore in the arms of sheltered coves. At the village of Svolvær, which is built upon a pile of bare stones, we took on board a number of ladies in fashionable dresses, with bonnets on the backs of their heads and a sufficiency of cumbrous petticoats to make up for the absence of hoops, which have not yet got further north than Dronthiem. In seeing these unexpected apparitions emerge from such a wild corner of chaos I could not but wonder at the march of modern civilisation. Pianos in Lapland, Parisian dresses among the Lofodens, billiard-tables in Hammerfest—whither shall we turn to find the romance of the North!

We sailed, in the lovely nocturnal sunshine, through the long, river-like channel—the Rasksund, I believe, it is called—between the islands of East-Vaagöe and Hindöe, the largest of the Lofodens. For a distance of fifteen miles the strait was in no place more than a mile in breadth, while it was frequently less than a quarter. The smooth water was a perfect mirror, reflecting on one side the giant cliffs, with their gorges choked with snow, their arrowy pinnacles and white lines of falling water—on the other, hills turfed to the summit with emerald velvet, sprinkled with pale groves of birch and alder, and dotted, along their bases, with the dwellings of the fishermen. It was impossible to believe that we were floating on an arm of the Atlantic—it was some unknown river, or a lake high up among the Alpine peaks. The silence of these shores added to the impression. Now and then a white sea-gull fluttered about the cliffs, or an eider duck paddled across some glassy cove, but no sound was heard: there was no sail on the water, no human being on the shore. Emerging at last from this wild and enchanting strait, we stood across a bay, opening southward to the Atlantic, to the port of Steilo, on one of the outer islands. Here the broad front of the island, rising against the roseate sky, was one swell of the most glorious green, down to the very edge of the sea, while the hills of East-Vaagöe, across the bay, showed only naked and defiant rock, with summit-fields of purple-tinted snow. In splendour of coloring, the tropics were again surpassed, but the keen north wind obliged us to enjoy it in an overcoat.

Toward midnight, the sun was evidently above the horizon, though hidden by intervening mountains. Braisted and another American made various exertions to see it, such as climbing the foremast, but did not succeed until about one o'clock, when they were favoured by a break in the hills. Although we had daylight the whole twenty-four hours, travellers do not consider that their duty is fulfilled unless they see the sun itself, exactly at midnight. In the morning, we touched at Throndenaes, on the northern side of Hindöe, a beautiful bay with green and wooded shores, and then, leaving the Lofodens behind us, entered the archipelago of large islands which lines the coast of Finmark. Though built on the same grand and imposing scale as the Lofodens, these islands are somewhat less jagged and abrupt in their forms, and exhibit a much more luxuriant vegetation. In fact, after leaving the Namsen Fjord, near Dronthiem, one sees very little timber until he reaches the parallel of 69°. The long straits between Senjen and Qvalö and the mainland are covered with forests of birch and turfy slopes greener than England has ever shown. At the same time the snow level was not more than 500 feet above the sea, and broad patches lay melting on all the lower hills. This abundance of snow seems a singular incongruity, when you look upon the warm summer sky and the dark, mellow, juicy green of the shores. One fancies that he is either sailing upon some lofty inland lake, or that the ocean-level in these latitudes must be many thousand feet higher than in the temperate zone. He cannot believe that he is on the same platform with Sicily and Ceylon.

After a trip up the magnificent Maans Fjord, and the sight of some sea-green glaciers, we approached Tromsöe, the capital of Finmark. This is a town of nearly 3000 inhabitants, on a small island in the strait between Qvalö and the mainland. It was just midnight when we dropped anchor, but, although the sun was hidden by a range of snowy hills in the north, the daylight was almost perfect. I immediately commenced making a sketch of the harbour, with its fleet of coasting vessels. Some Russian craft from Archangel, and a Norwegian cutter carrying six guns, were also at anchor before the town. Our French traveller, after amusing himself with the idea of my commencing a picture at sunset and finishing it at sunrise, started for a morning ramble over the hills. Boats swarmed around the steamer; the coal-lighters came off, our crew commenced their work, and when the sun's disc appeared, before one o'clock, there was another day inaugurated. The night had vanished mysteriously, no one could tell how.

CHAPTER XXV.

FINMARK AND HAMMERFEST.

THE steamer lay at Tromsöe all day, affording us an opportunity to visit an encampment of Lapps in Tromsdal, about four miles to the eastward. So far as the Lapps were concerned, I had seen enough of them, but I joined the party for the sake of the northern summer. The captain was kind enough to despatch a messenger to the Lapps, immediately on our arrival, that their herd of reindeer, pasturing on the mountains, might be driven down for our edification, and also exerted himself to procure a horse for the American lady. The horse came, in due time, but a side saddle is an article unknown in the arctic regions, and the lady was obliged to trust herself to a man's saddle and the guidance of a Norseman of the most remarkable health, strength, and stupidity.

Our path led up a deep valley, shut in by overhanging cliffs, and blocked up at the eastern end by the huge mass of the fjeld. The streams, poured down the crags from their snowy reservoirs, spread themselves over the steep side of the hill, making a succession of quagmires, over which we were obliged to spring and scramble in break-neck style

The sun was intensely hot in the enclosed valley, and we found the shade of the birchen groves very grateful. Some of the trees grew to a height of forty feet, with trunks the thickness of a man's body. There were also ash and alder trees, of smaller size, and a profusion of brilliant wild flowers. The little multeberry was in blossom; the ranunculus, the globe-flower, the purple geranium, the heath, and the blue forget-me-not spangled the ground, and on every hillock the young ferns unrolled their aromatic scrolls written with wonderful fables of the southern spring. For it was only spring here, or rather the very beginning of summer. The earth had only become warm enough to conceive and bring forth flowers, and she was now making the most of the little maternity vouchsafed to her. The air was full of winged insects, darting hither and thither in astonishment at finding themselves alive; the herbage seemed to be visibly growing under your eyes; even the wild shapes of the trees were expressive of haste, lest the winter might come on them unawares; and I noticed that the year's growth had been shot out at once, so that the young sprays might have time to harden and to protect the next year's buds. There was no lush, rollicking out-burst of foliage, no mellow, epicurean languor of the woods, no easy unfolding of leaf on leaf, as in the long security of our summers; but everywhere a feverish hurry on the part of nature to do something, even if it should only be half done. And above the valley, behind its mural ramparts, glowered the cold white snows, which had withdrawn for a little while, but lay in wait, ready to spring down as soon as the protecting sunshine should fail.

The lady had one harmless tumble into the mud, and we were all pretty well fatigued with our rough walk, when we reached the Lapp encampment. It consisted only of two families, who lived in their characteristic *gammes*, or huts of earth, which serve them also for winter dwellings. These burrows were thrown up on a grassy meadow, beside a rapid stream which came down from the fjeld; and at a little distance were two folds, or *corrals* for their reindeer, fenced with pickets slanting outward. A number of brown-haired, tailless dogs, so much resembling bear-cubs that at first sight we took them for such, were playing about the doors. A middle-aged Lapp, with two women and three or four children, were the inmates. They scented profit, and received us in a friendly way, allowing the curious strangers to go in and out at pleasure, to tease the dogs, drink the reindeer milk, inspect the children, rock the baby, and buy horn spoons to the extent of their desire. They were smaller than the Lapps of Kautokeino—or perhaps the latter appeared larger in their winter dresses—and astonishingly dirty. Their appearance is much more disgusting in summer than in winter, when the snow, to a certain extent, purifies everything. After waiting an hour or more, the herd appeared descending the fjeld, and driven toward the fold by two young Lapps, assisted by their dogs. There were about four hundred in all, nearly one-third being calves. Their hoarse bleating and the cracking noise made by their knee-joints, as they crowded together into a dense mass of grey, mossy backs, made a very peculiar sound; and this combined with their ragged look, from the process of shedding their coats of hair, did not very favourably impress those of our party who saw them for the first time. The old Lapp and his boy, a strapping fellow of fifteen, with a ruddy, olive complexion and almost Chinese features, caught a number of the cows with lassos, and proceeded to wean the young deer by anointing the mothers' dugs with cow-dung, which they carried in pails slung over their shoulders. In this delightful occupation we left them, and returned to Tromsöe.

As we crossed the mouth of the Ulvsfjord, that evening we had an open sea horizon toward the north, a clear sky, and so much sunshine at eleven o'clock that it was evident the Polar day had dawned upon us at last. The illumination of the shores was unearthly in its glory, and the wonderful effects of the orange sunlight, playing upon the dark hues of the island cliffs, can neither be told nor painted. The sun hung low between Fuglöe, rising like a double dome from the sea, and the tall mountains of Arnöe, both of which islands resembled immense masses of transparent purple glass, gradually melting into crimson fire at their bases. The glassy, leaden-coloured sea was powdered with a golden bloom, and the tremendous precipices at the mouth of the Lyngen Fjord, behind us, were steeped in a dark red, mellow flush, and touched with pencillings of pure, rose-coloured light, until their naked ribs seemed to be clothed in imperial velvet. As we turned into the Fjord and ran southward along their bases, a waterfall, struck by the sun, fell in fiery orange foam down the red walls, and the blue ice-pillars of a beautiful glacier filled up the ravine beyond it. We were all on deck, and all faces, excited by the divine splendour the scene, and tinged by the same wonderful aureole, shone as if transfigured. In my whole life I have never seen a spectacle so unearthly beautiful.

Our course brought the sun rapidly toward the ruby cliffs of Arnöe, and it was evident that he would soon be hidden from sight. It was not yet half-past eleven, and an enthusiastic passenger begged the captain to stop the vessel until midnight. " Why," said the latter, "it is midnight now, or very near it; you have Drontheim time, which is almost forty minutes in arrears." True enough, the real time lacked but five minutes of midnight, and those of us who had sharp eyes and strong imaginations saw the sun make his last dip and rise a little, before he vanished in a blaze of glory behind Arnöe. I turned away with my eyes full of dazzling spheres of crimson and gold, which danced before me wherever I looked, and it was a long time before they were blotted out by the semi-oblivion of a daylight sleep.

The next morning found us at the entrance of the long Alten Fjord. Here the gashed, hacked, split, scarred and shattered character of the mountains ceases, and they suddenly assume a long, rolling outline, full of bold features, but less wild and fantastic. On the southern side of the fjord many of them are clothed with birch and fir to the height of a thousand feet. The valleys here are cultivated to some extent, and produce, in good seasons, tolerable crops of potatoes, barley, and buckwheat. This is above lat. 70°, or parallel with the northern part of Greenland, and consequently the highest cultivated land in the world. In the valley of the Alten River, the Scotch fir sometimes reaches a height of seventy or eighty feet. This district is called the Paradise of Finmark, and no doubt floats in the imaginations of the settlers on Mageröe and the dreary Porsanger Fjord, as Andalusia and Syria float in ours. It is well that human bliss is so relative in its character.

At Talvik, a cheerful village with a very neat, pretty church, who should come on board but Pastor Hvoslef, our Kautokeino friend of the last winter! He had been made one of a Government Commission of four, appointed to investigate and report upon the dissensions between the nomadic Lapps and those who have settled habitations. A better person could not have been chosen than this good man, who has the welfare of the Lapps truly at heart, and in whose sincerity every one in the North confides.

We had on board Mr. Thomas, the superintendent of the copper works at Kaafjord, who had just resigned his seat in the Storthing and given up his situation for the purpose of taking charge of some mines at Copiapo, in Chili. Mr Thomas is an Englishman, who has been for twenty years past one of the leading men of Finmark, and no other man, I venture to say, has done more to improve and enlighten that neglected province. His loss will not be easily replaced. At Talvik, his wife, a pleasant, intelligent Norwegian lady came on board; and, as we passed the rocky portals guarding the entrance to the little harbour of Kaafjord, a gun, planted on a miniature battery above the landing-place, pealed forth a salute of welcome. I could partly understand Mr. Thomas's long residence in those regions, when I saw what a wild, picturesque spot he had chosen for his home. The cavernous entrances to the copper mines yawned in the face of the cliff above the outer bay below, on the water's edge, stood the smelting works, surrounded by labourers' cottages; a graceful white church crowned a rocky headland a little further on; and beyond, above a green lawn, decked with a few scattering birches, stood a comfortable mansion, with a garden in the rear. The flag of Norway and the cross of St. George floated from separate staffs on the lawn. There were a number of houses, surrounded with potato-fields on the slope stretching around the bay, and an opening of the hills at its head gave us a glimpse of the fir forests of the inland valleys. On such a cloudless day as we had, it was a cheerful and home-like spot.

We took a friendly leave of Mr. Thomas and departed, the little battery giving us I don't know how many three-gun salutes as we moved off. A number of whales spouted on all sides of us as we crossed the head of the fjord to Bosekop, near the mouth of the Alten River. This is a little village on a bare rocky headland, which completely shuts out from view the rich valley of the Alten, about which the Finmarkers speak with so much enthusiasm. "Ah, you should see the farms on the Alten," say they; "there we have large houses, fields, meadows, cattle, and the finest timber." This is Altengaard, familiar to all the readers of Mügge's "Afraja." The *gaard*, however, is a single large estate, and not a name applied to the whole district, as those unfamiliar with Norsk nomenclature might suppose. Here the Catholics have established a mission—ostensibly a missionary boarding-house, for the purpose of acclimating arctic apostles; but the people, who regard it with the greatest suspicion and distrust, suspect that the ultimate object is the overthrow of their inherited, venerated, and deeply-rooted Lutheran faith. At Bosekop we lost Pastor Hvoslef, and took on board the chief of the mission, the Catholic Bishop of the Arctic Zone—for I believe his diocese includes Greenland, Spitzbergen, and Polar America. Here is a Calmuck Tartar, thought I, as a short, strongly-built man, with sallow complexion, deep-set eyes, broad nostrils, heavy mouth, pointed chin, and high cheek-bones, stepped on board; but he proved to be a Russian baron, whose conversion cost him his estates. He had a massive head, however, in which intellect predominated, and his thoroughly polished manners went far to counteract the effect of one of the most unprepossessing countenances I ever saw.

M. Gay, who had known the bishop at Paris, at once entered into conversation with him. A short time afterwards, my attention was drawn to the spot where they stood by loud and angry exclamations. Two of our Norwegian *savans* stood before the bishop, and one of them, with a face white with rage, was furiously vociferating: "It is not true! it is not true! Norway is a free country!" "In this respect, it is not free," answered the bishop, with more coolness than I thought he could have shown, under such circumstances: "You know very well that no one can hold office except those who belong to your State Church—neither a Catholic, nor a Methodist, nor a Quaker: whereas in France, as I have said, a Protestant may even become a minister of the Government." "But we do not believe in the Catholic faith:—we will have nothing to do with it!" screamed the Norwegian. "We are not discussing our creeds," answered the bishop· "I say that, though Norway is a free country, politically, it does *not* secure equal rights to all its citizens, and so far as the toleration of religious beliefs is concerned, it is behind most other countries of Europe." He thereupon retreated to the cabin, for a crowd had gathered about the disputants, and the deck-passengers pressing aft, seemed more than usually excited by what was going on. The Norwegian shaking with fury, hissed through his set teeth: "How dare he come here to insult our national feeling!" Yes, but every word was true; and the scene was only another illustration of the intense vanity of the Norwegians in regard to their country. Woe to the man who says a word against Norway, though he say nothing but what everybody knows to be true! So long as you praise everything—scenery, people, climate, institutions, and customs — or keep silent where you cannot praise, you have the most genial conversation; but drop a word of honest dissent or censure, and you will see how quickly every one draws back into his shell. There are parts of our own country where a foreigner might make the same observation. Let a Norwegian travel in the Southern States, and dare to say a word in objection to slavery!

There is nothing of interest between Alten and Hammerfest, except the old sea-margins on the cliffs and a small glacier on the island of Seiland. The coast is dismally bleak and barren. Whales were very abundant; we sometimes saw a dozen spouting at one time. They were of the hump-backed species, and of only moderate size; yet the fishery would doubtless pay very well, if the natives had enterprise enough to undertake it. I believe, however, there is no whale fishery on the whole Norwegian coast. The desolate hills of Qvalö surmounted by the pointed peak of the Tjuve Fjeld, or "Thief Mountain,"—so called because it steals so much of the winter sunshine,—announced our approach to Hammerfest, and towards nine o'clock in the evening we were at anchor in the little harbour. The summer trade had just opened, and forty Russian vessels, which had arrived from the White Sea during the previous week or two, lay crowded before the large fish warehouses built along the water. They were all three-masted schooners the main and mizen masts set close together, and with very heavy, square hulls. Strong Muscovite faces, adorned with magnificent beards, stared at us from the decks, and a jabber of Russian, Finnish, Lapp, and Norwegian, came from the rough boats crowding about our gangways. The north wind, blowing to us off the land, was filled with the perfume of dried codfish, train oil, and burning whale-"scraps," with which, as we soon found, the whole place is thoroughly saturated.

There is one hotel in the place, containing half a dozen chambers of the size of a state-room. We secured quarters here with a great deal of difficulty, owing to slowness of comprehension on the part of an old lady who had charge of the house. The other American, who at first took rooms for himself and wife, gave them up again very prudently; for the noises of the billiard-room penetrated through the thin wooden partitions, and my bed, at least, had been slept in by one of the codfish aristocracy, for the salty odour was so pungent that it kept me awake for a long time. With our fare, we had less reason to complain. Fresh salmon, arctic ptarmigan, and reindeer's tongue were delicacies which would have delighted any palate, and the wine had really seen Bordeaux, although rainy weather had evidently prevailed during the voyage thence to Hammerfest. The town lies in a deep bight, inclosed by precipitous cliffs, on the south-western side of the island, whence the sun, by this time long past his midsummer altitude, was not visible at midnight. Those of our passengers who intended returning by the *Nordkap* climbed the hills to get another view of him, but unfortunately went upon the wrong summit, so that they did not see him after all. I was so fatigued, from the imperfect sleep of the sunshiny nights and the crowd of new and exciting impressions which the voyage had given me, that I went to bed; but my friend sat up until long past midnight, writing, with curtains drawn.

CHAPTER XXVI.

THE MIDNIGHT SUN.

Most of the travellers who push as far north as Hammerfest content themselves with one experience of the midnight sun, and return with the same steamer to Drontheim A few extend their journey to the North Cape, and, once a year, on an average, perhaps, some one is adventurous enough to strike across Lapland to Torneå. The steamers, nevertheless, pass the North Cape, and during the summer make weekly trips to the Varanger Fjord, the extreme eastern limit of the Norwegian territory. We were divided in opinion whether to devote our week of sunshine to the North Cape, or to make the entire trip and see something of the northern coast of Europe, but finally decided that the latter, on the whole, as being unfamiliar ground, would be most interesting. The screw-steamer Gyller (one of Odin's horses) was lying in the harbour when we arrived, and was to leave in the course of the next night; so we lost no time in securing places, as she had but a small cabin and no state-rooms. Nevertheless, we found her very comfortable, and in every respect far superior to the English vessels which ply between Hull and Christiania. Our fellow travellers were all returning to Drontheim—except three Norwegian officers on their way to make an official inspection of the fortress of Wardöhuus—and the last we saw of them was their return, an hour past midnight, from making a second attempt to see the sun from the hills. The night was somewhat obscured, and I doubt if they were successful.

When I went on deck on the morning after our departure, we were in the narrow strait between the island of Mageröe, the northern extremity of which forms the North Cape, and the mainland. On either side, the shores of bare bleak rock, spotted with patches of moss and stunted grass, rose precipitously from the water, the snow filling up their ravines from the summit to the sea. Not a tree nor a shrub, nor a sign of human habitation was visible; there was no fisher's sail on the lonely waters, and only the cries of some sea-gulls, wheeling about the cliffs, broke the silence. As the strait opened to the eastward, a boat appeared, beating into Kjelvik, on the south-eastern corner of the island; but the place itself was concealed from us by an intervening cape. This is the spot which Von Buch visited in the summer of 1807, just fifty years ago, and his description would be equally correct at the present day. Here, where the scurvy carries off half the inhabitants,—where pastors coming from Southern Norway die within a year,—where no trees grow, no vegetables come to maturity, and gales from every quarter of the Icy Sea beat the last faint life out of nature, men will still persist in living, in apparent defiance of all natural laws. Yet they have at least an excuse for it, in the miraculous provision which Providence has made for their food and fuel. The sea and fjords are alive with fish, which are not only a means of existence but of profit to them, while the wonderful Gulf Stream, which crosses 5000 miles of the Atlantic to die upon this Ultima Thule in a last struggle with the Polar Sea, casts up the spoils of tropical forests to feed their fires. Think of arctic fishers burning upon their hearths the palms of Hayti, the mahogany of Honduras, and the precious woods of the Amazon and the Orinoco!

In the spring months, there are on an average 800 vessels on the northern coast, between the North Cape and Vadsö, with a fishing population of 5000 men on board, whose average gains, even at the scanty prices they receive amount to $30 apiece, making a total yield of $150,000. It is only within a very few years that the Norwegian Government has paid any attention to this far corner of the peninsula. At present, considering the slender population, the means of communication are well kept up during eight months in the year, and the result is an increase (perceptible to an old resident, no doubt) in the activity and prosperity of the country.

On issuing from the strait, we turned southward into the great Porsanger Fjord, which stretches nearly a hundred miles into the heart of Lapland, dividing Western from Eastern Finmark. Its shores are high monotonous hills, half covered with snow, and barren of vegetation except patches of grass and moss. If once wooded, like the hills of the Alten Fjord, the trees have long since disappeared, and now nothing can be more bleak and desolate. The wind blew violently from the east, gradually lifting a veil of grey clouds from the cold pale sky, and our slow little steamer with jib and fore-topsail set, made somewhat better progress. Toward evening (if there is such a time in the arctic summer), we reached Kistrand, the principal settlement on the fjord. It has eight or nine houses, scattered along a gentle slope a mile in length, and a little red church, but neither gardens, fields, nor potato patches. A strip of grazing ground before the principal house was yellow with dandelions, the slope behind showed patches of brownish-green grass, and above this melancholy attempt at summer stretched the cold, grey, snow-streaked ridge of the hill. Two boats, manned by sea-Lapps, with square blue caps, and long ragged locks of yellow hair fluttering in the wind, brought off the only passenger and the mails, and we put about for the mouth of the fjord.

Running along under the eastern shore, we exchanged the dreadful monotony through which we had been sailing for more rugged and picturesque scenery. Before us rose a wall of dark cliff, from five to six hundred feet in height, gaping here and there with sharp clefts or gashes, as if it had cracked in cooling, after the primeval fires. The summit of these cliffs was the average level of the country; and this peculiarity, I found, applies to all the northern shore of Finmark, distinguishing the forms of the capes and islands from those about Alten and Hammerfest, which, again, are quite different from those of the Lofodens. "On returning from Spitzbergen," said a Hammerfest merchant to me, "I do not need to look at chart or compass, when I get sight of the coast; I know, from the formation of the cliffs, exactly where I am." There is some general resemblance to the chalk bluffs of England, especially about

Beachy Head, but the rock here appears to be mica-slate, disposed in thin, vertical strata, with many violent transverse breaks.

As we approached the end of the promontory which divides the Porsanger from the Laxe Fjord, the rocks became more abrupt and violently shattered. Huge masses, fallen from the summit, lined the base of the precipice, which was hollowed into cavernous arches, the home of myriads of sea-gulls. The rock of Sværholtklub, off the point, resembled a massive fortress in ruins. Its walls of smooth masonry rested on three enormous vaults, the piers of which were buttressed with slanting piles of rocky fragments. The ramparts, crenelated in some places, had mouldered away in others, and one fancied he saw in the rents and scars of the giant pile the marks of the shot and shell which had wrought its ruin. Thousands of white gulls, gone to their nightly roost, rested on every ledge and cornice of the rock; but preparations were already made to disturb their slumbers. The steamer's cannon was directed towards the largest vault, and discharged. The fortress shook with the crashing reverberation; "then rose a shriek, as of a city sacked"—a wild, piercing, maddening, myriad-tongued cry, which still rings in my ears. With the cry, came a rushing sound, as of a tempest among the woods; a white cloud burst out of the hollow arch-way, like the smoke of an answering shot, and, in the space of a second, the air was filled with birds, thicker than autumn leaves, and rang with one universal, clanging shriek. A second shot, followed by a second outcry and an answering discharge from the other caverns, almost darkened the sky. The whirring, rustling and screaming, as the birds circled overhead, or dropped like thick scurries of snow-flakes on the water, was truly awful. There could not have been less than fifty thousand in the air at one time, while as many more clung to the face of the rock, or screamed from the depth of the vaults. Such an indignation meeting I never attended before; but, like many others I have heard of, the time for action was passed before they had decided what to do.

It was now eleven o'clock, and Sværholt glowed in fiery bronze lustre as we rounded it, the eddies of returning birds gleaming golden in the nocturnal sun, like drifts of beech leaves in the October air. Far to the north, the sun lay in a bed of saffron light over the clear horizon of the Arctic Ocean. A few bars of dazzling orange cloud floated above him, and still higher in the sky, where the saffron melted through delicate rose-colour into blue, hung light wreaths of vapour, touched with pearly, opaline flushes of pink and golden grey. The sea was a web of pale slate-colour, shot through and through with threads of orange and saffron, from the dance of a myriad shifting and twinkling ripples. The air was filled and permeated with the soft, mysterious glow, and even the very azure of the southern sky seemed to shine through a net of golden gauze. The headlands of this deeply-indented coast—the capes of the Laxe and Porsanger Fjords, and of Mageröe—lay around us, in different degrees of distance, but all with foreheads touched with supernatural glory. Far to the north-east was Nordkyn, the most northern point of the mainland of Europe, gleaming rosily and faint in the full beams of the sun, and just as our watches denoted midnight the North Cape appeared to the westward

—a long line of purple bluff, presenting a vertical front of nine hundred feet in height to the Polar Sea. Midway between those two magnificent headlands stood the Midnight Sun, shining on us with subdued fires, and with the gorgeous colouring of an hour for which we have no name, since it is neither sunset nor sunrise, but the blended loveliness of both —but shining at the same moment, in the heat and splendour of noonday, on the Pacific Isles.

This was the midnight sun as I had dreamed it—as I had hoped to see it.

Within fifteen minutes after midnight, there was a perceptible increase of altitude, and in less than half an hour the whole tone of the sky had changed, the yellow brightening into orange, and the saffron melting into the pale vermilion of dawn. Yet it was neither the colours, nor the same character of light as we had had, half an hour *before* midnight. The difference was so slight as scarcely to be described; but it was the difference between evening and morning. The faintest transfusion of one prevailing tint into another had changed the whole expression of heaven and earth, and so imperceptibly and miraculously that a new day was already present to our consciousness. Our view of the wild cliffs of Sværholt, less than two hours before, belonged to yesterday, though we had stood on deck, in full sunshine, during all the intervening time. Had the sensation of a night slipped through our brains in the momentary winking of the eyes? Or was the old routine of consciousness so firmly stereotyped in our natures, that the view of a morning was sufficient proof to them of the preëxistence of a night? Let those explain the phenomenon who can—but I found my physical senses utterly at war with those mental perceptions wherewith they should harmonise. The eye saw but one unending day; the mind notched the twenty-four hours on its calendar, as before.

Before one o'clock we reached the entrance of the Kiöllefjord, which in the pre-diluvial times must have been a tremendous mountain gorge, like that of Gondo, on the Italian side of the Simplon. Its mouth is about half a mile in breadth, and its depth is not more than a mile and a half. It is completely walled in with sheer precipices of bare rock, from three to five hundred feet in height, except at the very head, where they subside into a stony heap, upon which some infatuated mortals have built two or three cabins. As we neared the southern headland, the face of which was touched with the purest orange light, while its yawning fissures lay in deep-blue gloom, a tall ruin, with shattered turrets and crumbling spires, detached itself from the mass, and stood alone at the foot of the precipice. This is the *Finnkirka*, or "Church of the Lapps," well known to all the northern coasters. At first it resembles a tall church with a massive square spire; but the two parts separate again, and you have a crag-perched castle of the middle-ages, with its watch-tower—the very counterpart of scores in Germany—and a quaint Gothic chapel on the point beyond. The vertical strata of the rock, worn into sharp points at the top and gradually broadening to the base, with numberless notched ornaments and channels fluted by the rain, make the resemblance marvellous, when seen under the proper effects of light and shade. The lustre in which we saw it had the effect of enchantment. There was a play of colours upon it, such as one sees in illuminated Moorish halls, and I am almost afraid to say how much I was enraptured by a scene which has not its equal on the whole Norwegian coast, yet of which none of us had ever heard before.

We landed a single passenger—a government surveyor apparently—on the heap of rocks beyond, and ran out under the northern headland, which again charmed us with a glory peculiarly its own. Here the colours were a part of the substance of the rock, and the sun but heightened and harmonised their tones. The huge projecting masses of pale yellow had a mellow gleam, like golden chalk; behind them were cliffs, violet in shadow; broad strata of soft red, tipped on the edges with vermilion; thinner layers, which shot up vertically to the height of four or five hundred feet, and striped the splendid sea-wall with lines of bronze, orange, brown, and dark red, while great rents and breaks interrupted these marvellous frescoes with their dashes of uncertain gloom. I have seen many wonderful aspects of nature, in many lands, but rock-painting such as this I never beheld. A part of its effect may have been owing to atmospheric conditions which must be rare, even in the North; but, without such embellishments, I think the sight of this coast will nobly repay any one for continuing his voyage beyond Hammerfest.

We lingered on deck, as point after point revealed some change in the dazzling diorama, uncertain which was finest, and whether something still grander might not be in store. But at last Nordkyn drew nigh, and at three o'clock the light became that of day, white and colourless. The northeast wind blew keenly across the Arctic Ocean, and we were both satisfied and fatigued enough to go to bed. It was the most northern point of our voyage—about 71° 20', which is further north than I ever was before, or ever wish to be again.

14*

CHAPTER XXVII.

THE VARANGER FJORD.—ARCTIC LIFE.

WHEN we awoke, after six hours' sleep, with curtains drawn to keep out the daylight, our steamer was deep in the Tana Fjord, which receives the waters of the Tana River, the lagest Lapland stream flowing into the Arctic Ocean. The greater part of the day was consumed in calling at two settlements of three houses each, and receiving and delivering mails of one letter, or less. The shores of this fjord are steep hills of bare rock, covered with patches of snow to the water's edge. The riven walls of cliff, with their wonderful configuration and marvellous colouring, were left behind us, and there was nothing of the grand or picturesque to redeem the savage desolation of the scenery The chill wind, blowing direct from Nova Zembla, made us shiver, and even the cabin saloon was uncomfortable without a fire. After passing the most northern point of Europe, the coast falls away to the south-east, so that on the second night we were again in the latitude of Hammerfest, but still within the sphere of perpetual sunshine. Our second night of sun was not so rich in colouring as the first, yet we remained on deck long enough to see the orb rise again from his lowest dip, and change evening into morning by the same incomprehensible process. There was no golden transfiguration of the dreadful shore; a wan lustre played over the rocks—pictures of eternal death—like a settled pallor of despair on Nature's stony face.

One of the stations on this coast, named Makur, consisted of a few fishermen's huts, at the bottom of a dismal rocky bight. There was no grass to be seen, except some tufts springing from the earth with which the roofs were covered, and it was even difficult to see where so much earth had been scraped together. The background was a hopelessly barren hill, more than half enveloped in snow. And this was midsummer—and human beings passed their lives here! "Those people surely deserve to enter Paradise when they die," I remarked to my friend, "for they live in hell while upon earth." "Not for that," he answered, "but because it is impossible for them to commit sin. They cannot injure their neighbours, for they have none. They cannot steal, for there is nothing to tempt them. They cannot murder, for there are none of the usual incentives to hate and revenge. They have so hard a struggle merely *to live*, that they cannot fall into the indulgences of sense; so that if there is nothing recorded in their favour, there is also nothing against them, and they commence the next life with blank books."

"But what a life!" I exclaimed. "Men may be happy in poverty, in misfortune, under persecution, in life-long disease even, so that they are not wholly deprived of the genial influences of society and Nature—but what is there here?" "They know no other world," said he, "and this ignorance keeps them from being miserable. They do no more thinking than is necessary to make nets and boats, catch fish and cook them, and build their log-houses. Nature provides for their marrying and bringing up their children, and the pastor, whom they see once in a long time, gives them their religion ready made." God keep them ignorant, then! was my involuntary prayer. May they never lose their blessed stupidity, while they are chained to these rocks and icy seas! May no dreams of summer and verdure, no vision of happier social conditions, or of any higher sphere of thought and action, flash a painful light on the dumb-darkness of their lives!

The next day, we were in the Varanger Fjord, having passed the fortress of Vardöhuus and landed our military committee. The Norwegian shore was now low and tame, but no vegetation, except a little brown grass, was to be seen. The Russian shore, opposite, and some twenty-five or thirty miles distant, consisted of high, bold hills, which, through a glass, appeared to be partially wooded. The Varanger Fjord, to which so important a political interest has attached within the last few years, is about seventy miles in depth, with a general direction towards the southwest. The boundary-line between Norwegian and Russian Finmark strikes it upon the southern side, about half-way from the mouth, so that three-fourths, or more, of the waters of the fjord belong to Norway. There is, however, a wonderful boundary-line, in addition, drawn by Nature between the alien waters. That last wave of the Gulf Stream which washes the North Cape and keeps the fjords of Finmark open and unfrozen the whole year through, sweeps eastward along the coast, until it reaches the head of Varanger Fjord. Here its power is at last spent, and from this point commences that belt of solid ice which locks up the harbours of the northern coast of Russia for six months in the year. The change from open water to ice is no less abrupt than permanent. Pastor Hvoslef informed me that in crossing from Vadsö, on the northern coast, to Pasvik, the last Norwegian settlement, close upon the Russian frontier, as late as the end of May, he got out of his boat upon the ice, and drove three or four miles over the frozen sea, to reach his destination.

The little fort of Vardöhuus, on an island at the northern entrance of the fjord, is not a recent defence, meant to check Russian plans in this quarter. It was established by Christian IV. nearly two and a half centuries ago. The king himself made a voyage hither, and no doubt at that time foresaw the necessity of establishing, by military occupation, the claims of Denmark to this part of the coast. The little fortress has actually done this service; and though a single frigate might easily batter it to pieces, its existence has kept Russia from the ownership of the Varanger Fjord and the creation (as is diplomatically supposed,) of an immense naval station, which, though within the Arctic waters, would at all times of the year be ready for service. It is well known that Russia has endeavoured to obtain possession of the northern side of the fjord, as well as of the Lyngen Fjord, near Tromsö, towards which her Lapland territory stretches out a long arm. England is particularly suspicious of these attempts, and the treaty recently concluded between the Allied Powers and Sweden had a special reference thereto

The importance of such an acquisition to Russia is too obvious to be pointed out, and the jealous watchfulness of England is, therefore, easy to understand. But it is a singular thing that the conflicting forces of Europe find a fulcrum on a little corner of this dead, desolate, God-forsaken shore.

About ten o'clock we reached Vadsö, the limit of the steamer's route. Here we had intended taking a boat, continuing our voyage to Nyborg, at the head of the fjord, crossing thence to the Tana, and descending that river in season to meet the steamer in the Tana Fjord on her return. We were behind time, however, and the wind was light; the people informed us that we could scarcely carry out the project; so we reluctantly gave it up, and went ashore to spend the day. Vadsö is a town of about 800 inhabitants, with a secure though shallow harbour, which was crowded with fishing vessels and Russian traders from the White Sea. It lies on the bleak hill-side, without a tree or bush, or a patch of grass large enough to be seen without close inspection, and its only summer perfume is that of dried fish. I saw in gardens attached to one or two houses a few courageous radishes and some fool-hardy potatoes, which had ventured above ground without the least chance of living long enough to blossom. The snow had been four feet deep in the streets in the beginning of June, and in six weeks it would begin to fall again. A few forlorn cows were hunting pasture over the hills, now and then looking with melancholy resignation at the strings of codfish heads hanging up to dry, on the broth of which they are fed during the winter. I took a walk and made a sketch during the afternoon, but the wind was so chill that I was glad to come back shivering to our quarters.

We obtained lodgings at the house of a baker, named Aas, who had learned the art of charging, and was therefore competent to conduct a hotel. In order to reach our room, we were obliged to pass successively through the family dwelling-room, kitchen, and a carpenter's workshop, but our windows commanded a full view of a grogshop across the way, where drunken Lapps were turned out with astonishing rapidity. It was the marriage month of the Lapps, and the town was full of young couples who had come down to be joined, with their relatives and friends, all in their gayest costumes. Through the intervention of the postmaster, I procured two women and a child, as subjects for a sketch. They were dressed in their best, and it was impossible not to copy the leer of gratified vanity lurking in the corners of their broad mouths. The summer dress consisted of a loose gown of bright green cloth, trimmed on the neck and sleeves with bands of scarlet and yellow, and a peculiar head-dress, shaped like a helmet, but with a broader and flatter crest, rounded in front. This, also, was covered with scarlet cloth, and trimmed with yellow and blue. They were greatly gratified with the distinction, and all the other Lapps, as in Kautokeino, would have willingly offered themselves. I found the same physical characteristics here as there—a fresh, ruddy complexion, inclining to tawny; bright blue eyes, brown hair, high cheek bones, and mouths of enormous width. They are not strikingly below the average size. Heine says, in one of his mad songs:

"In Lapland the people are dirty,
  Flat-headed, and broad-mouthed, and small·
They squat round the fire while roasting
  Their fishes, and chatter and squall;"

which is as good a description of them as can be packed into a stanza. On the present occasion they were all drunk, in addition. One of them lay for a long time at the door, with his legs doubled under him as he fell, the others stepping over his body as they went in and out. These poor creatures were openly and shamelessly allowed to drug themselves, as long as their money lasted. No wonder the race is becoming extinct, when the means of destruction is so freely offered.

Vadsö, although only forty miles from Vardö, at the mouth of the fjord, has a much drier and more agreeable climate, and the inhabitants are therefore loud in praise of their place. "We have no such fogs as at Vardö," say they; "our fish dry much better, and some years we can raise potatoes." For the last four or five years, however, the winters have been getting more and more severe, and now it is impossible to procure hay enough to keep their few cattle through the winter. We had on board a German who had been living there five years, and who appeared well satisfied with his lot. "I have married here," said he; "I make a good living with less trouble than in Germany, and have no wish to return." Singularly enough, there were also two Italian organ grinders on board, whom I accosted in their native language; but they seemed neither surprised nor particularly pleased. They dropped hints of having been engaged in some political conspiracy; and one of them said, with a curious mixture of Italian and Norsk words "*Jeg voglio ikke ritornare.*" I said the same thing ("I shall not return") as I left Vadsö.

We sailed early the next morning, and in the afternoon reached Vardö, where we lay three hours. Here we took on board the three officers, who had in the meantime made their inspection. Vardöhuus is a single star-shaped fort, with six guns and a garrison of twenty-seven men. During the recent war, the garrison was increased to three hundred—an unnecessary precaution, if there was really any danger of an attack to be apprehended, so long as the defences of the place were not strengthened. One of the officers, who had gone out fishing the night previous, caught eighty-three splendid cod in the space of two hours. It was idle sport, however, for no one would take his fish as a gift, and they were thrown on the shore to rot. The difficulty is not in catching but in curing them. Owing to the dampness of the climate they cannot be hung up on poles to dry slowly, like the *stock-fish* of the Lofodens, but must be first salted and then laid on the rocks to dry, whence the term *klip* (cliff) fish, by which they are known in trade.

At the mouth of the Tana we picked up four Englishmen, who had been salmon fishing on the river. They were sun-burnt, spotted with mosquito bites, and had had little luck, the river being full of nets and the fjord of seals, between which the best of the salmon are either caught or devoured but they spoke of their experience with true English relish. "Oh, it was very jolly!" said one: "we were so awfully bitten by mosquitoes. Then our interpreter always lost everything just before we wanted it—think of his losing our frying-pan, so that we had to fry in the lids of our kettles; He had a habit of falling overboard and getting nearly drowned before we could pull him in. We had a rough time of it, but it was very jolly, I assure you!" The young fellows meant what they said; they were all the better for their roughing, and I wish the spindle-shanked youths who polk and flirt at Newport and Saratoga had manliness enough for such undertakings.

We reached Hammerfest on the last day of July, and reoccupied our old quarters. That night the sun went below the horizon for the first time in eight days, but his depth was too slight to make any darkness visible. I was quite tired of the unending daylight, and would willingly have exchanged the pomp of the arctic midnight for the starlit darkness of home. We were confused by the loss of night; we lost the perception of time. One is never sleepy, but simply tired, and after a sleep of eight hours by sunshine, wakes up as tired as ever. His sleep at last is broken and irregular; he substitutes a number of short naps, distributed through the twenty-four hours, for the one natural repose, and finally gets into a state of general uneasiness and discomfort. A Hammerfest merchant, who has made frequent voyages to Spitzbergen, told me that in the latitude of 80° he never knew certainly whether it was day or night, and the cook was the only person on board who could tell him.

At first the nocturnal sunshine strikes you as being wonderfully convenient. You lose nothing of the scenery; you can read and write as usual; you never need be in a hurry, because there is time enough for everything It is not necessary to do your day's work in the daytime, for no night cometh. You are never belated, and somewhat of the stress of life is lifted from your shoulders; but, after a time, you would be glad of an excuse to stop seeing, and observing, and thinking, and even enjoying. There is no *compulsive* rest such as darkness brings—no sweet isolation, which is the best refreshment of sleep. You lie down in the broad day, and the summons, " Arise !" attends on every re-opening of your eyes. I never went below and saw my fellow-passengers all asleep around me without a sudden feeling that something was wrong: they were drugged, or under some unnatural influence, that they thus slept so fast while the sunshine streamed in through the port-holes.

There are some advantages of this northern summer which have presented themselves to me in rather a grotesque light. Think what an aid and shelter is removed from crime—how many vices which can only flourish in the deceptive atmosphere of night, must be checked by the sober reality of daylight! No assassin can dog the steps of his victim; no burglar can work in sunshine; no guilty lover can hold stolen interviews by moonlight—all concealment is removed, for the sun, like the eye of God, sees everything, and the secret vices of the earth must be bold indeed, if they can bear his gaze. Morally, as well as physically, there is safety in light and danger in darkness; and yet give me the darkness and the danger! Let the patrolling sun go off his beat for awhile, and show a little confidence in my ability to behave properly, rather than worry me with his sleepless vigilance.

I have described the smells of Hammerfest, which are its principal characteristic. It seemed to me the dreariest place in the world on first landing, a week previous; but, by contrast with what we had in the meantime seen, it became rather cheerful and comfortable. I was visiting a merchant after our return, and noticed with pleasure a stunted ash about eight feet high, in an adjoining garden. "Oh!" said he, in a tone of irritated pride, "we have plenty of trees here; there is quite a forest up the valley." This forest, after some search, I found. The trees were about six feet high, and some of them might have been as thick as my wrist. In the square before the merchant's house lay a crowd of drunken Lapps, who were supplied with as much bad brandy as they wanted by a licensed grog-shop. The Russian sailors made use of the same privilege, and we frequently heard them singing and wrangling on board their White Sea junks. They were *unapproachably* picturesque, especially after the day's work was over, when they generally engaged in hunting in the extensive forests of their beards, and exercised the law of retaliation on all the game they caught.

A long street of turf-roofed houses, whose inhabitants may be said to be under the sod even before they die, leads along the shore of the bay to a range of flakes redolent of drying codfish. Beyond this you clamber over rocks and shingles to a low grassy headland, whereon stands a pillar commemorating the measurement of a meridian line of 25° 20′, from the Danube to the Polar Sea, which was accomplished by the Governments of Austria, Russia, and Sweden, between the years 1816 and 1852. The pillar marks the northern terminus of the line, and stands in lat. 70° 40′ 11·3″. It is a plain shaft of polished red granite, standing on a base of grey granite, and surmounted by a bronze globe, on which a map of the earth is roughly outlined.

CHAPTER XXVIII.

THE RETURN TO DARKNESS.—NORWEGIAN CHARACTER.

I DO not intend to trace our return, step by step, down the Norwegian coast. The splendid weather which prevailed during our upward voyage, enabled us to see all the interesting points, leaving only those parts which we missed in the few hours devoted to sleep, to give a little novelty to our return. During the whole trip we had not a drop of rain, —the rarest good fortune in these latitudes,—and were therefore twice enabled to enjoy, to the fullest extent, the sublime scenery of the Lofoden Isles and the coast of Nordland. This voyage has not its like in the world. The traveller, to whom all other lands are familiar, has here a new volume of the most wonderful originality and variety, opened to him. The days are illuminated pages, crowded with pictures, the forms and hues of which he can never forget. After I returned to the zone of darkness, and recovered from the stress and tension of three weeks of daylight, I first fully appreciated the splendours of the arctic sun. My eyes were still dazzled with the pomp of colour, and the thousand miles of coast, as I reviewed them in memory, with their chaos of island-pyramids of shattered rock, their colossal cliffs, their twisted fjords, and long fjeld-levels of eternal snow, swam in a sea of saffron and rosy light, in comparison with which the pale blue day around me seemed dull and dead. My dream of the North, in becoming a reality, has retained the magical atmosphere of dreams, and basks in the same gorgeous twilight which irradiates the Scandinavian sagas.

I was particularly struck during the return, with the rapid progress of summer—the flying leaps with which she clears her short course. Among the Lofodens, the potatoes were coming into blossom, and the rye and barley into head; the grass was already cut, in many places, and drying on poles, and the green of the woods and meadows showed the dark, rich character of southern lands. Owing to this rapidity of growth, all the more hardy varieties of vegetables may be successfully cultivated. Mr. Thomas informed me that his peas and beans at Kaafjord (lat. 70° N.) grew three inches in twenty-four hours, and, though planted six weeks later than those about Christiania, came to maturity at the same time. He has even succeeded in raising excellent cauliflowers. But very few of the farmers have vegetable gardens, and those which I saw contained only radishes and lettuce, with a few useful herbs. One finds the same passion for flowers, however, as in Northern Sweden, and the poorest are rarely without a rose or a geranium in their windows.

Pastor Hvoslef, who was again our fellow-traveller for a few hours, gave me some interesting information concerning the Lapps. They are, it seems, entitled to the right of suffrage, and to representation in the Storthing, equally with the Norwegians. The local jurisdiction repeats on a small scale what the Storthing transacts on a large one, being entirely popular in its character, except that the *vogts* and *länsmen* (whose powers are somewhat similar to those of our judges and country magistrates) are not elected. But each district chooses from among its inhabitants a committee to confer upon and arrange all ordinary local matters. These committees, in turn, choose persons to constitute a higher body, who control the reciprocal relations of the several districts, and intervene in case of difficulties between them. The system is necessarily simpler and somewhat more primitive in its character than our local organisations in America; but it appears at present to answer every purpose. The heavy responsibility resting upon judges in Norway—the severity of the checks and penalties by which their probity is insured—probably contributes to make the administration of the laws more efficacious and easy. The Lapps are not a difficult people to govern, and much of the former antagonism between them and the poorer classes of the Norwegians has passed away. There is little, if any, amalgamation of the two races, nor will there ever be, but there is probably as little conflict between them as is compatible with the difference of blood.

At Tromsöe, a tall, strong, clerical gentleman came on board, who proved to be the noted Pastor Lamers, one of the first if not the very first clergyman in Norway, who has refused to receive the government support—or, in other words, has seceded from the Church, as a State establishment, while adhering to all its fundamental doctrines. It is the first step towards the separation of Church and State, which must sooner or later come, in Norway and in Sweden He has a congregation of three hundred members, in Tromsöe, and is about organising a church at Gibostad, on the island of Senjen. He has some peculiar views, I believe, in relation to the baptism of children, and insists that the usual absolution dealt out by the Pastors is of no effect without full confession and the specification of particular sins—but in other respects he is entirely orthodox, retaining even the ceremonial of the Eucharist. This, in the Lutheran church of Norway, comes so near to the Roman Catholic doctrine of transubstantiation, that one cannot easily perceive any difference. Instead of bread, an unleavened wafer is administered to the communicants, the priest saying, as he gives it, "This is the *true* body and blood of Jesus Christ." Mr. Forrester, a devout admirer of the Church, which he thinks identical with that of England in all its essentials, says, "The Lutherans reject the Romish doctrine of transubstantiation, but they hold that of a spiritual and ineffable union of the divine nature with the elements, the substance of which remains unchanged. This is called *consubstantiation*." Verily, the difference between tweedledum and tweedledee—one being as absurd as the other.

No one, coming from a land where all sects stand upon an equal footing, and where every church must depend for existence on its own inherent vitality, can fail to be struck with the effete and decrepit state of religion in Sweden and Norway. It is a body of frigid mechanical forms and ceremonies, animated here and there with a feeble spark of spiritual life, but diffusing no quickening and animating glow. I have often been particularly struck with the horror with which the omission of certain forms was regarded by persons in whom I could discover no trace of any religious principle. The Church has a few dissensions to combat; she has not been weakened by schism; but she is slowly ossifying from sheer inertia. The Reformation needs to be reformed again, and perhaps the tardy privileges granted to the *Haugianer* and *Läsare*—the northern Methodists—may result in producing a body of Dissenters large enough to excite emulation, action, and improvement. In Norway, the pastors have the best salaries and the easiest places of all government officials. Those who conscientiously discharge their duties have enough to do; but were this universally the case, one would expect to find the people less filthy, stupid, and dishonest than they are in many parts of the country. A specimen of the intelligence of one, who is now a member of the Storthing, was communicated to me by a gentleman who heard it. The clergyman advocated the establishment of telegraph lines in Norway, "not for the sake of sending news," said he, "that is of no consequence. But it is well known that no wolf can pass under a telegraph wire, and if we can get lines put up throughout the country, all the wolves will be obliged to leave!" Of course, I do not mean to assert that the Norwegian clergymen, as a body, are not sincere, zealous, well-informed men. The evil lies rather in that system which makes religion as much a branch of government service as law or diplomacy; and which, until very recently, has given one sect an exclusive monopoly of the care of human souls.

I had a strong desire to converse with Pastor Lamers in relation to the stand he has taken, but he was surrounded by a crowd of persons during his stay on board, and no opportunity presented itself. The sensation which his presence produced, showed that there are restless elements at work in the mind of the people. The stony crust is beginning to heave and split at last. Even the deck-passengers gathered into little groups and talked earnestly. Two gentlemen near me were discussing the question of an Established Church, one contending, that a variety of sects tended only to confuse, perplex, and unchristianise the uneducated, unthinking class, while the other asserted that this very class adhered most tenaciously to whatever faith had been taught them. At this moment a woman standing near us exclaimed: "There were false prophets in all times, and there are false prophets now! We must beware of them!"—the earnestness of her speech affording a good comment on the argument just produced. Whatever may be the popular opinion concerning the course of Pastor Lamers, I could not but notice the marked respect displayed by every one who approached him.

In passing Hindoë, we saw two magnificent golden eagles wheeling around one of the loftiest cliffs. The wind blew strongly from the south-west, increasing until we had what sailors call a dry gale in crossing the West Fjord, but it abated the next day and by the late twilight we recrossed the arctic circle. This night there was great rejoicing on board, at the discovery of a star. We had not seen one for a month, and some of the passengers coming from Finmark had been more than two months in daylight. While we were all gazing upon it as upon some extraordinary phenomenon, a flood of yellow lamp-light suddenly streamed through the cabin skylight. The sky was still brilliant with sunset in the north, but it was dark enough to see to sleep. We could not yet cover ourselves all over, even as with a cloak; still there was a shelter and friendly covering for the helpless body. Our sleep became sound and regular, and its old power of restoration was doubly sweet, since we had known what it was to be deprived of it.

Our fellow-passengers, after leaving Carlsoe, where the young Englishmen stopped to hunt, were almost exclusively Norwegian, and this gave us further opportunities of becoming acquainted with some peculiarities of the national character. Intelligent Norwegians, especially those who have travelled, are exceedingly courteous, gentlemanly, and agreeable persons. The three officers on board were men of unusual intelligence and refinement, and we considered ourselves fortunate in having their company during the entire voyage. The *landhand lare*, or country merchants, and government officials of the lower ranks, exhibit more reserve, and not unfrequently a considerable amount of ignorance and prejudice. Perhaps the most general feature of the Norwegian character is an excessive national vanity, which is always on the alert, and fires up on the slightest provocation. Say everything you like, except that Norway in any respect is surpassed by any other country. One is assailed with questions about his impressions of the scenery, people, government, &c.—a very natural and pardonable curiosity, it is true, and one only demands in return that his candour be respected, and no offence taken. This, however, is rarely the case. If there is no retaliatory answer on the spot, you hear a remark days afterwards which shows how your mild censure has rankled in the mind of the hearer. My friend was asked by a passenger whether he did not think the women of Finmark very beautiful. It was impossible to answer in the affirmative: the questioner went off in high dudgeon, and did not speak to him again for several days.

In the Varanger Fjord, we had pretty freely expressed our impressions of the desolate coast. Afterwards on returning past the grand cliff scenery of Nordkyn, we were admiring some bold formation of the rocks, when a Norwegian came up and said, in a tone of angry irony: " Ah, you find a little to admire at last, do you? You find *some* beauty in our country, after all?" So in regard to the government. The Norwegians may be justly proud of their constitution, which is as republican in its character as our own. There is so much in the administration of the government which every one must heartly commend, that they should be less sensitive in regard to minor faults. This sensitiveness, however, is partly accounted for, when we remember that for four hundred years Norway was a Danish province, and that only forty-three years ago she leaped at once from subjection to a freedom such as no other country in Europe enjoys. The intense pride and self-glorification of the people resembles that of a youth who for the first time assumes a dress-coat and standing collar. King Oscar, on his accession to the throne, gave the country a separate national flag, and nowhere does one see such a display of flags. All over the land and all along the shores, the colours of Norway are flying.

Jealousy of Sweden and dislike of the Swedes are inherited feelings, and are kept alive by a mutual prejudice on the part of the latter people. One cannot but smile a little at the present union of Sweden and Norway, when he finds that the countries have separate currencies, neither of which will pass at its full value in the other—separate tariffs, and of course Custom-house examinations between the two, and, if the Norwegians had their way, would have separate diplomatic representatives abroad. Yet the strength of Norway is undoubtedly in her alliance with Sweden: alone, she would be but a fourth-rate power. Enough has been done to satisfy her national feeling and secure her liberties against assault, and it is now time that this unnecessary jealousy and mistrust of a kindred race should cease. The Swedes have all the honesty which the Norwegians claim for themselves, more warmth and geniality of character, and less selfish sharpness and shrewdness. Mügge tells a story of a number of Swedes who were at a dinner party in Paris, where the health of "the King of Sweden and Norway" was proposed and drunk with great enthusiasm. One glass was observed to be untouched. It belonged to a Norwegian, who, when called upon for an explanation, said: "I cannot drink such a toast as this, but I will drink the health of the King of Norway, who is also King of Sweden!"

One cannot find fault with a people for their patriotism. I have always admired that love of *Gamle Norge* which shines through Norwegian history, song, and saga—but when it is manifested in such ridiculous extremes, one doubts the genuineness of the feeling, and suspects it of being alloyed with some degree of personal vanity. There are still evils to be eradicated,—reproaches to be removed,—reforms to be achieved, which claim all the best energies of the best men of the country, and positive harm is done by concealing or denying the true state of things.

CHAPTER XXIX.

DRONTHIEM AND BERGEN.

WE spent another day and a half in Dronthiem, before reshipping in the steamer for Bergen. With the exception of a trip to the Lierfoss, or falls of the Nid, however, it was by no means a satisfactory sojourn. The hotel was full, and we could only get quarters in the billiard-room, through which other guests were continually passing and repassing. Two small boys were quite inadequate to the service; the table d'hote was the scantiest I ever saw, and the charges at the rate of three dollars a day. The whole of Sunday was consumed in an attempt to recover our carrioles, which we left behind us on embarking for Hammerfest. The servants neglected to get them on Saturday evening, as we had ordered, and in the morning the man who had the key of the warehouse went into the country, taking it with him. The whole day was spent in searching and waiting, and it was only by unremitting exertions that we succeeded in putting them on board in the evening. Owing to this annoyance, I was unable to attend service in the cathedral, or even to see the inside of it.

Our drive to the Lierfoss, in the evening, was an exquisits enjoyment. The valley of the Nid, behind Drontheim, is one of the most carefully cultivated spots in Norway. Our road led up the stream, overlooking rich levels of grain and hay fields, studded with large and handsome farm-houses, while the lower slopes of the hills and the mound-like knolls scattered along their bases, were framed to the very summit, steep as they were. The whole scene was like a piece of landscape gardening, full of the loveliest effects, which were enhanced by the contrast of the grey, sterile mountains by which the picture was framed. The soft, level sunshine, streaming through the rifts of broken thunder-clouds in the west, slowly wandered over the peaceful valley, here lighting up a red-roofed homestead, there a grove in full summer foliage, or a meadow of so brilliant an emerald that it seemed to shine by its own lustre. As we approached the Lierfoss, the road was barred with a great number of gates, before which waited a troop of ragged boys, who accompanied us the whole of the way, with a pertinacity equal to that of the little Swiss beggars.

The Nid here makes two falls about half a mile apart, the lower one being eighty, and the upper one ninety feet in height. The water is of a dark olive-green colour, and glassy transparency, and so deep that at the brink it makes huge curves over the masses of rock in its bed without breaking into the faintest ripple. As you stand on a giant boulder above it, and contrast the swift, silent rush with the thundering volume of amber-tinted spray which follows, you feel in its full force the strange fascination of falling water—the temptation to plunge in and join in its headlong revelry. Here, however, I must admit that the useful is not always the beautiful. The range of smoky mills driven by a sluice from the fall had better be away. The upper fall is divided in the centre by a mass of rock, and presents a broader and more imposing picture, though the impetus of the water is not so great.

The coast between Drontheim and Bergen is, on the whole, much less striking than that further north; but it has some very grand features. The outer islands are, with few exceptions, low and barren, but the coast, deeply indented with winding fjords, towers here and there into sublime headlands, and precipitous barriers of rock. Christiansund, where we touched the first afternoon, is a singularly picturesque place, built on four islands, separated by channels in the form of a cross. The bare, rounded masses of grey rock heave up on all sides behind the houses, which are built along the water's edge; here and there a tree of superb greenness shines against the colourless background, and the mountains of the mainland, with their tints of pink and purple, complete the picture. The sun was burningly hot, and the pale-green water reflected the shores in its oily gloss; but in severe storms, I was told, it is quite impossible to cross from one island to another, and the different parts of the town sometimes remain for days in a state of complete isolation. I rose very early next morning, to have a view of Molde and the enchanting scenery of the Romsdals-fjord. The prosperous-looking town, with its large square houses, its suburban cottages and gardens, on the slope of a long green hill, crowned with woods, was wholly Swiss in its appearance, but the luminous morning vapors hovering around the Alpine peaks in the east, entirely hid them from our view. In this direction lies the famous Romsdal, which many travellers consider the grandest specimen of Norwegian scenery. Unfortunately we could not have visited it without taking an entire week, and we were apprehensive lest the fine weather, which we had now enjoyed for twenty-four days, should come to an end before we were done with the Bergenstift. It is almost unexampled that travellers make the voyage from Drontheim to the Varanger Fjord and back without a cloudy day. While we had perpetual daylight, the tourists whom we left behind were drenched with continual rains.

Aalesund is another island port, smaller than Christiansund, but full as picturesque. The intense heat and clearness of the day, the splendour of the sunshine, which turned the grassy patches on the rocks into lustrous velvet, and the dark, dazzling blue of the sea belonged rather to southern Italy than to Norway. As we approached Bergen, however, the sky became gradually overcast, and the evening brought us clouds and showers. Not far from Aalesund was the castle of Rollo, the conqueror of Normandy. All this part of the coast is Viking ground: from these fjords went forth their piratical dragons, and hither they returned, laden with booty, to rest and carouse in their strongholds. They were the buccaneers of the north in their time, bold, brave, with the virtues which belong to courage and hardihood, but coarse, cruel, and brutal. The Viking of Scandinavian song is a splendid fellow; but his original, if we may judge from his descendants, was a stupid, hard-headed, lustful, and dirty giant, whom we should rather not have had for a companion. Harold Haarfager may have learnt in Constantinople to wash his face, and comb his beautiful hair, but I doubt if many of his followers imitated him. Let us hope that Ingeborg changed her dress occasionally, and that Balder's temple was not full of fleas; that Thorsten Vikingsson placed before his guests something better than *fladbröd* and rancid butter; and that Björn and Frithiof acted as honestly towards strangers as towards each other. The Viking chiefs, undoubtedly, must have learned the comfort of cleanliness and the delights of good living, but if such habits were general, the nation has greatly degenerated since their time.

We stayed on deck until midnight, notwithstanding the rain, to see the grand rock of Hornelen, a precipice 1200 feet high. The clouds lifted a little, and there was a dim, lurid light in the sky as our steamer swept under the awful cliff. A vast, indistinct mass, reaching apparently to the zenith, the summit crowned with a pointed tour, resembling the Cathedral of Drontheim, and the sides scarred with deep fissures, loomed over us. Now a splintered spire disengaged itself from the gloom, and stood defined against the sky; lighter streaks marked the spots where portions had slid away; but all else was dark, uncertain, and sublime. Our friendly captain had the steamer's guns discharged as we were abreast of the highest part. There were no separate echoes, but one tremendous peal of sound, prolonged like the note of an organ-pipe, and gradually dying away at the summit in humming vibrations.

Next morning, we were sailing in a narrow strait, between perpendicular cliffs, fluted like basaltic pillars. It was raining dismally, but we expected nothing else in the neighbourhood of Bergen. In this city the average number of rainy days in a year is *two hundred*. Bergen weather has become a by-word throughout the north, and no traveller ventures to hope for sunshine when he turns his face thither. "Is it still raining at Bergen?" ask the Dutch skippers when they meet a Norwegian captain. "Yes, blast you; is it still blowing at the Texel?" is generally the response.

We took on board four or five lepers, on their way to the hospital at Bergen. A piece of oil-cloth had been thrown over some spars to shield them from the rain, and they sat on deck, avoided by the other passengers, a melancholy picture of disease and shame. One was a boy of fourteen, upon whose face wart-like excrescences were beginning to appear; while a woman, who seemed to be his mother, was hideously swollen and disfigured. A man, crouching down with his head between his hands, endeavoured to hide the seamed and knotted mass of protruding blue flesh, which had once been a human face. The forms of leprosy, elephantiasis, and other kindred diseases, which I have seen in the East, and in tropical countries, are not nearly so horrible. For these unfortunates there was no hope. Some years, more or less, of a life which is worse than death, was all to which they could look forward. No cure has yet been discovered for this terrible disease. There are two hospitals in Bergen, one of which contains about five hundred patients; while the other, which has recently been erected for the reception of cases in the earlier stages, who may be subjected to experimental courses of treatment, has already one hundred. This form of leprosy is supposed to be produced partly by an exclusive diet of salt fish, and partly by want of personal cleanliness. The latter is the most probable cause, and one does not wonder at the result, after he has had a little experience of Norwegian filth. It is the awful curse which falls upon such beastly habits of life. I wish the Norwegians could be made Mussulmen for awhile, for the sake of learning that cleanliness is not only next to godliness, but a necessary part of it. I doubt the existence of filthy Christians, and have always believed that St. Jerome was atrociously slandered by the Italian painters. But is there no responsibility resting upon the clergymen of the country, who have so much influence over their flocks, and who are themselves clean and proper persons?

Bergen is also, as I was informed, terribly scourged by venereal diseases. Certainly, I do not remember a place, where there are so few men—tall, strong, and well-made as the people generally are—without some visible mark of disease or deformity. A physician of the city has recently endeavoured to cure syphilis in its secondary stage, by means of inoculation, having first tried the experiment upon himself; and there is now a hospital where this form of treatment is practised upon two or three hundred patients, with the greatest success, as another physician informed me. I intended to have visited it, as well as the hospital for lepers; but the sight of a few cases, around the door of the latter establishment, so sickened me, that I had no courage to undertake the task.

Let me leave these disagreeable themes, and say that Bergen is one of the most charmingly picturesque towns in all the

North. Its name, "The Mountain," denotes one of its most striking features. It is built upon two low capes, which project from the foot of a low mountain, two thousand feet high, while directly in its rear lies a lovely little lake, about three miles in circumference. On the end of the northern headland stands the fortress of Berghenhuus, with the tall square mass of Walkendorf's Tower, built upon the foundations of the former palace of King Olaf Kyrre, the founder of the city. The narrow harbour between is crowded with fishing-vessels,—during the season often numbering from six to eight hundred,—and beyond it the southern promontory, quite covered with houses, rises steeply from the water. A public grove, behind the fortress, delights the eye with its dark-green mounds of foliage; near it rise the twin towers of the German Church, which boasts an age of nearly seven hundred years, and the suburbs on the steep mountain-sides gradually vanish among gardens and country-villas, which are succeeded by farms and grazing fields, lying under the topmost ridges of the bare rock. The lake in the rear is surrounded with the country residences of the rich merchants —a succession of tasteful dwellings, each with its garden and leafy arbours, its flowers and fountains, forming a rich frame to the beautiful sheet of water. Avenues of fine old lindens thread this suburban paradise, and seats, placed at the proper points, command views of which one knows not the loveliest. Everything has an air of ancient comfort, taste, and repose. One sees yet, the footsteps of mighty Hansa, who for three centuries reigned here supreme. The northern half of Bergen is still called the "German Quarter," and there are very few citizens of education who do not speak the language.

With one or two exceptions, the streets are rough and narrow. There are no quaint peculiarities in the architecture, the houses being all of wood, painted white or some light colour. At every door stands a barrel filled with water, to be ready in case of fire. Owing to the great number of fishing-vessels and its considerable foreign trade, Bergen is a much more lively and bustling place than either Christiania or Drontheim. The streets are well populated, and the great square at the head of the harbour is always thronged with a motley concourse of fishermen, traders, and country people. Drunkenness seems to be a leading vice. I saw, at least, fifty people, more or less intoxicated, in the course of a short walk, one afternoon. The grog-shops, however, are rigidly closed at six o'clock on Saturday evening, and remain so until Monday morning, any violation or evasion of the law being severely punished. The same course has been adopted here as in Sweden; the price of brandy has been doubled, by restrictions on its manufacture, and every encouragement has been afforded to breweries. The beer of Christiania is equal in flavour and purity to any in the world, and it is now in great demand all over Norway.

The day after our arrival the sky cleared again, and we were favoured with superb weather; which might well be the case, as the people told me it had previously been raining every day for a month. The gardens, groves, and lawns of velvet turf, so long moistened, now blazed out with splendid effect in the hot August sunshine. "Is there such a green anywhere else in the world?" asked my friend. "If anywhere, only in England—but scarcely there," I was obliged to confess. Yet there was an acquaintance of mine in

Bergen, a Hammerfest merchant, who, in this rare climax of summer beauty, looked melancholy and dissatisfied. "I want to get back to the north," said he, "I miss our Arctic summer. These dark nights are so disagreeable, that I am very tired of them. There is nothing equal to our three months of daylight, and they alone reconcile us to the winter." Who will say, after this, that anything more than the fundamental qualities of human nature are the same in all climates? But from the same foundation you may build either a Grecian temple or a Chinese pagoda.

The lions of Bergen are soon disposed of. After you have visited the fortress and admired the sturdy solidity of Walkendorf's Tower, you may walk into the German church which stands open (or did, when we were there), without a soul to prevent you from carrying off some of the queer old carved work and pictures. The latter are hideous enough to be perfectly safe, and the church, though exceedingly quaint and interesting, is not beautiful. Then you may visit the museum, which contains an excellent collection of northern fish, and some very curious old furniture. The collection of antiquities is not remarkable; but it should be remembered that the museum has been created within the last twenty years, and is entirely the result of private taste and enterprise. One of the most singular things I saw was a specimen (said to be the only one in existence) of a fish called the "herring-king," about twelve feet in length by one in thickness, and with something of the serpent in its appearance. The old Kraaken has not shown himself for a number of years, possibly frightened away by the appearance of steamers in his native waters. In spite of all the testimony which Capell Brooke has collected in favour of his existence, he is fast becoming a myth.

Bergen, we found, is antiquated in more respects than one. On sending for horses, on the morning fixed for our departure, we were coolly told that we should have to wait twenty-four hours; but after threatening to put the law in force against the *skyds-skaffer*, he promised to bring them by one o'clock in the afternoon. In this city of 30,000 inhabitants, no horses are kept in readiness at the post-station; but are furnished by farmers somewhere at a distance. In the matter of hotels, however, Bergen stands in the front rank of progress, rivalling Christiania and Drontheim. The fare is not so good, and the charges are equally high. There are two little inns, with five or six rooms each, and one boarding-house of the same size. We could only get one small room, into which all three were packed, at a charge of a dollar and a quarter per day; while for two wretched meals we paid a dollar and a half each. The reader may judge of our fare from the fact that one day our soup was raspberry juice and water, and another time, cold beer, flavoured with pepper and cinnamon. Add tough beafsteaks swimming in grease and rancid butter, and you have the principal ingredients. For the first time in my life I found my digestive powers unequal to the task of mastering a new national diet.

CHAPTER XXX.

A TRIP TO THE VÖRING-FOSS.

AFTER waiting only five hours, we obtained three horses and drove away from Bergen. It was a superb afternoon, spotlessly blue overhead, with still bluer water below, and hills of dark, velvety verdure throbbing and sparkling in the sunshine, and the breezes from off the fjord. We sped past the long line of suburban gardens, through the linden avenues, which, somehow or other, suggested to me the days of the Hanseatic League, past Tivoli, the Hoboken of Bergen, and on the summit of the hill beyond stopped to take a parting look at the beautiful city. She sat at the foot of her guardian mountain, across the lake, her white towers and red roofs rising in sharp relief against the purple background of the islands which protect her from the sea. In colour, form, and atmospheric effect, the picture was perfect. Norway is particularly fortunate in the position and surroundings of her three chief cities. Bergen bears away the palm, truly, but either of them has few rivals in Europe.

Our road led at first over well-cultivated hills dotted

with comfortable farmhouses—a rolling, broken country enclosed by rugged and sterile groups of hills. After some miles we turned northward into a narrow valley running parallel to the coast line. The afternoon sun shining over the shoulder of the mountain-ridge on our left, illuminated with dazzling effect the green pastures in the bosom of the valley, and the groves of twinkling birch and sombre fir on the opposite slope. I have never seen purer tints in the sunshine—never a softer transparency in the shadows. The landscape was ideal in its beauty, except the houses, whose squalor and discomfort were real. Our first station lay off the road, on a hill. A very friendly old man promised to get us horses as soon as possible, and his wife set before us the best fare the house afforded—milk, oaten shingles, and bad cheese. The house was dirty, and the aspect of the family bed, which occupied one end of the room, merely divided by boards into separate compartments for the parents, children and servants was sufficient to banish sleep. Notwithstanding the poverty of the place, the old woman set a good value upon her choice provender. The horses were soon forthcoming, and the man, whose apparent kindness increased every moment, said to me, "Have I not done well? Is it not very well that I have brought you horses so soon?" I assented cheerfully, but he still repeated the same questions, and I was stupid enough not to discover their meaning, until he added; "I have done everything so well, that you ought to give me something for it." The naive manner of this request made it seem reasonable, and I gave him something accordingly, though a little disappointed, for I had congratulated myself on finding at last a friendly and obliging *skyds-skaffer* (Postmaster) in Norway.

Towards evening we reached a little village on the shore of the Osterfjord. Here the road terminated, and a water station of eighteen miles in length lay before us. The fjords on the western coast of Norway are narrow, shut in by lofty and abrupt mountains, and penetrate far into the land—frequently to the distance of a hundred miles. The general direction of the valleys is parallel to the line of the coast, intersecting the fjords at nearly a right angle, so that they, in connection with these watery defiles, divide the mountains into immense irregular blocks, with very precipitous sides and a summit table-land varying from two to four thousand feet above the sea level. For this reason there is no continuous road in all western Norway, but alternate links of land and water—boats and post-horses. The deepest fjords reach very nearly to the spinal ridge of the mountain region, and a land-road from Bergen to this line would be more difficult to construct than any of the great highways across the Alps. In proportion to her population and means, Norway has done more for roads than any country in the world. Not only her main thoroughfares, but even her by-ways, give evidence of astonishing skill, industry, and perseverance. The Storthing has recently appropriated a sum of $188,000 for the improvement of roads, in addition to the repairs which the farmers are obliged to make, and which constitute almost their only tax, as there is no assessment whatever upon landed property. There seems a singular incongruity, however, in finding such an evidence of the highest civilization, in connection with the semi-barbaric condition of the people. Generally, the improvement of the means of communication in a country is in the ratio of its social progress.

As we were obliged to wait until morning before commencing our voyage, we set about procuring supper and lodging. Some dirty beds in a dirty upper room constituted the latter, but the former was a doubtful affair. The landlord, who persisted in calling me "Dock," made a foraging excursion among the houses, and, after some time, laid before us a salted and smoked leg of mutton, some rancid butter, hard oaten bread, and pestilential cheese. I ate as a matter of duty towards my body, but my companions were less conscientious. We deserve no credit for having risen early the next morning, neither was there any self-denial in the fact of our being content with a single cup of coffee. The boatmen, five in number, who had been engaged the evening before, took our carrioles apart and stowed them in the stern, while we three disposed ourselves very uneasily in the narrow bow. As we were about pushing off, one of the men stepped upon a stone and shouted in a loud voice, "Come and help us, fairies!"—whereat the others laughed heartily. The wind was against us, but I thought the men hugged the shore much more than was necessary. I noticed the same thing afterwards, and spoke of it, but they stated that there were strong currents in these fjords, setting towards the sea. The water, in fact, is but slightly brackish, and the ebb and flow of the tides is hardly felt.

The scenery in the Osterfjord is superb. Mountains, 2000 feet high, inclose and twist it between their interlocking bases. Cliffs of naked rock overhang it, and cataracts fall into it in long zigzag chains of foam. Here and there a little embayed dell rejoices with settlement and cultivation, and even on the wildest steeps, where it seems almost impossible for a human foot to find hold, the people scramble at the hazard of their lives, to reap a scanty harvest of grass for the winter. Goats pasture everywhere, and our boatmen took delight in making the ewes follow us along the cliffs, by imitating the bleating of kids. Towards noon we left the main body of the fjord and entered a narrow arm which lay in eternal shadow under tremendous walls of dark rock. The light and heat of noonday were tropical in their silent intensity, painting the summits far above with dashes of fierce colour, while their bases sank in blue gloom to meet the green darkness of the water. Again and again the heights enclosed us, so that there was no outlet; but they opened as if purposely to make way for us, until our keel grated the pebbly barrier of a narrow valley, where the land road was resumed. Four miles through this gap brought us to another branch of the same fjord, where we were obliged to have our carrioles taken to pieces and shipped for a short voyage.

At its extremity the fjord narrowed, and still loftier mountains overhung it. Shut in by these, like some palmy dell in the heart of the porphyry mountains of the Sahara, lay Bolstadören, a miracle of greenness and beauty. A mantle of emerald velvet, falling in the softest slopes and swells to the water's edge, was thrown upon the valley; the barley had been cut and bound to long upright poles to dry, rising like golden pillars from the shaven stubble; and, to crown all, above the landing-place stood a two-story house, with a jolly fat landlord smoking in the shade, and half-a-dozen pleasant-looking women gossipping in-doors. 'Can we get anything to eat?" was the first question. "The gentlemen can have fresh salmon and potatoes, and red wine if they wish it," answered the mistress. Of course we wished it; we wished for any food clean enough to be eatable, and the promise of such fare was like the falling of manna n the desert. The salmon, fresh from the stream, was particularly fine; the fish here is so abundant that the land lord had caught 962, as he informed us, in the course of one season.

We had but two miles of land before another sheet of water intervened, and our carrioles were again taken to pieces. The postillions and boatmen along this route were great scamps, frequently asking more than the legal fare, and in one instance threatened to prevent us from going on unless we paid it. I shall not bore the reader with accounts of our various little squabbles on the road, all of which tended more and more to convince us, that unless the Norwegians were a great deal more friendly, kind, and honest a few years ago than they are now, they have been more over-praised than any people in the world. I must say, however, that they are bungling swindlers, and could only be successful with the greenest of travellers. The moment an imposition is resisted, and the stranger shows himself familiar with the true charges and methods of travel, they give up the attempt; but the desire to cheat is only less annoying to one than cheating itself. The fees for travelling by *skyds* are, it is true, disproportionably low, and in many instances the obligation to furnish horses is no doubt an actual loss to the farmer. Very often we would have willingly paid a small increase upon the legal rates if it had been asked for as a favour; but when it was boldly demanded as a right, and backed by a falsehood, we went not a stiver beyond the letter of the law.

Landing at Evanger, an intelligent landlord, who had four brothers in America, gave us return horses to Vossevangen, and we enjoyed the long twilight of the warm summer evening, while driving along the hills which overlook the valley connecting the lakes of Vossevangen and Evanger. It was a lovely landscape, ripe with harvest, and the air full of mellow, balmy odours from the flowers and grain. The black spire of Vossevangen church, standing dark against the dawning moonlight, was the welcome termination of our long day's journey, and not less welcome were our clean and comfortable quarters in the house of a merchant there. Here we left the main road across Norway, and made an excursion to the Vöring-Foss, which lies beyond the Hardanger Fjord, about fifty miles distant, in a south-eastern direction.

Vossevangen, in the splendour of a cloudless morning, was even more beautiful than as a moonlit haven of repose. The compact little village lay half buried in trees, clustered about the massive old church, with its black, pointed tower, and roof covered with pitched shingles, in the centre of the valley, while the mountains around shone bald and bright through floating veils of vapour which had risen from the lake. The people were all at work in the fields betimes, cutting and stacking the barley. The grass-fields, cut smooth and close, and of the softest and evenest green, seemed kept for show rather than for use. The bottom of the valley along which we drove, was filled with an unbroken pine forest, inclosing here and there a lake,

> "Where Heaven itself, brought down to Earth,
> Seemed fairer than above;"

while the opposite mountain rose rich with harvest fields and farmhouses. There are similar landscapes between Fribourg and Vevay, in Switzerland—finer, perhaps, except that all cultivated scenery in Norway gains wonderfully in effect from the savage environment of the barren fjelds. Here, cultivation is somewhat of a phenomenon, and a rich, thickly settled valley strikes one with a certain surprise. The Norwegians have been accused of neglecting agriculture; but I do not see that much more could be expected of them. The subjugation of virgin soil, as we had occasion to notice, is a serious work. At the best, the grain harvests are uncertain, while fish are almost as sure as the season; and so the surplus agricultural population either emigrates or removes to the fishing grounds on the coast. There is, undoubtedly, a considerable quantity of wild land which could be made arable, but the same means, applied to the improvement of that which is at present under cultivation, would accomplish far more beneficent results.

Leaving the valley, we drove for some time through pine forests, and here, as elsewhere, had occasion to notice the manner in which this source of wealth has been drained of late years. The trees were very straight and beautiful, but there were none of more than middle age. All the fine old timber had been cut away; all Norway, in fact, has been despoiled in like manner, and the people are but just awaking to the fact, that they are killing a goose which lays golden eggs. The government, so prudently economical that it only allows $100,000 worth of silver to be quarried annually in the mines of Kongsberg, lest the supply should be exhausted, has, I believe, adopted measures for the preservation of the forests; but I am not able to state their precise character. Except in valleys remote from the rivers and fjords, one now finds very little mature timber.

> "The tallest pine,
> Hewn on Norwegian hills, to be the mast
> Of some great admiral,"

I have not yet seen.

We at last came upon a little lake, in a close glen with walls 1000 feet high. Not suspecting that we had ascended much above the sea-level, we were surprised to see the gorge all at once open below us, revealing a dark-blue lake, far down among the mountains. We stood on the brink of a wall, over which the stream at our side fell in a "hank" of divided cataracts. Our road was engineered with great difficulty to the bottom of the steep, whence a gentler descent took us to the hamlet of Vasenden, at the head of the lake. Beyond this there was no road for carrioles, and we accordingly gave ours in charge of a bright, active and intelligent little post-master, twelve years old. He and his mother then rowed us across the lake to the village of Graven, whence there was a bridle-road across the mountains to a branch of the Hardanger Fjord. They demanded only twelve skillings (ten cents) for the row of three miles, and then posted off to a neighbouring farmhouse to engage horses for us.

There was a neat white dwelling on the hill, which we took to be the parsonage, but which proved to be the residence of an army captain on leave, whom we found sitting in the door, cleaning his gun, as we approached. He courteously ushered us into the house, and made his appearance soon afterwards in a clean shirt, followed by his wife, with wine and cakes upon a tray. I found him to be a man of more than ordinary intelligence, and of an earnest and reflective turn of mind, rare in men of his profession. He spoke chiefly of the passion for emigration which now possesses the Norwegian farmers, considering it not rendered necessary by their actual condition, but rather one of those contagions which spread through communities and nations, overcoming alike prudence and prejudice. He deplored it as retarding the development of Norway. Personal interest, however, is everywhere stronger than patriotism, and I see no signs of the emigration decreasing for some years to come.

After waiting a considerable time, we obtained two horses and a strapping farmer's son for guide. The fellow was delighted to find out where we came from, and was continually shouting to the people in the fields: "Here these are Americans: they were born there!" whereat the people stared, saluted, and then stared again. He shouldered our packs and marched beside the horses with the greatest ease. "You are strong," I remarked. "Yes," he replied, "I am a strong Normand," making his patriotism an excuse for his personal pride. We had a terribly tough pull up the mountain, through fine woods, to the summit level of the fjeld. The view backwards, over the lake, was enchanting, and we lingered long on the steep, loth to lose it. Turning again, a desolate lake lay before us, heathery swells of the bleak table-land and distant peaks, touched with snow. Once upon the broad, level summit of a Norwegian fjeld, one would never guess what lovely valleys lie under those misty breaks which separate its immense lobes—what gashes of life and beauty penetrate its stony heart. There are, in fact, two Norways: one above—a series of detached, irregular masses, bleak, snowy, wind-swept and heather-grown, inhabited by herdsmen and hunters: and one below—a ramification of narrow veins of land and water, with fields and forests, highways and villages.

So, when we had traversed the upper land for several miles, we came to a brink overlooking another branch of the lower land, and descended through thick woods to the farms of Ulvik, on the Eyfjord, an arm of the Hardanger. The shores were gloriously beautiful: slopes of dazzling turf inclosed the bright blue water, and clumps of oak, ash, and linden, in park-like groups, studded the fields. Low red farmhouses, each with its hollow square of stables and granaries, dotted the hill-sides, and the people, male and female, were everywhere out reaping the ripe barley and piling it, pillar-wise, upon tall stakes. Owing to this circumstance we were obliged to wait some time for oarsmen. There was no milk to be had, nor indeed anything to eat, notwithstanding the signs of plenty on all sides. My friend, wandering from house to house, at last discovered an old man, who brought him a bowl of mead in exchange for a cigar. Late in the afternoon two men came, put us into a shabby and leaky boat, and pulled away slowly for Vik, ten miles distant.

The fjord was shut in by lofty and abrupt mountains, often interrupted by deep lateral gorges. This is the general character of the Hardanger Fjord, a broad winding sheet of water, with many arms, but whose extent is diminished to the eye by the grandeur of its shores. Nothing can be wilder or more desolate than this scenery, especially at the junction of the two branches, where all signs of habitation are shut out of sight, and one is surrounded by mighty precipices of dark-red rock, vanishing away to the eastward in a gloomy defile. It was three hours and a half before we reached Vik, at the head of a bay on the southern side. Here, however, some English fishermen were quartered and we made sure of a supper. The landlord, of course, received their superfluous salmon, and they were not the men to spare a potato-field, so both were forthcoming, and in the satisfaction of appeased hunger, we were willing to indorse the opinion of a former English traveller in the guest's book: " This place seems to me a paradise, although very probably it is not one." The luxury of fishing, which I never could understand, has taught the Norwegians to regard travellers as their proper prey. Why should a man, they think, pay 50*l*. for the privilege of catching fish, which he gives away as soon as caught, unless he don't know how else to get rid of his money? Were it not that fishing in Norway includes pure air, hard fare, and healthy exercise, I should agree with somebody's definition of angling, " a rod with a fly at one end and a fool at the other ;" but it is all that, and besides furnished us with a good meal more than once; wherefore I respect it.

We were now but eight miles from the Vöring-Foss, and set out betimes the next morning, taking with us a bottle of red wine, some dry bread, and Peder Halstensen as guide. I mention Peder particularly, because he is the only jolly, lively, wide-awake, open-hearted Norwegian I have ever seen. As rollicking as a Neapolitan, as chatty as an Andalusian, and as frank as a Tyrolese, he formed a remarkable contrast to the men with whom we had hitherto come in contact. He had long black hair, wicked black eyes, and a mouth which laughed even when his face was at rest. Add a capital tenor voice, a lithe, active frame, and something irresistibly odd and droll in his motions, and you have his principal points. We walked across the birch-wooded isthmus behind Vik to the Eyfjordsvand, a lake about three miles long, which completely cuts off the further valley, the mountains on either side falling to it in sheer precipices 1000 feet high.

We embarked in a crazy, leaky boat, Peder pulling vigorously and singing, "*Frie dig ved lifve*" ("Life let us cherish"), with all the contentment on his face which is expressed in Mozart's immortal melody. "Peder," said I, "do you know the national song of Norway?" "I should think so," was his answer, stopping short in the midst of a wild fjeld-song, clearing his throat, and singing with a fervour and enthusiasm which rang wide over the lonely lake:—

> "Minstrel, awaken the harp from its slumbers,
>   Strike for old Norway, the land of the free!
> High and heroic, in soul-stirring numbers,
>   Clime of our fathers, we strike it for thee!

> Old recollections awake our affections—
> Hallow the name of the land of our birth;
> Each heart beats its loudest, each cheek glows its proudest,
> For Norway the ancient, the throne of the earth!" *

"Dost thou know," said he, becoming more familiar in his address, " that a lawyer (by the name of Bjerregaard) wrote this song, and the Storthing at Christiania gave him a hundred specie dollars for it. That was not too much, was it ?" " No," said I; " five hundred dollars would have been little enough for such a song." " Yes, yes, that it would," was his earnest assent ; and as I happened at that moment to ask whether we could see the peaks of the Halling Jökeln, he commenced a sœter-song of life on the lofty fjeld—a song of snow, and free winds, and blue sky. By this time we had reached the other end of the lake, where, in the midst of a little valley of rich alluvial soil, covered with patches of barley and potatoes, stood the hamlet of Sæbö. Here Peder procured a horse for my friend, and we entered the mouth of a sublime gorge which opened to the eastward—a mere split in the mighty ramparts of the Hardanger-Fjeld. Peder was continually shouting to the people in the fields: "Look here! These are Americans, these two, and the other one is a German ! This one talks Norsk, and the others don't."

We ascended the defile by a rough footpath, at first through alder thickets, but afterwards over immense masses of rocky ruin, which had tumbled from the crags far above, and almost blocked up the valley. For silence, desolation, and awful grandeur, this defile equals any of the Alpine passes. In the spring, when the rocks, split by wedges of

* Latham's translation.

ice, disengage themselves from the summit, and thunder down upon the piled wrecks of ages, it must be terribly sublime. A bridge, consisting of two logs spanned across abutments of loose stones, and vibrating strongly under our tread, took us over the torrent. Our road, for some distance, was now a mere staircase, scrambling up, down, under, over, and between the chaos of sundered rocks. A little further, and the defile shut in altogether, forming a *cul de sac* of apparently perpendicular walls, from 2000 to 3000 feet high. "How are we to get out of this?" I asked Peder. "Yonder," said he, pointing to the inaccessible summit in front. "But where does the stream come from?" "That you will soon see." Lo! all at once a clean split from top to bottom disclosed itself in the wall on our left, and in passing its mouth we had a glimpse up the monstrous chasm, whose dark-blue sides, falling sheer 3000 feet, vanished at the bottom in eternal gloom and spray.

Crossing the stream again, we commenced ascending over the débris of stony avalanches, the path becoming steeper and steeper, until the far-off summit almost hung over our heads. It was now a zigzag ladder, roughly thrown together, but very firm. The red mare which my friend rode climbed it like a cat, never hesitating, even at an angle of 50°, and never making a false step. The performance of this noble animal was almost incredible. I should never have believed a horse capable of such gymnastics, had I not seen it with my own eyes, had I not mounted her myself at the most difficult points, in order to test her powers. You, who have climbed the *Mayenwand*, in going from the glacier of the Rhone to the Grimsel, imagine a slant higher, steeper, and composed of loose rocks, and you will have an exact picture of our ascent. We climbed well; and yet it took us just an hour and a half to reach the summit.

We were now on the great plateau of the Hardanger Fjeld, 2500 feet above the sea. A wild region lay before us —great swells, covered with heather, sweeping into the distance and given up to solitude and silence. A few isolated peaks, streaked with snow, rose from this upper level; and a deep break on our left revealed the top of the chasm through which the torrent made its way. At its extremity, a mile or more distant, rose a light cloud of vapour, seeming close at hand in the thin mountain air. The thick, spongy soil, not more than two feet deep, rests on a solid bed of rock,—the entire Hardanger Fjeld, in fact, is but a single rock,—and is therefore always swampy. Whortleberries were abundant, as well as the multeberry (*Rubus chamæmorus*), which I have found growing in Newfoundland; and Peder, running off on the hunt of them, was continually leading us astray. But at last, we approached the wreath of whirling spray, and heard the hollow roar of the Vöring-Foss. The great chasm yawned before us; another step, and we stood on the brink. I seized the branch of a tough pine sapling as a support and leaned over. My head did not swim; the height was too great for that, the impression too grand and wonderful. The shelf of rock on which I stood projected far out over a gulf 1200 feet deep, whose opposite side rose in one great escarpment from the bottom to a height of 800 feet above my head. On this black wall, wet with eternal spray, was painted a splendid rainbow, forming two thirds of a circle before it melted into the gloom below. A little stream fell in one long thread of silver from the very summit, like a plumb-line dropped to measure the 2000 feet. On my right hand the river, coming down from the level of the fjeld in a torn, twisted, and boiling mass, reached the brink of the gulf at a point about 400 feet below me, whence it fell in a single sheet to the bottom, a depth of between 800 and 900 feet.

Could one view it from below, this fall would present one of the grandest spectacles in the world. In height, volume of water, and sublime surroundings it has no equal. The spectator, however, looks down upon it from a great height above its brink, whence it is so foreshortened that he can only guess its majesty and beauty. By lying upon your belly and thrusting your head out beyond the roots of the pines, you can safely peer into the dread abyss, and watch, through the vortex of whirling spray in its tortured womb, the starry coruscations which radiate from the bottom of the fall, like rockets of water incessantly exploding. But this view, sublime as it is, only whets your desire to stand below, and see the river, with its sprayey crest shining against the sky, make but one leap from heaven to hell. Some persons have succeeded, by entering the chasm at its mouth in the valley below, in getting far enough to see a portion of the fall, the remainder being concealed by a projecting rock; and the time will come, no doubt, when somebody will have energy enough to carry a path to its very foot. I envy the travellers who will then visit the Vöring-Foss.

A short distance above the fall there are a few cabins inhabited by sœters, or herdsmen, whither we repaired to procure some fresh milk. The house was rude and dirty: but

16*

the people received us in a friendly manner. The powerful housewife laid aside her hay-rake, and brought us milk which was actually sweet (a rare thing in Norway,) dirty, but not rancid butter, and tolerable cheese. When my friend asked for water, she dipped a pailful from a neighbouring stream, thick with decayed moss and vegetable mould, and handed it to him. He was nice enough to pick out a rotten root before drinking, which one of the children snatched up from the floor and ate. Yet these people did not appear to be in want; they were healthy, cheerful, and contented; and their filthy manner of living was the result of sheer indolence and slovenliness. There was nothing to prevent them from being neat and comfortable, even with their scanty means; but the good gifts of God are always spoiled and wasted in dirty hands.

When we opened our bottle of wine, an exquisite aroma diffused itself through the room—a mingled smell of vine blossoms and ripe grapes. How could the coarse vintage sent to the North, watered and chemically doctored as it is, produce such a miracle? We tasted—superb old Chateau Latour, from the sunniest hill of Bordeaux! By whatever accident it had wandered thither, it did not fall into unappreciative hands. Even Brita Halstendsdatter Höl, the strong housewife, smacked her lips over the glass which she drank after sitting to me for her portrait.

When the sketch was completed, we filled the empty bottle with milk and set out on our return.

CHAPTER XXXI.

SKETCHES FROM THE BERGENSTIFT.

OUR return from the Vöring-Foss to the hamlet of Sæbö was accomplished without accident or particular incident. As we were crossing the Eyfjordsvand, the stillness of the savage glen, yet more profound in the dusk of evening, was broken by the sudden thunder of a slide in some valley to the eastward. Peder stopped in the midst of "*Frie dig ved lifvet,*" and listened. "Ho!" said he, "the spring is the time when the rocks come down, but that sounds like a big fellow, too." Peder was not so lively on the way back, not because he was fatigued, for in showing us how they danced on the fjeld, he flung himself into the air in a marvellous manner, and turned over twice before coming down, but partly because he had broken our bottle of milk, and partly because there was something on his mind. I waited patiently, knowing that it would come out at last, as indeed it did. "You see," said he, hesitatingly, "some travellers give a drink-money to the guide. It is n't an obligation, you know; but then some give it. Now, if you should choose to give me anything, do n't pay it to the landlord for me, because then I won't get it You are not bound to do so you know but *some* travellers do it, and I do n't know but you might also. Now, if you should, give it directly to me, and then I will have it." When we reached Vik, we called Peder aside and gave him three marks. "Oh, you must pay your bill to the landlord," said he. "But that is your drink-money," I explained. "That?" he exclaimed; "it is not possible! *Frie dig ved lifvet*," &c., and so he sang, cut a pigeon-wing or two, and proceeded to knot and double knot the money in a corner of his pocket-handkerchief.

"Come and take a swim!" said Peder, reappearing. "I can swim ever since I fell into the water. I tumbled off the pier, you must know, and down I went. Everything became black before my eyes; and I thought to myself, 'Peder, this is the end of you.' But I kicked and splashed nevertheless, until my eyes opened again, wide enough to see where a rope was. Well, after I found I could fall into the water without drowning, I was not afraid to swim." In fact, Peder now swam very well, and floundered about with great satisfaction in the ice cold water. A single plunge was all I could endure. After supper the landlady came in to talk to me about America. She had a son in California, and a daughter in Wisconsin, and showed me their daguerrotypes and some bits of gold with great pride. She was a stout, kindly, motherly body, and paid especial attention to our wants on finding where we came from. Indeed we were treated in the most friendly manner by these good people, and had no reason to complain of our reckoning on leaving. This experience confirms me in the belief that honesty and simplicity may still be characteristics of the Norwegians in the more remote parts of the country.

We bade a cordial farewell to Vik next morning, and set off on our return, in splendid sunshine. Peder was in the boat, rejoiced to be with us again; and we had no sooner gotten under way, than he began singing, "*Frie dig ved lifvet.*" It was an intensely hot day, and the shores of Ulvik were perfectly dazzling. The turf had a silken gloss; the trees stood darkly and richly green, and the water was purest sapphire. "It is a beautiful bay, is it not?" said the farmer who furnished us with horses, after we had left the boat and were slowly climbing the fjeld. I thought I had never seen a finer; but when heaven and earth are in entire harmony, when form, colour and atmosphere accord like some rich swell of music, whatever one sees is perfect. Hence I shall not say how beautiful the bay of Ulvik was to me, since under other aspects the description would not be true.

The farmer's little daughter, however, who came along to take back one of the horses, would have been a pleasant apparition at any time and in any season. She wore her Sunday dress, consisting of a scarlet bodice over a white chemise, green petticoat, and white apron, while her shining flaxen hair was plaited into one long braid with narrow strips of crimson and yellow cloth and then twisted like a garland around her head. She was not more than twelve or thirteen years old, but tall, straight as a young pine, and beautifully formed, with the promise of early maidenhood in the gentle swell of her bosom. Her complexion was lovely —pink, brightened with sunburnt gold,—and her eyes like the blossoms of the forget-me-not, in hue. In watching her firm yet graceful tread, as she easily kept pace with the horse, I could not realise that in a few more years she would probably be no more graceful and beautiful than the women at work in the fields—coarse, clumsy shapes, with frowzy air, leathery faces, and enormous hanging breasts.

In the Bergenstift, however, one sometimes sees a pretty face; and the natural grace of the form is not always lost. About Vossevangen, for instance, the farmers' daughters are often quite handsome; but beauty, either male or female, is in Norway the rarest apparition. The grown-up women, especially after marriage, are in general remarkably plain. Except among some of the native tribes of Africa, I have nowhere seen such overgrown, loose, pendant breasts as among them. This is not the case in Sweden, where, if there are few beauties, there are at least a great many passable faces. There are marked differences in the blood of the two nations; and the greater variety of feature and complexion in Norway seems to indicate a less complete fusion of the original stocks.

We were rowed across the Graven Lake by an old farmer, who wore the costume of the last century,—a red coat, *à la* Frederic the Great, long waistcoat, and white knee-breeches. He demanded double the lawful fare, which, indeed, was shamefully small; and we paid him without demur. At Vasenden we found our carrioles and harness in good condition, nothing having been abstracted except a ball of twine. Horses were in waiting, apparently belonging to some well-to-do farmer; for the boys were well dressed, and took especial care of them. We reached the merchant's comfortable residence at Vossevangen before sunset, and made amends on his sumptuous fare for the privations of the past three days.

We now resumed the main road between Christiania and Bergen. The same cloudless days continued to dawn upon us. For one summer, Norway had changed climates with Spain. Our oil-cloths were burnt up and cracked by the heat, our clothes covered with dust, and our faces became as brown as those of Bedouins. For a week we had not a cloud in the sky; the superbly clear days belied the old saying of "weather-breeders."

Our road, on leaving Vossevangen, led through pine-forests, following the course of a stream up a wild valley, enclosed by lofty mountains. Some lovely cataracts fell from the steep on our left; but this is the land of cataracts and there is many a one, not even distinguished by a name, which would be renowned in Switzerland. I asked my postillion the name of the stream beside us. "Oh," said he, "it has none; it is not big enough!" He wanted to take us all the way through to Gudvangen, twenty-eight miles, on our paying double fare, predicting that we would be obliged to wait three hours for fresh horses at each intermediate station. He waited some time at Tvinde, the first station, in the hope that we would yield, but departed suddenly in a rage on seeing that the horses were already coming. At this place, a stout young fellow, who had evidently been asleep, came out of the house and stood in the door staring at us with open mouth for a full hour. The post-master sat on the step and did likewise. It was the height of harvest-time, and the weather favourable almost to a miracle; yet most of the harvesters lay upon their backs under the trees as we passed. The women appeared to do most of the out-door, as well as the inn-door work. They are certainly far more industrious than the men, who, judging from what I saw of them, are downright indolent Evidences of slow, patient, plodding toil, one sees truly; but active industry, thrift, and honest ambition, nowhere.

The scenery increased in wildness and roughness as we proceeded. The summit of Hvitnaset (White-nose) lifted its pinnacles of grey rock over the brow of the mountains on the north, and in front, pale, blue-grey peaks, 5000 feet high, appeared on either hand. The next station was a village of huts on the side of a hill. Everybody was in the fields except one woman, who remained to take charge of the station. She was a stupid creature, but had a proper sense of her duty; for she started at full speed to order horses, and we afterwards found that she must have run full three English miles in the space of half an hour. The emigration to America from this part of Bergenstift has been very great, and the people exhibited much curiosity to see and speak with us.

The scenery became at the same time more barren and more magnificent, as we approached the last station, Stalheim, which is a miserable little village at the head of the famous Naerödal. Our farmer-postillion wished to take us on to Gudvangen with the same horses, urging the same reasons as the former one. It would have been better if we had accepted his proposal; but our previous experience had made us mistrustful. The man spoke truth, however; hour after hour passed away, and the horses came not. A few miserable people collected about us, and begged money. I sketched the oldest, ugliest and dirtiest of them, as a specimen, but regretted it afterwards, as his gratitude on receiving a trifle for sitting, obliged me to give him my hand. Hereupon another old fellow, not quite so hideous, wanted to be taken also. "Lars," said a woman to the former, "are you not ashamed to have so ugly a face as yours go to America?" "Oh,' said he, "it does not look so ugly in the book." His delight on getting the money created some amusement. "Indeed," he protested, "I am poor, and want it; and you need not laugh."

The last gush of sunset was brightening the tops of the savage fjeld when the horses arrived. We had waited two hours and three quarters and I therefore wrote a complaint in the post-book in my best Norsk. From the top of a hill beyond the village, we looked down into the Naerödal. We stood on the brink of a tremendous wall about a thousand feet above the valley. On one side, the stream we had been following fell in a single cascade 400 feet; on the other, a second stream, issuing from some unseen defile, flung its several ribbons of foam from nearly an equal height. The valley, or rather gorge, disappeared in front between mountains of sheer rock, which rose to the height of 3000 feet. The road—a splendid specimen of engineering—was doubled back and forth around the edge of a spur projecting from the wall on which we stood, and so descended to the bottom. Once below, our carrioles rolled rapidly down the gorge, which was already dusky with twilight. The stream, of the most exquisite translucent azure-green colour, rolled between us; and the mountain crests towered so far above, that our necks ached as we looked upwards. I have seen but one valley which in depth and sublimity can equal the Naerdöl—the pass of the Taurus, in Asia Minor, leading from Cappadocia into Cilicia. In many places the precipices were 2000 feet in perpendicular height; and the streams of the upper fjeld, falling from the summits, lost themselves in evanescent water-dust before they reached the bottom. The bed of the valley was heaped with fragments of rock; which are loosed from above with every returning spring.

It was quite dark before we reached Gudvangen, thoroughly tired and as hungry as wolves. My postillion, on hearing me complain, pulled a piece of dry mutton out of his pocket and gave it to me. He was very anxious to learn whether brandy and tobacco were as dear in America as in Norway; if so, he did not wish to emigrate. A stout girl had charge of Braisted's horse; the female postillions always fell to his lot. She complained of hard work and poor pay, and would emigrate if she had the money. At Gudvangen we had a boat journey of thirty-five miles before us, and therefore engaged two boats with eight oarsmen for the morrow. The people tried hard to make us take more, but we had more than the number actually required by law, and, as it turned out, quite as many as were necessary. Travellers generally supply themselves with brandy for the use of their boatmen, from an idea that they will be stubborn and dilatory without it. We did so in no single instance; yet our men were always steady and cheerful.

We shipped our carrioles and sent them off in the larger boat, delaying our own departure until we had fortified ourselves with a good breakfast, and laid in some hard bread and pork omelette, for the day. The Gudvangen Fjord, down which we now glided over the glassy water is a narrow mountain avenue of glorious scenery. The unseen plateaus of the Blaa and Graa Fjelds, on either hand, spilled their streams over precipices from 1000 to 2000 feet in height, above whose cornices shot the pointed summits of bare grey rock, wreathed in shifting clouds, 4000 feet above the sea. Pine-trees feathered the less abrupt steeps, with patches of dazzling turf here and there; and wherever a gentler slope could be found in the coves, stood cottages surrounded by potato-fields and ripe barley stacked on poles. Not a breath of air rippled the dark water, which was a perfect mirror to the mountains and the strip of sky between them, while broad sheets of morning sunshine, streaming down the breaks in the line of precipices, interrupted with patches of fiery colour the deep, rich, transparent gloom of the shadows. It was an enchanted voyage until we reached the mouth of the Aurlands Fjord, divided from that of Gudvangen by a single rocky buttress 1000 feet high. Beyond this point the watery channel is much broader, and the shores diminish in grandeur as they approach the Sogne Fjord, of which this is but a lateral branch.

I was a little disappointed in the scenery of Sogne Fjord. The mountains which enclose it are masses of sterile rock, neither lofty nor bold enough in their forms to make impression, after the unrivalled scenery through which we had passed. The point of Vangnæs, a short distance to the westward, is the "Framnæs" of Frithiof's Saga, and I therefore looked towards it with some interest, for the sake of that hero and his northern lily, Ingeborg. There are many bauta-stones still standing on the shore, but one who is familiar with Tegner's poem must not except to find his descriptions verified, either in scenery or tradition. On turning eastward, around the point of Fronningen, we were surprised by the sudden appearance of two handsome houses, with orchards and gardens, on the sunny side of the bank. The vegetation, protected in some degree from the sea-winds, was wonderfully rich and luxuriant. There were now occasional pine-woods on the southern shore, but the general aspect of this fjord is bleak and desolate. In the heat and breathless silence of noonday, the water was like solid crystal. A faint line, as if drawn with a pencil along the bases of the opposite mountains, divided them from the equally perfect and palpable mountains inverted below them. In the shadows near us, it was quite impossible to detect the boundary between the substance and its counterpart. In the afternoon we passed the mouth of the northern arms of the fjord, which strike into the heart of the wildest and grandest region of Norway; the valley of Justedal, with its tremendous glaciers, the snowy teeth of the Hurunger, and the crowning peaks of the Skagtolstind. Our course lay down the other arm, to Lærdalsören, at the head of the fjord. By five o'clock it came in sight, at the mouth of a valley opening through the barren flanks on the Fille Fjeld. We landed, after a voyage of ten hours, and found welcome signs of civilisation in a neat but exorbitant inn.

Our boatmen, with the exception of stopping half an hour for breakfast, had pulled steadily the whole time. We had no cause to be dissatisfied with them, while they were delighted with the moderate gratuity we gave them. They were tough, well-made fellows, possessing a considerable amount of endurance, but less actual strength than one would suspect. Braisted, who occasionally tried his hand at an oar, could pull them around with the greatest ease. English travellers whom I have met inform me that in almost every trial they find themselves stronger than the Norwegians. This is probably to be accounted for by their insufficient nourishment. Sour milk and oaten bread never yet fed an athlete. The proportions of their bodies would admit of fine muscular development; and if they cannot do what their Viking ancestors once did, it is because they no longer live upon the spoils of other lands, as they.

CHAPTER XXXII.

HALLINGDAL—THE COUNTRY-PEOPLE OF NORWAY.

THERE are two roads from Lærdalsören to Christiania, the eastern one passing through the districts of Valders and Hadeland, by way of the Little Miösen Lake and the Randsfjord, while the western, after crossing the Fille Fjeld, descends the long Hallingdal to Ringerike. In point of scenery there is little difference between them; but as we intended visiting the province of Tellemark, in Southern Norway, we chose the latter. The valley of the Fille Fjeld, which we entered on leaving Lærdalsören, is enclosed by wild, barren mountains, more isolated and irregular in their forms than the Hardanger and Dovre Fjelds. There were occasional precipices and dancing waterfalls, but in general the same tameness and monotony we had found on the Sogne Fjord. Down the bed of the valley flowed a large rapid stream, clear as crystal, and of a beautiful beryl tint. The cultivation was scanty; and the potato fields, utterly ruined by disease, tainted the air with sickening effluvia. The occasional forests on the hillsides were of fir and birch, while poplar, ash, and linden grew in the valley. The only fruit-trees I saw were some sour red cherries.

But in the splendour of the day, this unfriendly valley shone like a dell of the Apennines. Not a cloud disturbed the serenity of the sky; the brown grass and yellow moss on the mountains were painted with sunny gold, and the gloss and sparkle of the foliage equalled that of the Italian ilex and laurel. On the second stage a new and superb road carried us through the rugged defile of Saltenaaset. This pass is evidently the effect of some mighty avalanche thousands of ages ago. The valley is blocked up by tremendous masses of rock, hurled one upon the other in the wildest confusion, while the shattered peaks from which they fell still tower far above. Threading this chaos in the shadow of the rocks, we looked across the glen upon a braided chain of foam, twisted together at the end into a long white cascade, which dropped into the gulf below. In another place, a rainbow meteor suddenly flashed across the face of a dark crag, betraying the dusty spray of a fall, else invisible.

On the third stage the road, after mounting a difficult steep, descended into the valley of Borgund, in which stands most probably the most ancient church in Norway. It is a singular, fantastic structure, bristling with spiky spires and covered with a scale armour of black pitched shingles. It is certainly of no more recent date than the twelfth century, and possibly of the close of the eleventh. The architecture shows the Byzantine style in the rounded choir and the arched galleries along the sides, the Gothic in the windows and pointed gables, and the horned ornaments on the roof suggest the pagan temples of the ante-Christian period. A more grotesque affair could hardly be found in Christendom; it could only be matched among the monstrosities of Chinese art. With the exception of the church of Hitterdal, in Tellemark, a building of similar date, this is the best preserved of the few antiquities of Norway. The entire absence of feudal castles is a thing to be noticed. Serfdom never existed here, and one result of this circumstance, perhaps, is the ease with which institutions of a purely republican stamp have been introduced.

Our road still proceeded up the bottom of a rough barren valley, crossing stony headlands on either side. At the station of Haug our course turned to the south-east, climbing a slope leading to the plateau of the Fille Fjeld—a severe pull for our horses in the intense heat. The birch woods gradually diminished in size until they ceased altogether, and the naked plain stretched before us. In this upper land the air was delicious and inspiring. We were more than 3000 feet above the sea, but the summits to the right and left, with their soft gleams of pale gray, lilac and purple hues in the sunshine, and pure blue in shadow, rose to the height of 6000. The heat of the previous ten days had stripped them bare of snow, and the landscape was drear and monotonous. The summits of the Norwegian Fjelds have only the charm of wildness and bleakness. I doubt whether any mountains of equal height exhibit less grandeur in their upper regions. The most imposing features of Norwegian scenery are its deep valleys, its tremendous gorges with their cataracts, flung like banners from steeps which seem to lean against the very sky, and, most of all, its winding, labryinthine fjords—valleys of the sea, in which the phenomena of the valleys of the land are repeated. I found no scenery in the Bergenstift of so original and impressive a character as that of the Lofoden Isles.

The day was Sunday, and we, of course, expect to see some evidence of it in the appearance of the people. Yet, during the whole day, we found but one clean person—the hostess of an inn on the summit of Fille Fjeld, where we stopped to bait our horses. She was a young fresh-faced woman, in the first year of her wifehood, and her snowy chemise and tidy petticoat made her shine like a star among the dirty and frowzy creatures in the kitchen. I should not forget a boy, who was washing his face in a brook as we passed; but he was young, and didn't know any better. Otherwise the people lounged about the houses, or sat on the rocks in the sun, filthy, and something else, to judge from certain signs. At Haug, forgetting that it was a fast station, where there is no *tilsigelse* (money for ordering horses) to be paid, I handed the usual sum to the landlady, saying: "This is for *tilsigelse*." "It is quite right," said she, pocketing the coin.

Skirting an azure lake, we crossed the highest part of the pass, nearly four thousand feet above the sea, and descended a naked valley to the inn of Bjöberg. The landlord received us very cordially; and as the inn promised tolerable accommodation, he easily persuaded us to stop there for the night. His wife wore a frightful costume, which we afterwards found to prevail throughout all Hemsedal and Hallingdal. It consisted simply of a band across the shoulders, above the breasts, passing around the arms and over the back of the neck, with an immense baggy, dangling skirt hanging therefrom to the ancles. Whether she was fat or lean, straight or crooked, symmetrical or deformed, it was impossible to discern, except when the wind blew. The only thing to be said in favour of such a costume is, that it does not impede the development and expansion of the body in any direction. Hence I would strongly recommend its adoption to the advocates of reform in feminine dress at home. There is certainly none of that weight upon the hips, of which they complain in the fashionable costume. It is far more baggy, loose, and hideous than the Bloomer, with the additional advantage of making all ages and styles of beauty equally repulsive, while on the score of health and convenience, there is still less to be said against it. Do not stop at half-way measures, oh, fair reformers!

It seems incredible that, in a pastoral country like Norway, it should be almost impossible to procure sweet milk and good butter. The cattle are of good quality, there is no better grass in the world; and the only explanation of the fact is to be found in the general want of cleanliness, especially among the inhabitants of the mountain districts, which are devoted to pasturage alone. Knowing this, one wonders the less to see no measures taken for a supply of water in the richer grain-growing valleys, where it is so easily procurable. At Björberg, for instance, there was a stream of delicious water flowing down the hill, close beside the inn, and four bored pine-trunks would have brought it to the very door; but, instead of that, the landlady whirled off to the stream in her revolving dress, to wash the dishes, or to bring us half a pint to wash ourselves. We found water much more abundant the previous winter in Swedish Lapland.

Leaving Bjöberg betimes, we drove rapidly down Hemsedal, enjoying the pure delicious airs of the upper fjeld. The scenery was bleak and grey; and even the soft pencil of the morning sun failed to impart any charm to it, except the nameless fascination of utter solitude and silence. The valley descends so gradually that we had driven two Norsk miles before the fir-forests in its bed began to creep up the mountain-sides. During the second stage we passed the remarkable peak of Saaten, on the opposite side of the valley— the end or cape of a long projecting ridge, terminating in a scarped cliff, from the very summit of which fell a cascade from three to four hundred feet in height. Where the water came from, it was impossible to guess, unless there were a large deposit of snow in the rear; for the mountains fell away behind Saaten, and the jagged, cleft headland rose alone above the valley. It was a strange and fantastic feature of the landscape, and, to me, a new form in the repertory of mountain aspects.

We now drove, through fir-woods balmy with warm resinous odours, to Ekre, where we had ordered breakfast by *forbud*. The morning air had given us a healthy appetite; but our spirits sank when the only person at the station, a stupid girl of twenty, dressed in the same bulging, hideous sack, informed us that nothing was to be had. After some persuasion she promised us coffee, cheese, and bread, which came in due time; but with the best will we found it impossible to eat anything. The butter was rather black than yellow, the cheese as detestable to the taste as to the smell, the bread made apparently of saw-dust, with a slight mixture of oat-bran, and the coffee muddy dregs, with some sour cream in a cup, and sugar-candy which appeared to have been sucked and then dropped in the ashes. The original colour of the girl's hands was barely to be distinguished through their coating of dirt; and all of us, tough old travellers as we were, sickened at the sight of her. I verily believe that the poorer classes of the Norwegians are the filthiest people in Europe. They are even worse than the Lapps, for their habits of life allow them to be clean.

After passing Ekre, our view opened down the valley, over a wild stretch of wooded hills, to the blue mountain folds of the Hallingdal, which crosses the Hemsedal almost at right angles, and receives its tributary waters. The forms of the mountains are here more gradual; and those grand sweeps and breaks which constitute the peculiar charms of the scenery of the Bergenstift are met with no longer. We had a hot ride to the next station, where we were obliged to wait nearly an hour in the kitchen, our *forbud* not having been forwarded from the former station as soon as the law allowed us to expect. A strapping boy of eighteen acted as station master. His trowsers reached considerably above his shoulder blades, leaving barely room for a waistcoat, six inches long, to be buttoned over his collar bone. The characteristic costumes of Norway are more quaint and picturesque in the published illustrations than in the reality, particularly those of Hemsedal. My postillion to this station was a communicative fellow, and gave me some information about the value of labour. A harvest-hand gets from one mark (twenty-one cents) to one and a half daily, with food, or two marks without. Most work is paid by the job; a strong lumber-man may make two and a half marks when the days are long, at six skillings (five cents) a tree—a plowman two marks. In the winter the usual wages of labourers are two marks a week, with board. Shoemakers, tailors, and other mechanics average about the same daily. When one considers the scarcity of good food, and the high price of all luxuries, especially tobacco and brandy, it does not seem strange that the emigration fever should be so prevalent. The Norwegians have two traits in common with a large class of Americans—rampant patriotism and love of gain; but they cannot so easily satisfy the latter without sacrificing the former.

From the village of Göl, with its dark pretty church, we descended a steep of many hundred feet, into Hallingdal, whose broad stream flashed blue in the sunshine far below us. The mountains were now wooded to their very summits; and over the less abrupt slopes, ripe oats and barley-fields made yellow spots of harvest among the dark forests. By this time we were out of smoking material, and stopped at the house of a *landhandlare*, or country merchant, to procure a supply. A riotous sound came from the door as we approached. Six or eight men, all more or less drunk, and one woman, were inside, singing, jumping, and howling like a pack of Bedlamites. We bought the whole stock of tobacco, consisting of two cigars, and hastened out of the len. The last station of ten miles was down the beautiful Hallingdal, through a country which seemed rich by contrast with Hemsedel and the barren fjeld. Our stopping-place was the village of Næs, which we reached in a famished condition, having eaten nothing all day. There were two *landhandlare* in the place, with one of whom we lodged

Here we found a few signs of Christianity such as gardens and decent dresses; but both of the merchant's shops swarmed with rum-drinkers.

I had written, and sent off from Bjöborg, *forbud* tickets for every station as far as Kongsberg. By the legal regulations, the *skyds-skaffer* is obliged to send forward such tickets as soon as received, the traveller paying the cost thereof on his arrival. Notwithstanding we had given our *forbud* twelve hours' start, and had punctually paid the expense at every station, we overtook it at Næs. The postmaster came to know whether we would have it sent on by special express, or wait until some traveller bound the same way would take it for us. I ordered it to be sent immediately, astounded at such a question, until, making the acquaintance of a Scotchman and his wife, who had arrived in advance of us, the mystery was solved. They had spent the night at the first station beyond Bjöberg, where our *forbud* tickets were given to them, with the request that they would deliver them. They had punctually done so as far as Næs, where the people had endeavoured to prevent them from stopping for the night, insisting that they were bound to go on and carry the *forbud*. The cool impudence of this transaction reached the sublime. At every station that day, pay had been taken for service unperformed, and it was more than once demanded twice over.

We trusted the repeated assurance of the post-master at Næs, that our tickets had been forwarded at once, and paid him accordingly. But at the first station next morning we found that he had not done so; and this interlinked chain of swindling lasted the whole day. We were obliged to wait an hour or two at every post, to pay for messengers who probably never went, and then to resist a demand for repayment at the other end of the station. What redress was there? We might indeed have written a complaint in imperfect Norsk, which would be read by an inspector a month afterwards; or perhaps it would be crossed out as soon as we left, as we saw done in several cases. Unless a traveller is very well versed in the language and in the laws relating to the *skyds* system, he has no defence against imposition, and even in such a case, he can only obtain redress through delay. The system can only work equitably when the people are honest; and perhaps they were so when it was first adopted.

Here I must tell an unpleasant truth. There must have been some foundation in the beginning for the wide reputation which the Norwegians have for honest simplicity of character; but the accounts given by former travellers are undeserved praise if applied at present. The people are trading on fictitious capital. "Should I have a written contract?" I asked of a landlord, in relation to a man with whom I was making a bargain. "Oh, no," said he, "everybody is honest in Norway;" and the same man tried his best to cheat me. Said Braisted, "I once heard an old sailor say,—'when a man has a reputation for honesty, watch him!'" —and there is some knowledge of human nature in the remark. Norway was a fresh field when Laing went thither; opportunities for imposition were so rare, that the faculty had not been developed; he found the people honest, and later travellers have been content with echoing his opinion. "When I first came to the country," said an Irish gentleman who for ten years past has spent his summers there, "I was advised, as I did not understand the currency, to offer a handful in payment, and let the people take what was due to them." "Would you do it now?" I asked. "No, indeed," said he, "and the man who then advised me, a Norwegian merchant, now says he would not do it either." An English salmon-fisher told me very much the same thing. "I believe they are honest in their intercourse with each other," said he; "but they do not scruple to take advantage of travellers whenever they can." For my own part, I must say that in no country of Europe, except Italy, have I experienced so many attempts at imposition. Another Englishman, who has been farming in Norway for several years, and who employs about forty labourers, has been obliged to procure Swedes, on account of the peculations of native hands. I came to Norway with the popular impression concerning the people, and would not confess myself so disagreeably undeceived, could I suppose that my own experiences were exceptional. I found, however, that they tallied with those of other travellers; and the conclusion is too flagrant to be concealed.

As a general rule, I have found the people honest in proportion as they are stupid. They are quick-witted whenever the spirit of gain is aroused; and the ease with which they pick up little arts of acquisitiveness does not suggest an integrity proof against temptation. It is but a negative virtue, rather than that stable quality rooted in the very core of a man's nature. I may, perhaps, judge a little harshly; but when one finds the love of gain so strongly developed, so keen and grasping, in combination with the four capital vices of the Norwegians—indolence, filth, drunkenness, and licentiousness,—the descent to such dishonest arts as I have described is scarcely a single step. There are, no doubt, many districts where the people are still untempted by rich tourists and sportsmen, and retain the virtues once ascribed to the whole population: but that there has been a general and rapid deterioration of character cannot be denied. The statistics of morality, for instance, show that one child out of every ten is illegitimate; and the ratio has been steadily increasing for the past fifty years. Would that the more intelligent classes would seriously set themselves to work for the good of "*Gamle Norge*" instead of being content with the poetical flourish of her name!

The following day, from Naes to Green, was a continuation of our journey down the Hallingdal. There was little change in the scenery,—high fir-wooded mountains on either hand, the lower slopes spotted with farms. The houses showed some slight improvement as we advanced. The people were all at work in the fields, cutting the year's satisfactory harvest. A scorching sun blazed in a cloudless sky; the earth was baked and dry, and suffocating clouds of dust rose from under our horses' hoofs. Most of the women in the fields, on account of the heat, had pulled off their body-sacks, and were working in shifts made on the same principle, which reached to the knees. Other garments they had none. A few, recognising us as strangers, hastily threw on their sacks or got behind a barley-stack until we had passed; the others were quite unconcerned. One, whose garment was exceedingly short, no sooner saw us than she commenced a fjeld dance, full of astonishing leaps and whirls to the great diversion of the other hands. "Weel done, cutty sark!" I cried; but the quotation was thrown away upon her.

Green, on the Kröder Lake, which we did not reach until long after dark, was an oasis after our previous experience. Such clean, refined, friendly people, such a neat table, such excellent fare, and such delicious beds we had certainly never seen before. Blessed be decency! blessed be humanity! was our fervent ejaculation. And when in the morning we paid an honest reckoning and received a hearty "*lycksame resa!*" (a lucky journey!) at parting, we vowed that the place should always be green in our memories. Thence to Kongsberg we had fast stations and civilised people; the country was open, well settled, and cultivated, the scenery pleasant and picturesque, and, except the insufferable heat and dust, we could complain of nothing.

CHAPTER XXXIII.

TELLEMARK AND THE RIUKAN FOSS.

KONGSBERG, where we arrived on the 26th of August, is celebrated for its extensive silver mines, which were first opened by Christian IV in 1624, and are now worked by the Government. They are doubtless interesting to mineralogists; but we did not visit them. The guide-book says, "The principal entrance to the mines is through a level nearly two English miles in length; from this level you descend by thirty-eight perpendicular ladders, of the average length of five fathoms each, a very fatiguing task, and then find yourself at the bottom of the shaft, and are rewarded by the sight of the veins of native silver"—not a bit of which, after all, are you allowed to put into your pocket. Thank you! I prefer remaining above ground, and was content with having in my possession smelted specimens of the ore, stamped with the head of Oscar I.

The goal of our journey was the Riukan Foss, which lies in Upper Tellemark, on the south-eastern edge of the great plateau of the Hardanger Fjeld. This cascade disputes with the Vöring Foss the supremacy of the thousand waterfalls of Norway. There are several ways from Kongsberg thither; and in our ignorance of the country, we suffered ourselves to be guided by the landlord of our hotel. Let no traveller follow our example! The road he recommended was almost impassable for carrioles, and miserably supplied with horses, while that through Hitterdal, by which we returned, is broad, smooth, and excellent. We left on the morning after our arrival, taking a road which led up the valley of the Lauven for some distance, and then struck westward through the hills to a little station called Moen. Here, as the place was rarely visited by travellers, the people were simple, honest, and friendly. Horses could not be had in less than two hours; and my postillion, an intelligent fellow far gone in consumption, proposed taking the same horse to the next station, fifteen miles further. He accepted my offer of increased pay; but another, who appeared to be the owner of the horses, refused, demanding more than double the usual rates. "How is it?" said I, "that you were willing to bring us to Moen for one and a half marks, and will not take us to Bolkesjö for less than five?" "It was my turn," he answered, "to furnish post-horses. I am bound by law to bring you here at the price fixed by the law; but now I can make my own bargain, and I want a price that will leave me some profit." This was reasonable enough; and we finally agreed to retain two of the horses taking the postmaster's for a third.

The region we now traversed was almost a wilderness. There were grazing-farms in the valley, with a few fields of oats or barley; but these soon ceased, and an interminable forest enclosed us. The road, terribly rough and stony, crossed spurs of the hills, slowly climbing to a wild summit-level, whence we caught glimpses of lakes far below us, and the blue mountain-ranges in the west, with the pyramidal peak of the Gousta Fjeld crowning them. Bolkesjö, which we reached in a little more than two hours, is a small hamlet on the western slope of the mountain, overlooking a wide tract of lake and forest. Most of the inhabitants were away in the harvest-fields; but the *skyds-shaffer*, a tall powerful fellow, with a grin of ineffable stupidity on his face, came forward as we pulled in our horses on the turfy square between the rows of magazines. "Can we get horses at once?" "Ne-e-ey!" was his drawling answer, accompanied with a still broader grin, as if the thing were a good joke. "How soon?" "In three hours." "But if we pay fast prices?" He hesitated, scratched his head, and drawled, "In a *liten stund*" (a "short time"), which may mean any time from five minutes to as many hours. "Can we get fresh milk?" "Ne-e-ey!" "Can we get butter?" "Ne-e-ey!" "What can we get?" "Nothing." Fortunately we had foreseen this emergency, and had brought a meal with us from Kongsberg.

We took possession of the kitchen, a spacious and tolerably clean apartment, with ponderous benches against two sides of it, and two bedsteads, as huge and ugly as those of kings, built along the third. Enormous platters of pewter, earthen and stone ware, were ranged on shelves, while a cupboard, fantastically painted, contained the smaller crockery. There was a heavy red and green cornice above the bed, upon which the names of the host and his wife, with the date of their marriage, were painted in yellow letters. The worthy couple lay so high that several steps were necessary to enable them to reach the bed, in which process their eyes encountered words of admonition, painted upon triangular boards, introduced to strengthen the pillars at the head and foot. One of these inscriptions ran, "This is my bed: here I take my rest in the night, and when morning comes I get up cheerfully and go to work;" and the other, " When thou liest down to sleep think on thy last hour, pray that God will guard thy sleep, and be ready for thy last hour when it comes." On the bottom of the cupboard was a representation of two individuals with chalk-white faces and inky eyes, smoking their pipes and clinking glasses. The same fondness for decorations and inscriptions is seen in all the houses in Tellemark and a great part of Hallingdal. Some of them are thoroughly Chinese in gaudy colour and grotesque design.

In the course of an hour and a half we obtained three strong and spirited stallions, and continued our journey towards the Tind-Sö. During this stage of twelve or thirteen miles, the quality of our carrioles was tested in the most satisfactory manner. Up-hill and down, over stock and stone, jolted on rock and wrenched in gulley, they were whirled at a smashing rate; but the tough ash and firmly-welded iron resisted every shock. For any other than Norwegian horses and vehicles, it would have been hazardous travelling. We were anxious to retain the same animals for the remaining stage to Tinoset, at the foot of the lake; but the postillions refused, and a further delay of two hours was the consequence. It was dark when the new horses came; and ten miles of forest lay before us. We were ferried one by one across the Tind Elv, on a weak, loose raft and got our carrioles up a frightful bank on the opposite side by miraculous luck. Fortunately we struck the post-road from Hitterdal at this place; for it would have been impossible to ride over such rocky by-ways as we had left behind us. A white streak was all that was visible in the gloom of the forest. We kept in the middle of it, not knowing whether the road went up, down, or on a level, until we had gone over it. At last, however, the forest came to an end, and we saw Tind Lake lying still and black in the starlight. All were in bed at Tinoset; but we went into the common sleeping-room, and stirred the people up promiscuously until we found the housewife, who gave us the only supper the house afforded—hard oaten bread and milk. We three then made the most of two small beds.

In the morning we took a boat, with four oarsmen, for Mael, at the mouth of the Westfjord-dal, in which lies the Riukan Foss. There was no end to our wonderful weather. In rainy Norway the sky had for once forgotten its clouds. One after another dawned the bright Egyptian days, followed by nights soft, starry, and dewless. The wooded shores of the long Tind Lake were illuminated with perfect sunshine, and its mirror of translucent beryl broke into light waves under the northern breeze. Yet, with every advantage of sun and air, I found this lake undeserving of its reputation for picturesque beauty. The highest peaks rise to the height of 2000 feet, but there is nothing bold and decided in their forms, and after the splendid fjords of the western coast the scenery appears tame and common-place. Our boatmen pulled well, and by noon brought us to Hakenaes, a distance of twenty-one miles. Here we stopped to engage horses to the Riukan Foss, as there is no post-station at Mael. While the old man put off in his boat to notify the farmers whose turn it was to supply the animals, we entered the farm-house, a substantial two-story building. The rooms were tolerably clean and well stocked with the clumsy, heavy furniture of the country, which is mostly made by the farmers themselves, every man being his own carpenter, cooper, and blacksmith. There were some odd old stools, made of segments of the trunk of a tree, the upper part hollowed out so as to receive the body, and form a support for the back. I have no doubt that this fashion of seat is as old as the time of the Vikings. The owner was evidently a man in tolerable circumstances, and we therefore cherished the hope of getting a good meal; but all that the old woman, with the best will in the world, was able to furnish, was milk, butter, oaten bread, and an egg apiece. The upper rooms were all supplied with beds, one of which displayed remarkable portraits of the Crown Prince of Denmark and his spouse, upon the head-board. In another room was a loom of primitive construction.

It was nearly two hours before the old farmer returned with the information that the horses would be at Mael as soon as we; but we lay upon the bank for some time after arriving there, watching the postillions swim them across the mouth of the Maan Elv. Leaving the boat, which was to await our return the next day, we set off up the Westfjord-dal, towards the broad cone-like mass of the Gousta-Fjeld, whose huge bulk, 6000 feet in height, loomed grandly over the valley. The houses of Mael, clustered about its little church, were scattered over the slope above the lake;

and across the river, amid the fields of grass and grain stood another village of equal size. The bed of the valley dotted with farms and groups of farm-houses, appeared to be thickly populated; but as a farmer's residence rarely consists of less than six buildings—sometimes even eight—a stranger would naturally overrate the number of inhabitants. The production of grain, also, is much less than would be supposed from the amount of land under cultivation, owing to the heads being so light. The valley of the Maan, apparently a rich and populous region, is in reality rather the reverse. In relation to its beauty, however, there can be no two opinions. Deeply sunken between the Gousta and another bold spur of the Hardanger, its golden harvest-fields and groves of birch, ash, and pine seem doubly charming from the contrast of the savage steeps overhanging them, at first scantily feathered with fir-trees, and scarred with the tracks of cataracts and slides, then streaked only with patches of grey moss, and at last bleak and sublimely bare. The deeply-channelled cone of the Gousta, with its indented summit, rose far above us, sharp and clear in the thin ether; but its base, wrapped in forests and wet by many a waterfall —sank into the bed of blue vapour which filled the valley.

There was no Arabian, nor even Byzantine blood in our horses; and our attendants—a stout full-grown farmer and a boy of sixteen—easily kept pace with their slow rough trot. In order to reach Tinoset the next day, we had determined to push on to the Riukan Foss the same evening Our quarters for the night were to be in the house of the old farmer, Ole Torgensen, in the village of Däl, half-way between Mael and the cataract, which we did not reach until five o'clock, when the sun was already resting his chin on the shoulder of the Gousta. On a turfy slope surrounded with groves, above the pretty little church of Dâl, we found Ole's *gaard*. There was no one at home except the daughter, a blooming lass of twenty, whose neat dress, and graceful, friendly deportment, after the hideous feminines of Hallingdal, in their ungirdled sacks and shifts, so charmed us that if we had been younger, more sentimental, and less experienced in such matters, I should not answer for the consequences. She ushered us into the guests' room, which was neatness itself, set before us a bottle of Bavarian beer and promised to have a supper ready on our return.

There were still ten miles to the Riukan, and consequently no time to be lost. The valley contracted, squeezing the Maan between the interlocking bases of the mountains, through which, in the course of uncounted centuries, it had worn itself a deep groove, cut straight and clean into the heart of the rock. The loud, perpetual roar of the vexed waters filled the glen; the only sound except the bleating of goats clinging to the steep pastures above us. The mountain walls on either hand were now so high and precipitous, that the bed of the valley lay wholly in shadow; and on looking back, its further foldings were dimly seen through purple mist. Only the peak of the Gousta, which from this point appeared an entire and perfect pyramid, 1500 feet in perpendicular height above the mountain platform from which it rose, gleamed with a rich bronze lustre in the setting sun. The valley was now a mere ascending gorge, along the sides of which our road climbed. Before us extended a slanting shelf thrust out from the mountain and affording room for a few cottages and fields; but all else was naked rock and ragged pine. From one of the huts we passed, a crippled, distorted form crawled out on its hands and knees to beg of us. It was a boy of sixteen, struck with another and scarcely less frightful form of leprosy. In this case, instead of hideous swellings and fungous excrescences, the limbs gradually dry up and drop off piecemeal at the joints. Well may the victims of both these forms of hopeless disease curse the hour in which they were begotten. I know of no more awful example of that visitation of the sins of the parents upon the children, which almost always attends confirmed drunkenness, filth, and licentiousness.

When we reached the little hamlet on the shelf of the mountain, the last rays of the sun were playing on the summits above. We had mounted about 2000 feet since leaving the Tind Lake, and the dusky valley yawned far beneath us, its termination invisible, as if leading downward into a lower world. Many hundreds of feet below the edge of the wild little platform on which we stood, thundered the Maan in a cleft, the bottom of which the sun has never beheld. Beyond this the path was impracticable for horses; we walked, climbed, or scrambled along the side of the dizzy steep, where, in many places, a false step would have sent us to the brink of gulfs whose mysteries we had no desire to explore. After we had advanced nearly two miles in this manner, ascending rapidly all the time, a hollow reverberation, and a glimpse of profounder abysses ahead, revealed the neighbourhood of the Riukan. All at once patches of lurid gloom appeared through the openings of the birch thicket we were threading, and we came abruptly upon the brink of the great chasm into which the river falls.

The Riukan lay before us, a miracle of sprayey splendour, an apparition of unearthly loveliness, set in a framework of darkness and terror befitting the jaws of hell. Before us, so high against the sky as to shut out the colours of sunset, rose the top of the valley—the level of the Hardanger table land, on which, a short distance further, lies the Miös-Vand, a lovely lake, in which the Maan Elv is born. The river first comes into sight a mass of boiling foam, shooting around the corner of a line of black cliffs which are rent for its passage, curves to the right as it descends, and then drops in a single fall of 500 feet in a hollow caldron of bare black rock. The water is already foam as it leaps from the summit; and the successive waves, as they are whirled into the air, and feel the gusts which for ever revolve around the abyss, drop into beaded fringes in falling, and go fluttering down like scarfs of the richest lace. It is not water, but the spirit of water. The bottom is lost in a shifting snowy film, with starry rays of foam radiating from its heart, below which, as the clouds shifts, break momentary gleams of perfect emerald light. What fairy bowers of some Northern Undine are suggested in those sudden flashes of silver and green! In that dim profound, which human eye can but partially explore, in which human foot shall never be set, what secret wonders may still lie hidden! And around this vision of perfect loveliness, rise the awful walls wet with spray which never dries, and crossed by ledges of dazzling turf, from the gulf so far below our feet, until, still further above our heads, they lift their irregular cornices against the sky.

I do not think I am extravagant when I say that the Riukan Foss is the most beautiful cataract in the world. I looked upon it with that involuntary suspension of the breath and quickening of the pulse, which is the surest recognition of beauty. The whole scene, with its breadth and grandeur of form, and its superb gloom of colouring, enshrining this one glorious flash of grace, and brightness, and loveliness, is indelibly impressed upon my mind. Not alone during that half hour of fading sunset, but day after day, and night after night, the embroidered spray-wreaths of the Riukan were falling before me.

We turned away reluctantly at last, when the emerald pavement of Undine's palace was no longer visible through the shooting meteors of silver foam. The depths of Westfjord dal were filled with purple darkness: only the perfect pyramid of the Gousta, lifted upon a mountain basement more than 4000 feet in height, shone like a colossal wedge of fire against the violet sky. By the time we reached our horses we discovered that we were hungry, and, leaving the attendants to follow at their leisure, we urged the tired animals down the rocky road. The smell of fresh-cut grain and sweet mountain hay filled the cool evening air; darkness crept under the birches and pines, and we no longer met the home-going harvesters. Between nine and ten our horses took the way to a *gaard* standing a little off the road; but it did not appear to be Ole Torgensen's, so we kept on. In the darkness, however, we began to doubt our memory, and finally turned back again. This time there could be no mistake: it was *not* Ole Torgensen's. I knocked at various doors, and hallooed loudly, until a sleepy farmer made his appearance, and started us forward again. He kindly offered to accompany us, but we did not think it necessary. Terribly fatigued and hungry, we at last saw a star of promise—the light of Ole's kitchen window. There was a white cloth on the table in the guests' house, and Ole's charming daughter—the Rose of Westfjord-dalen—did not keep us long waiting. Roast mutton, tender as her own heart, potatoes plump as her cheeks, and beer sparkling as her eyes, graced the board; but emptiness, void as our own celibate lives, was there when we arose. In the upper room there were beds, with linen fresh as youth and aromatic as spring; and the peace of a full stomach and a clear conscience descended upon our sleep.

In the morning we prepared for an early return to Mael, as the boatmen were anxious to get back to their barley-fields. I found but one expression in the guests' book—that of satisfaction with Ole Torgensen, and cheerfully added our amen to the previous declarations. Ole's bill proved his honesty, no less than his worthy face. He brightened up on learning that we were Americans. "Why," said he, "there have only been two Americans here before in all my life; and you cannot be a *born* American, because you speak Norsk so well." "Oh," said I, "I have learned the language in travelling." "Is it possible?" he exclaimed: "then you must have a powerful intellect." "By no means," said I, "it is a very easy thing; I have travelled much, and can speak six other languages." Now, God help us!" cried he; "*seven* languages! It is truly wonderful how much comprehension God has given unto man, that he can keep seven languages in his head at one time. Here am I, and I am not a fool; yet I do not see how it would be possible for me to speak anything but Norsk; and when I think of you, it shows me what wonders God has done. Will you not make a mark under your name, in the book, so that I may distinguish you from the other two?" I cheerfully complied, and hereby notify future visitors why my name is italicised in Ole's book.

We bade farewell to the good old man, and rode down the valley of the Maan, through the morning shadow of the Gousta. Our boat was in readiness; and its couch of fir boughs in the stern became a pleasant divan of indolence, after our hard horses and rough roads. We reached Tinoset by one o'clock, but were obliged to wait until four for horses. The only refreshment we could obtain was oaten bread, and weak spruce beer. Off at last, we took the postroad to Hitterdal, a smooth, excellent highway, through interminable forests of fir and pine. Towards the close of the stage, glimpses of a broad, beautiful, and thickly-settled valley glimmered through the woods, and we found ourselves on the edge of a tremendous gully, apparently the bed of an extinct river. The banks on both sides were composed entirely of gravel and huge rounded pebbles, masses of which we loosened at the top, and sent down the sides, gathering as they rolled, until in a cloud of dust they crashed with a sound like thunder upon the loose shingles of the bottom 200 feet below. It was scarcely possible to account for this phenomenon by the action of spring torrents from the melted snow. The immense banks of gravel, which we found to extend for a considerable distance along the northern side of the valley, seemed rather to be the deposit of an ocean-flood.

Hitterdal, with its enclosed fields, its harvests, and groups of picturesque, substantial farm-houses, gave us promise of good quarters for the night; and when our postillions stopped at the door of a prosperous-looking establishment, we congratulated ourselves on our luck. But (—) never whistle until you are out of the woods. The people seemed decidedly not to like the idea of our remaining, but promised to give us supper and beds. They were stupid, but not unfriendly; and our causes of dissatisfaction were, first, that they were so outrageously filthy, and secondly, that they lived so miserably when their means evidently allowed them to do better. The family room, with its two cumbrous bedsteads built against the wall, and indescribably dirty beds, was given up to us, the family betaking themselves to the stable. As they issued thence in the morning, in single garments, we were involuntary observers of their degree of bodily neatness; and the impression was one we would willingly forget. Yet a great painted desk in the room contained, amid many flourishes, the names and character of the host and hostess, as follows:—"Andres Svennogsen Bamble, and Ragnil Thorkilsdatter Bamble, Which These Two Are Respectable People." Over the cupboard, studded with earthen-ware dishes, was an inscription in misspelt Latin: "Solli Deo Glorria." Our supper consisted of boiled potatoes and fried salt pork, which, having seen the respectable hosts, it required considerable courage to eat, although we had not seen the cooking. Fleas darkened the floor; and they, with the fear of something worse, prevented us from sleeping much. We did not ask for coffee in the morning, but, as soon as we could procure horses, drove away hungry and disgusted from Bamble-Kaasa and its respectable inhabitants.

The church of Hitterdal, larger than that of Borgund, dates from about the same period, probably the twelfth century. Its style is similar, although it has not the same horned ornaments upon the roof, and the Byzantine features being simpler, produce a more harmonious effect. It is a charmingly quaint and picturesque building, and the people of the valley are justly proud of it. The interior has been renovated, not in the best style.

Well, to make this very long chapter short, we passed the beautiful falls of the Tind Elv, drove for more than twenty miles over wild piny hills, and then descended to Kongsberg, where Fru Hansen comforted us with a good dinner. The next day we breakfasted in Drammen, and, in baking heat and stifling dust, traversed the civilised country between that city and Christiania. Our Norwegian travel was now at an end; and, as a snobby Englishman once said to me of the Nile, "it is a good thing to have gotten over."

CHAPTER XXXIV.

NORWAY AND SWEDEN.

WE spent four days in Christiania, after completing our Norwegian travels. The sky was still perfectly clear, and up to the day of our departure no rain fell. Out of sixty days which we had devoted to Norway, only four were rainy—a degree of good fortune which rarely falls to the lot of travellers in the North.

Christiania, from its proximity to the continent, and its character as capital of the country, is sufficiently advanced in the arts of living, to be a pleasant resting-place after the *désagrêmens* and privations of travel in the interior. It has two or three tolerably good and very exorbitant hotels, and some bankers with less than the usual amount of conscience. One of them offered to change some Prussian thalers for my friend, at only ten per cent. less than their current value. The *vognmand* from whom we purchased our carrioles, endeavoured to evade his bargain, and protested that he had not money enough to repurchase them. I insisted, however, and with such good effect that he finally pulled a roll of notes, amounting to several hundred dollars out of his pocket, and paid me the amount in full. The

English travellers whom I met had not fared any better; and one and all of us were obliged to recede from our preconceived ideas of Norwegian character. But enough of an unpleasant theme; I would rather praise than blame, any day, but I can neither praise nor be silent when censure is a part of the truth.

I had a long conversation with a distinguished Norwegian, on the condition of the country people. He differed with me in the opinion that the clergy were to some extent responsible for their filthy and licentious habits, asserting that, though the latter were *petits seigneurs*, with considerable privileges and powers, the people were jealously suspicious of any attempt to exert an influence upon their lives. But is not this a natural result of the preaching of doctrinal religion, of giving an undue value to external forms and ceremonies? "We have a stubborn people," said my informant; "their excessive self-esteem makes them difficult to manage. Besides, their morals are perhaps better than would be inferred from the statistics. Old habits have been retained, in many districts, which are certainly reprehensible, but which spring from custom rather than depravity. I wish they were less vain and sensitive, since in that case they would improve more rapidly." He stated also that the surprising number of illegitimate births is partly accounted for by the fact that there are a great number of connections which have all the character of marriage except the actual ceremony. This is an affair of considerable cost and show; and many of the poorer people, unable to afford it, live together rather than wait, hoping that a time may come when they will be able to defray the expenses, and legitimate the children who may meanwhile be born. In some cases the parties disagree, the connection is broken off, and each one seeks a new mate. Whatever palliation there may be in particular instances, the moral effect of this custom is unquestionably bad; and the volume of statistics recently published by Herr Sundt, who was appointed by the Storthing to investigate the subject, shows that there is no agricultural population in the world which stands lower in the scale of chastity, than that of Norway.

In the course of our conversation, the gentleman gave an amusing instance of the very sensitiveness which he condemned. I happened, casually, to speak of the Icelandic language. "The *Icelandic* language!" he exclaimed. "So you also in America call it Icelandic; but you ought to know that it is Norwegian. It is the same language spoken by the Norwegian Vikings who colonised Iceland—the old Norsk, which originated here, and was merely carried thither." "We certainly have some reason," I replied, "seeing that it now only exists in Iceland, and has not been spoken in Norway for centuries; but let me ask why you, speaking Danish, call your language Norsk." "Our language, as written and printed, is certainly pure Danish," said he; "but there is some difference of accent in speaking it." He did not add that this difference is strenuously preserved and even increased by the Norwegians, that they may not be suspected of speaking Danish, while they resist with equal zeal, any approach to the Swedish. Often, in thoughtlessly speaking of the language as Danish, I have heard the ill-humoured reply, " Our language is not Danish, but Norsk." As well might we say at home, "We speak American, not English."

I had the good fortune to find Professor Munck, the historian of Norway, at home, though on the eve of leaving for Italy. He is one of the few distinguished literary names the country has produced. Holberg the comedian was born in Bergen; but he is generally classed among the Danish authors. In art, however, Norway takes no mean rank, the names of her painters Dahl, Gude, and Tidemand having a European reputation. Professor Munck is about fifty years of age, and a fine specimen of the Viking stock. He speaks English fluently, and I regretted that the shortness of my stay did not allow me to make further drafts on his surplus intelligence. In the Museum of Northern Antiquities, which is small, as compared with that of Copenhagen, but admirably arranged, I made the acquaintance of Professor Keyser, the author of a very interesting work, on the "Religion of Northmen," a translation of which by Mr. Barclay Pennock, appeared in New York, some three years ago.

I was indebted to Professor Munck, for a sight of the Storthing, or National Legislative Assembly, which was then in session. The large hall of the University, a semicircular room, something like our Senate Chamber, has been given up to its use, until an appropriate building shall be erected. The appearance and conduct of the body strikingly reminded me of one of our State Legislatures. The members were plain, practical-looking men, chosen from all classes, and without any distinguishing mark of dress. The speaker was quite a young man, with a moustache. Schweigaard, the first jurist in Norway, was speaking as we entered. The hall is very badly constructed for sound, and I could not understand the drift of his speech, but was exceedingly struck by the dryness of his manner. The Norwegian Constitution has been in operation forty-three years, and its provisions, in most respects so just and liberal, have been most thoroughly and satisfactorily tested. The Swedes and a small conservative party in Norway, would willingly see the powers of the Storthing curtailed a little; but the people now know what they have got, and are further than ever from yielding any part of it. In the house of almost every Norwegian farmer, one sees the constitution, with the *facsimile* autographs of its signers, framed and conspicuously hung up. The reproach has been made, that it is not an original instrument—that it is merely a translation of the Spanish Constitution of 1812, a copy of the French Constitution of 1791, &c.; but it is none the worse for that. Its framers at least had the wisdom to produce the right thing at the right time, and by their resolution and determined attitude to change a subject province into a free and independent state: for, carefully guarded as it is, the union with Sweden is only a source of strength and security.

One peculiarity of the Storthing is, that a majority of its members are, and necessarily must be, farmers; whence Norway is sometimes nicknamed the *Farmer State*. Naturally, they take very good care of their own interests, one of their first steps being to abolish all taxes on landed property; but in other respects I cannot learn that their rule is not as equitable as that of most legislative bodies. Mügge, in his recently published *Nordisches Bilderbuch* (Northern

Picture Book), gives an account of a conversation which he had with a Swedish statesman on this subject. The latter was complaining of the stubbornness and ignorance of the Norwegian farmers. Mügge asked, (the remainder of the dialogue is too good to be omitted) :—

"The Storthing, then, consists of a majority of coarse and ignorant people?"

STATESMAN. "I will not assert that. A certain practical understanding cannot be denied to most of these farmers, and they often bestow on their sons a good education before giving them the charge of the paternal fields. One, therefore, finds in the country many accomplished men: how could there be 700 students in Christiania, if there were not many farmers' sons among them?"

AUTHOR. "But does this majority of farmers in the Storthing commit absurdities? does it govern the country badly, burden it with debts or enact unjust laws?"

STATESMAN. "That cannot exactly be admitted, although this majority naturally gives its own interests the preference, and shapes the government accordingly. The state has no debts; on the contrary, its treasury is full, an abundance of silver, its bank-notes in demand, order everywhere, and, as you see, an increase of prosperity, with a flourishing commerce. Here lies a statement before me, according to which, in the last six months alone, more than a hundred vessels have been launched in different ports."

AUTHOR. "The Farmer-Legislature, then, as I remark, takes care of itself, but is niggardly and avaricious when its own interests are not concerned?"

STATESMAN. "It is a peculiar state of affairs. In very

many respects this reproach cannot be made against the farmers. If anything is to be done for science, or for so-called utilitarian objects, they are always ready to give money. If a deserving man is to be assisted, if means are wanted for beneficial purposes, insane asylums, hospitals, schools, and such like institutions, the Council of State is always sure that it will encounter no opposition. On other occasions however, these lords of the land are as hard and tough a Norwegian pines, and button up their pockets so tight that not a dollar drops out."

"AUTHOR. "On what occasions?"

STATESMAN. "Why, you see (shrugging his shoulders), those farmers have not the least *comprehension of statesmanship!* As soon as there is any talk of appropriations for increasing the army, or the number of officers, or the pay of foreign ministers, or the salaries of high official persons, or anything of that sort, you can't do anything with them."

AUTHOR. (To himself.) "God keep them a long time without a comprehension of statesmanship! If I were a member of the Storthing, I would have as thick a head as the rest of them."

On the 5th of September, Braisted and I took passage for Gottenburg, my friend having already gone home by way of Kiel. We had a smooth sea and an agreeable voyage, and awoke the next morning in Sweden. On the day after our arrival, a fire broke out in the suburb of Haga, which consumed thirteen large houses, and turned more than two hundred poor people out of doors. This gave me an opportunity to see how fires are managed here. It was full half an hour after the alarm-bell was rung before the first engine began to play; the water had to be hauled from the canal, and the machine, of a very small and antiquated pattern, contributed little towards stopping the progress of the flames. The intervention of a row of gardens alone saved the whole suburb from destruction. There must have been from six to eight thousand spectators present,' scattered all over the rocky knolls which surround Gottenburg. The fields were covered with piles of household furniture and clothing, yet no guard seemed to be necessary for their protection, and the owners showed no concern for their security.

There is a degree of confidence exhibited towards strangers in Sweden, especially in hotels, at post-stations, and on board the inland steamers, which tells well for the general honesty of the people. We went on board the steamer *Werner* on the morning of the 8th, but first paid our passage two days afterwards, just before reaching Carlstad. An account book hangs up in the cabin, in which each passenger enters the number of meals or other refreshments he has had, makes his own bill and hands over the amount to the stewardess. In posting, the *skjutsbonder* very often do not know the rates, and take implicitly what the traveller gives them. I have yet to experience the first attempt at imposition in Sweden. The only instances I heard of were related to me by Swedes themselves, a large class of whom make a point of depreciating their own country and character. This habit of detraction is carried to quite as great an extreme as the vanity of the Norwegians, and is the less pardonable vice of the two.

It was a pleasant thing to hear again the musical Swed-
18*

ish tongue, and to exchange the indifference and reserve of Norway for the friendly, genial, courteous manner of Sweden. What I have said about the formality and affectation of manners, and the rigidity of social etiquette, in the chapters relating to Stockholm, was meant to apply especially to the capital. Far be it from me to censure that natural and spontaneous courtesy which is a characteristic of the whole eople. The more I see of the Swedes, the more I am convinced that there is no kinder, simpler, and honester people in the world. With a liberal common school system, a fairer representation, and release from the burden of a state church, they would develope rapidly and nobly.

Our voyage from Gottenburg to Carlstad, on the Wener Lake, had but one noteworthy point—the Falls of Trollhätten. Even had I not not been fresh from the Riukan-Foss, which was still flashing in my memory, I should have been disappointed in this renowned cataract. It is not a single fall, but four successive descents, within the distance of half a mile, none of them being over twenty feet in perpendicular height. The Toppö Fall is the only one which at all impressed me, and that principally through its remarkable form. The huge mass of the Götha River, squeezed between two rocks, slides down a plane with an inclination of about 50°, strikes a projecting rock at the bottom, and takes an upward curve, flinging tremendous volumes of spray, or rather broken water, into the air. The bright emerald face of the watery plane is covered with a network of silver threads of shifting spray, and gleams of pale blue and purple light play among the shadows of the rising globes of foam below.

CHAPTER XXXV.

A TRAMP THROUGH WERMELAND AND DALECARLIA.

On leaving Carlstad our route lay northward up the valley of the Klar Elv, in the province of Wermeland, and thence over the hills, by way of Westerdale, in Dalecarlia, to the head of the Siljan Lake. The greater part of this region is almost unknown to travellers, and belongs to the poorest and wildest parts of Sweden. We made choice of it for this reason, that we might become acquainted with the people in their true character, and compare them with the same class in Norway. Our heavy luggage had all been sent on to Stockholm, in the charge of an Irish friend, and we retained no more than could be carried easily in two packs, as we anticipated being obliged to perform part of the journey on foot.

It rained in torrents during the day we spent in Carlstad, and some lumber merchants of Gottenburg, who were on their way to Fryxendal, to superintend the getting down of their rafts, predicted that the deluge would last an entire month. There was always a month of rainy weather at this season they said, and we had better give up our proposed journey. We trusted to our combined good luck however, and were not deceived, for, with the exception of two days, we had charming weather during the remainder of our stay in Sweden. Having engaged a two-horse cart for the first post-station, we left Carlstad on the morning of the 11th of September. The clouds were still heavy, but gradually rolled into compacter masses, giving promise of breaking away. The city is built upon a little island at the head of the lake, whence we crossed to the mainland by a strong old bridge. Our road led eastward through a slightly undulating country, where broad woods of fir and birch divided the large, well cultivated farms. The *gårds*, or mansions, which we passed, with their gardens and ornamental shrubbery, gave evidence of comfort and competence. The people were in the harvest-fields, cutting oats, which they piled upon stakes to dry. Every one we met saluted us courteously, with a cheerful and friendly air, which was all the more agreeable by contrast with the Norwegian reserve.

At the station, Prestegård, we procured a good breakfast of ham, eggs, and potatoes, and engaged two carts to take us further. We now turned northward over a lovely rolling country, watered with frequent streams,—a land of soft outlines, of woods and swelling knolls, to which the stately old houses gave an expression of contentment and household happiness. At Deye we left our carts, shouldered our packs, and trudged off on foot up the valley of the Klar Elv, which is here a broad lazy stream, filled with tens of thousands of pine-logs, waiting to be carried down to the Wener by the first freshet. The scenery charmed us by its rich and quiet beauty; it was without grand or striking features, but gently undulating, peaceful, and home-like. We found walking very fatiguing in the hot sun, which blazed upon us all the afternoon with a summer heat. The handsome residences and gardens, which we occasionally passed, gave evidence of taste and refinement in their possessors, and there was a pleasant grace in the courteous greetings of the country people whom we met. Towards evening we reached a post-station, and were tired enough to take horses again. It was after dark before we drew up at Ohlsäter, in the heart of Wermeland. Here we found a neat, comfortable room, with clean beds, and procured a supper of superb potatoes. The landlord was a tall, handsome fellow, whose friendly manners, and frank face, breathing honesty and kindness in every lineament, quite won my heart. Were there more such persons in the world, it would be a pleasanter place of residence.

We took horses and bone-shattering carts in the morning, for a distance of thirteen miles up the valley of the Klar Elv. The country was very picturesque and beautiful, well cultivated, and quite thickly settled. The wood in the sheltered bed of the valley was of remarkably fine growth; the birch trees were the largest I ever saw, some of them being over one hundred feet in height. Comfortable residences, with orchards and well-kept gardens attached, were quite frequent, and large saw-mills along the river, which in some places was entirely concealed by floating rafts of lumber, gave an air of industry and animation to the landscape. In one place the road was spanned, for a considerable distance, with triumphal arches of foliage. I inquired the meaning of this display of the boy who accompanied us. "Why,"

said he, " there was a wedding a week ago, at the *herregård*
(gentleman's residence); the young Herr got married, and
these arches were put up for him and his bride." The herregård, which we passed soon afterwards, was an imposing
mansion, upon an eminence overlooking the valley. Beside it was a *jernbruk*, or iron-works, from which a tram-
way, some miles in length, led to the mines.

Resuming our knapsacks, we walked on up the valley.
The hills on either side increased in height, and gloomed
darkly under a threatening sky. The aspect of the country
gradually became wilder, though, wherever there was cultivation, it bore the same evidence of thrift and prosperity.
After a steady walk of four hours, we reached the village of
Råda, where our road left the beautiful Klar Elv, and struck
northwards towards Westerdal, in Dalecarlia. We procured
a dinner of potatoes and bacon, with excellent ale, enjoying,
meanwhile, a lovely view over a lake to the eastward, which
stretched away for ten miles between the wooded hills. The
evening was cold and raw: we drove through pine-woods,
around the head of the lake, and by six o'clock reached Asplund, a miserable little hamlet on a dreary hill. The post-
station was a forlorn cottage with a single room, not of the
most inviting appearance. I asked if we could get quarters
for the night. "If you *will* stay, of course you *can*," said
the occupant, an old woman; "but there is no bed, and I
can get you horses directly to go on." It was a distance of
thirteen miles to the next station, but we yielded to the old
woman's hint, and set forward. The road led through woods
which seemed interminable. We were jammed together into
a little two-wheeled cart, with the boy between our knees

He seemed much disinclined to hurry the horse, but soon fell asleep, and one of us held him by the collar to prevent his tumbling out, while the other took the lines, and urged on our slow beast. The night was so dark that we had great difficulty in keeping the road, but towards eleven o'clock we emerged from the woods, and found, by shaking the boy, that we were approaching the station at last. This was a little place called Laggasen, on the nothern frontier of Wermeland.

Everybody had gone to bed in the hut at which we stopped. We entered the kitchen, which was at the same time the bed-room, and aroused the inmates, who consisted of a lonely woman, with two or three children. She got up in a very scanty chemise, lit a wooden splinter, and inspected us, and, in answer to our demand for a bed, informed us that we would have to lie upon the floor. We were about to do this, when she said we could get good quarters at the *Nore*, on the top of the hill. Her earnestness in persuading us to go made me suspect that she merely wanted to get rid of us, and I insisted that she should accompany us to show the way. After some hesitation she consented, and we set out. We first crossed a broad swamp, on a road made of loose logs, then climbed a hill, and trudged for some distance across stubble-fields, until my patience was quite worn out, and Braisted made use of some powerful maritime expressions. Finally, we reached a house, which we entered without more ado. The close, stifling atmosphere, and the sound of hard breathing on all sides, showed us that a whole family had been for some hours asleep there. Our guide thumped on the door, and hailed, and at length somebody awoke. "Can you give two travellers a bed?" she asked. "No," was the comfortable reply, followed by the yell of an aroused baby, and the noises of the older children. We retreated at once, and opened a battery of reproaches on the old woman for having brought us on a fool's errand. "There is Ohlsen's," she replied, very quietly, "I think I can get you a bed there." Whereupon we entered another house in the same unceremonious manner, but with a better result. A plump, good-natured housewife jumped out of bed, went to an opposite door, and thumped upon it. "Lars!" she cried, "come out of that this minute!" As we entered, with a torch of dry fir, Lars, who proved to be a middle-aged man, got out of bed sleepily, picked up his clothes and marched off. The hostess then brought clean sheets and pillow-cases, and by midnight we were sweetly and blissfully stowed away together in the place vacated by poor Lars.

Nothing could exceed the kindness and courtesy of the good people in the morning. The hostess brought us coffee, and her son went off to get us a horse and cart. She would make no charge, as we had had so little, she said, and was quite grateful for the moderate sum I gave her. We had a wild road over hills, covered with pine forests, through the breaks in which we now and then caught a glimpse of a long lake to the westward, shining with a steel-blue gleam in the morning sun. There were but few clearings along the road, and miles frequently intervened without a sign of human habitation. We met, however, with great numbers of travellers, mostly farmers, with laden hay-carts. It was Sunday morning, and I could not help contrasting these people with those we had seen on the same day three weeks previous whilst crossing the Fille Fjeld. Here, every one had evidently been washed and combed : the men wore clean shirts and stockings, and the women chemises of snowy whiteness under their gay boddices. They were mostly Dalecarlians, in the picturesque costume of the province. We entered Dalecarlia on this stage, and the frank fresh faces of these people, their unmistakeable expression of honesty and integrity, and the hearty cordiality of their greetings, welcomed us delightfully to the storied ground of Sweden.

Towards noon we reached the village of Tyngsjö, a little settlement buried in the heart of the wild woods. A mile or two of the southern slope of a hill had been cleared away, and over this a number of dark wooden farmhouses were scattered, with oats and potato-fields around them. An odd little church stood in midst, and the rich swell of a hymn, sung by sweet Swedish voices, floated to us over the fields as we drove up to the post-station. The master, a tall, slender man, with yellow locks falling upon his shoulders, and a face which might be trusted with millions, welcomed us with a fine antique courtesy, and at once sent off for horses. In a little while three farmers came, saluting us gracefully, and standing bareheaded while they spoke to us. One of them, who wore a dark brown jacket and knee-breeches, with a clean white shirt and stockings, had a strikingly beautiful head. The face was a perfect oval, the eyes large and dark, and the jet-black hair, parted on the forehead, fell in silky waves upon his shoulders. He was as handsome and graceful as one of Vandyk's cavaliers, and showed the born gentleman in his demeanour. He proposed that we should take one horse, as it could be gotten without delay, while two (which the law obliged us to take and pay for, if the farmers chose), would have detained us an hour. As the women were in church, the post-master himself cooked us some freshly-dug potatoes, which, with excellent butter, he set before us. "I have a kind of ale," said he, "which is called porter; if you will try it, perhaps you will like it." It was, in reality, so good, that we took a second bottle with us for refreshment on the road. When I asked how much we should pay, he said: "I don't think you should pay anything, there was so little." "Well," said I, "It is worth at least half a rigs-daler." "Oh, but that may be too much," he answered, hesitatingly.

Our postillion was a fine handsome fellow, so rosy and robust that it made one feel stronger and healthier to sit beside him. He did not spare the horse, which was a big, capable animal, and we rolled along through endless forests of fir and pine as rapidly as the sandy road would allow. After we had gone about eight miles he left us, taking a shorter foot-path through the woods. We guessed at our proper direction, sometimes taking the wrong road, but finally, after two hours or more, emerged from the woods into Westerdal, one of the two great valleys from which Dalecarlia (*Dalarne*, or The Dales) takes its name. The day was magnificent, clear, and with a cold north-east wind, resembling the latter part of October at home. The broad, level valley, with its fields and clustered villages, lay before us in the pale, cold autumnal sunshine, with low blue hills bounding it in the distance. We met many parties in carts, either returning from church, or on their way to visit neighbours. All were in brilliant Sunday costume, the men in blue jackets and knee-breeches, with vests of red or some other brilliant colour, and the women with gay embroidered boddices, white sleeves, and striped petticoats of blue, red, brown, and purple, and scarlet stockings. Some of them wore, in addition, an outer jacket of snowy sheepskin, with elaborate ornamental stitch-work on the back. Their faces were as frank and cheerful as their dresses were tidy, and they all greeted us with that spontaneous goodness of heart which recognises a brother in every man. We had again taken a wrong road, and a merry party carefully set us right again, one old lady even proposing to leave her friends and accompany us, for fear we should go astray again.

We crossed the Westerdal by a floating bridge, and towards sunset reached the inn of Rågsveden, our destination. It was a farmer's *gård*, standing a little distance off the road. An entrance through one of the buildings, closed with double doors, admitted us into the courtyard, a hollow square, surrounded with two story wooden dwellings, painted dark red. There seemed to be no one at home, but after knocking and calling for a time an old man made his appearance. He was in his second childhood, but knew enough to usher us into the kitchen and ask us to wait for the landlord's arrival. After half an hour our postillion arrived with four or five men in their gayest and trimmest costume, the landlord among them. They immediately asked who and what we were, and we were then obliged to give them an account of all our travels. Their questions were shrewd and intelligent, and their manner of asking, coupled as it was with their native courtesy, showed an earnest desire for information, which we were most willing to gratify. By and by the hostess came, and we were ushered into a very pleasant room, with two beds, and furnished with a supper of fresh meat, potatoes, and mead. The landlord and two or three of the neighbours sat with us before the fire until we were too sleepy to answer any more questions. A more naturally independent and manly bearing I have never seen than that of our host. He was a tall, powerful man, of middle age, with very handsome features, which were softened but not weakened in expression by his long blond hair, parted on his forehead. He had the proper pride which belongs to the consciousness of worth, and has no kinship with empty vanity. "We have come to Dalecarlia to see the descendants of the people who gave Gustavus Vasa his throne," said I, curious to see whether he would betray any signs of flattered pride. His blue eye flashed a little, as he sat with his hands clasped over one knee, gazing at the fire, a light flush ran over his temples—but he said nothing, Some time ago a proposition was made to place a portrait of Gustavus Vasa in the church at Mora. "No," said the Dalecarlians, "we will not have it: we do not need any picture to remind us of what our fathers have done."

The landlady was a little woman, who confessed to being forty-nine years old, although she did not appear to be more than forty. "I have had a great deal of headache," said she, "and I look much older than I am." Her teeth were superb, as were those of all the women we saw. I do not suppose a tooth-brush is known in the valley; yet the teeth one sees are perfect pearls. The use of so much sour milk is said to preserve them. There was a younger person in the house, whom we took to be a girl of sixteen, but who proved to be the son's wife, a woman of twenty-six, and the mother of two or three children. The Dalecarlians marry young when they are able, but even in opposite cases they rarely commit any violation of the laws of morality. Instances are frequent, I was told, where a man and woman, unable to defray the expense of marriage, live together for years in a state of mutual chastity, until they have saved a sum sufficient to enable them to assume the responsibilities of married life. I know there is no honester, and I doubt whether there is a purer, people on the earth than these Dalecarlians.

We awoke to another glorious autumnal day. The valley was white with frost in the morning, and the air deliciously keen and cold; but after sunrise heavy white vapours arose from the spangled grass, and the day gradually grew milder. I was amused at the *naïve* curiosity of the landlady and her daughter-in-law, who came into our room very early, that they might see the make of our garments and our manner of dressing. As they did not appear to be conscious of any impropriety, we did not think it necessary to feel embarrassed. Our Lapland journey had taught us habits of self-possession under such trying circumstances. We had coffee, paid an absurdly small sum for our entertainment, and took a cordial leave of the good people. A boy of fifteen, whose eyes, teeth and complexion kept my admiration on the stretch during the whole stage, drove us through unbroken woods to Skamhed, ten miles further down the valley. Here the inn was a little one story hut, miserable to behold externally but containing a neat guest's room and moreover, as we discovered in the course of time--a good breakfast. While we were waiting there, a man came up who greeted us in the name of our Lord Jesus Christ, on learning that we came from America. "Are you not afraid to travel so far from home?" he asked: "how could you cross the great sea?" "Oh," I answered, "there is no more danger in one part of the world than another." "Yes," said he, "God is as near on the water as on the land"—unconsciously repeating the last words of Sir Humphrey Gilbert: "Christ walked upon the waves and quieted them, and he walks yet, for them that believe in Him." Hereupon he began repeating some hymns, mingled with texts of Scripture, which process he continued until we became heartily tired. I took him at a venture, for an over-enthusiastic *Läsare*, or "Reader," the name given to the Swedish dissenters.

We had a station of twenty-three miles before us, to the village of Landbobyn, which lies in the wooded wilderness between Osterdal and Westerdal. Our postillion, a fine young fellow of twenty-two, over six feet in height, put on his best blue jacket and knee-breeches, with a leather apron reaching from his shoulders to below his knees. This is an article worn by almost all Dalecarlians for the purpose of saving their clothes while at work, and gives them an awkward and ungraceful air. This fellow, in spite of a little fear at the bare idea, expressed his willingness to go with us all over the world, but the spirit of wandering was evidently so easy to be kindled in him, that I rather discouraged him. We had a monotonous journey of five hours through a forest of pine, fir, and birch, in which deer and elk are frequently met with; while the wolf and the bear haunt its remoter valleys. The ground was but slightly undulating, and the scenery in general was as tame as it was savage.

Landbobyn was a wretched hamlet on the banks of a stream, with a few cleared fields about it. As the sun had not yet set, we determined to push on to Kettbo, eight or ten miles further, and engaged a boy to pilot us through the woods. The post-station was a miserable place, where we found it impossible to get anything to eat. I sat down and talked with the family while our guide recruited himself with a large dish of thick sour milk. "Why do you travel about the earth?" asked his mother: "is it that you may spy out the poverty of the people and see how miserably they live?" "No," said I, "it is that I may become acquainted with the people, whether they are poor or not." "But," she continued, "did you ever see a people poorer than we?" "Often," said I; "because you are contented, and no one can be entirely poor who does not complain." She shook her head with a sad smile and said nothing.

Our guide poled us across the river in a rickety boat, and then plunged into the woods. He was a tall, well grown boy of fifteen or sixteen, with a beautiful oval face, long fair hair parted in the middle and hanging upon his shoulders, and a fine, manly, resolute expression. With his jacket, girdle, knee-breeches, and the high crowned and broad brimmed felt hat he wore, he reminded me strongly of the picture of Gustavus Vasa in his Dalecarlian disguise, in the cathedral of Upsala. He was a splendid walker, and quite put me, old pedestrian as I am, out of countenance. The footpath we followed was terribly rough; we stumbled over stock and stone, leaped fallen trees, crossed swamps on tussocks of spongy moss, and climbed over heaps of granite boulders: yet, while we were panting and exhausted with our exertions to keep pace with him, he walked onward as quietly and easily as if the smoothest meadow turf were under his feet. I was quite puzzled by the speed he kept up on such a hard path, without seeming to put forth any extra strength. At sunset he pointed out some clearings on a hill side over the tree tops, a mile or two ahead, as our destination. Dusk was gathering as we came upon a pretty lake, with a village scattered along its hilly shore. The post-station, however, was beyond it, and after some delay the boy procured a boat and rowed us across. Telling us to go up the hill and we should find the inn, he bade us good bye and set out on his return.

We soon reached a *gård*, the owner whereof, after satisfying his curiosity concerning us by numerous questions, informed us that the inn was still further. After groping about in the dark for awhile, we found it. The landlord and his wife were sitting before the fire, and seemed, I thought, considerably embarrassed by our arrival. There was no bed, they said, and they had nothing that we could eat; their house was beyond the lake, and they only came over to take charge of the post-station when their turn arrived. We were devoured with hunger and thirst, and told them we should be satisfied with potatoes and a place on the floor. The wife's brother, who came in soon afterwards, was thereupon despatched across the lake to bring coffee for us, and the pleasant good-wife put our potatoes upon the fire to boil. We lit our pipes, meanwhile, and sat before the fire, talking with our host and some neighbours who came in. They had much to ask about America, none of them having ever before seen a native of that country. Their questions related principally to the cost of living, to the value of labour, the price of grain, the climate and productions, and the character of our laws. They informed me that the usual wages in Dalecarlia were 24 skillings (13 cents) a day, and that one *tunne* (about 480 lbs.) of rye cost 32 *rigsdaler* ($8.37½). "No doubt you write descriptions of your travels?" asked the landlord. I assented. "And then, perhaps, you make books of them?" he continued: whereupon one of the neighbours asked, "But do you get any money for your books?"

The potatoes were finally done, and they, with some delicious milk, constituted our supper. By this time the brother had returned, bringing with him coffee, a pillow, and a large coverlet made entirely of cat-skins. A deep bed of hay was spread upon the floor, a coarse linen sheet thrown over it, and, with the soft fur covering, we had a sumptuous bed. About midnight we were awakened by an arrival. Two tailors, one of them hump-backed, on their way to Wermeland, came in, with a tall, strong woman as postillion. The fire was rekindled, and every thing which the landlord had extracted from us was repeated to the new comers, together with a very genial criticism upon our personal appearance and character. After an hour or two, more hay was brought in and the two tailors and the postillioness lay down side by side. We had barely got to sleep again, when there was another arrival. "I am the post-girl," said a female voice. Hereupon everybody woke up, and the story of the two foreign travellers was told over again. In the course of the conversation I learned that the girl carried the post twenty English miles once a week, for which she received 24 *rigs* ($6.25) annually. " It is a hard business," said the hump-backed tailor. " Yes; but I am obliged to do it," answered the girl. After her departure we were not again disturbed, and managed to get some sleep at last.

We all completed our toilettes in the same room, without the least embarrassment; and, with a traveller's curiosity I may be pardoned for noticing the general bodily cleanliness of my various bed-fellows, especially as the city Swedes are in the habit of saying that the country people are shockingly dirty. We had coffee, and made arrangements with the girl who had brought the tailors to take us back in her cart. Our host would make no charge for the bed, and next to nothing for our fare, so I put a bank-note in the hand of little Pehr, his only child, telling him to take care of it, and spend it wisely when he grew up. The delight of the good people knew no bounds. Pehr must hold up his little mouth to be kissed, again and again; the mother shook us warmly by the hand, and the father harnessed his horse and started with us. May the blessing of God be upon all poor, honest, and contented people!

Our road led between wooded hills to the Siljan-Forss, a large iron-foundry upon a stream which flows into the Siljan Lake. It was a lovely morning, and our postillion who was a woman of good sense and some intelligence, chatted with me the whole way. She was delighted to find that we could so easily make ourselves understood. "When I saw you first in the night," said she, "I thought you must certainly be Swedes. All the foreigners I saw in Stockholm had something dark and cloudy in their countenances, but both of you have shining faces." She questioned me a great deal about the sacred localities of Palestine, and about the state of religion in America. She evidently belonged to the *Läsare*, who, she stated, were very numerous in Dalecarlia. "It is a shame," said she, "that we poor people are obliged to pay so much for the support of the Church, whether we belong to it or not. Our taxes amount to 40 *rigs* yearly, ten of which, in Mora parish, go to the priest. They say he has an income of half a *rigs* every hour of his life. King Oscar wishes to make religion free, and so it ought to be, but the clergy are all against him, and the clergy control the *Bondeständ* (House of Peasants), and so he can do nothing." The woman was thirty-one years old, and worn with hard labour. I asked her if she was married. "No," she answered, with a deep sigh, looking at the betrothal-ring on her finger. "Ah," she continued, "we are all poor, Sweden is a poor country; we have only iron and timber, not grain, and cotton, and silk, and sugar, like other countries."

As we descended towards the post-station of Vik we caught a glimpse of the Siljan Lake to the south, and the tall tower of Mora Church, far to the eastward. At Vik, where we found the same simple and honest race of people, we parted with the postillioness and with our host of Kettbo, who thanked us again in Pehr's name, as he shook hands for the last time. We now had fast horses, and a fine road over a long wooded hill, which was quite covered with the *lingon,* or Swedish cranberry. From the further slope we at last looked down upon Mora, at the head of the Siljan Lake, in the midst of a broad and fertile valley. Ten miles to the eastward arose the spire of Orsa, and southward, on an island in the lake, the tall church of Sollerön. "You can see three churches at once," said our postillion with great pride. So we could, and also the large, stately inn of Mora—a most welcome sight to us, after five days on potato diet.

CHAPTER XXXVI.

LAST DAYS IN THE NORTH.

Mora, in Dalecarlia, is classic ground. It was here that Gustavus Vasa first harangued the people, and kindled that spark of revolution, which in the end swept the Danes from Sweden. In the cellar of a house which was pointed out to us, on the southern shore of the Siljan Lake, he lay hidden three days; in the barn of Ivan Elfssen he threshed corn, disguised as a peasant; and on the road by which we had travelled from Kettbo, in descending to the lake, we had seen the mounds of stone, heaped over the Danes, who were slain in his first victorious engagement. This district is considered, also, one of the most beautiful in Sweden. It has, indeed, a quiet, tranquil beauty, which gradually grows upon the eye, so that if one is not particularly aroused on first acquaintance, he at least carries away a delightful picture in his memory. But in order to enjoy properly any Swedish landscape whatsoever, one should not be too fresh from Norway.

After dinner we called at the "Parsonage of Mora," which has given Miss Fredrika Bremer the materials for one of her stories of Swedish life.

The *Prost*, Herr Kjelström, was not at home, but his wife received us with great cordiality, and insisted upon our remaining to tea. The magister——, who called at the same time, gave us some information concerning the porphyry quarries at Elfdal, which we were debating whether we should visit. Very little is doing at present, not more than ten men in all being employed, and in his opinion we would hardly be repaid for the journey thither; so we determined to turn southward again, and gradually make our way to Stockholm. Fru Kjelström was one of the few Swedes I met, who was really an enthusiastic admirer of Tegner; she knew by heart the greater part of his "Frithiof's Saga."

The morning after our arrival in Mora dawned dark and cloudy, with a wailing wind and dashes of rain. There were threats of the equinoctial storm, and we remembered the prediction of the lumber merchants in Carlstad. During the night, however, a little steamer belonging to an iron company arrived, offering us the chance of a passage down the lake to Leksand. While we were waiting on the shore the magister, who had come to see us depart, gave me some information about the Läsare. He admitted that there were many in Dalecarlia, and said that the policy of persecution, which was practised against them in the beginning, was now dropped. They were, in general, ignored by the clerical authorities. He looked upon the movement rather as a transient hallucination than as a permanent secession from the Established Church, and seemed to think that it would gradually disappear, if left to itself. He admitted that the king was in favour of religious liberty, but was so guarded in speaking of the subject that I did not ascertain his own views.

We had on board about sixty passengers, mostly peasants from Upper Elfdel, bound on a peddling excursion through Sweden, with packs of articles which they manufacture at home. Their stock consisted mostly of pocket-books, purses, boxes, and various small articles of ornament and use. The little steamer was so well laden with their solid forms that she settled into the mud, and the crew had hard poling to get her off. There was service in Mora Church, and the sound of the organ and choir was heard along the lake. Many friends and relatives of the wandering Elfdalians were on the little wooden pier to bid them adieu. "God's peace be with thee!" was a parting salutation which I heard many times repeated. At last we got fairly clear and paddled off through the sepia-coloured water, watching the softly undulating shores, which soon sank low enough to show the blue, irregular hills in the distant background. Mora spire was the central point in the landscape, and remained visible until we had nearly reached the other end of the lake. The Siljan has a length of about twenty-five miles, with a breadth of from six to ten. The shores are hilly, but only moderately high, except in the neighborhood of Rättvik, where they were bold and beautiful. The soft slopes on either hand were covered with the yellow pillars of the ripe oats, bound to upright stakes to dry. From every village rose a tall midsummer pole, yet laden with the withered garlands of Sweden's fairest festival, and bearing aloft its patriotic symbol, the crossed arrows of Dalecarlia. The threatened storm broke and dispersed as we left Mora, and strong sun-bursts between the clouds flashed across these pastoral pictures.

Soon after we left, a number of the men and women collected together on the after-deck, and commenced singing hymns, which occupation they kept up with untiring fervour during the whole voyage. The young girls were remarkable for weight and solidity of figure, ugliness of face, and sweetness of voice. The clear, ringing tones, with a bell-like purity and delicious *timbre*, issued without effort from between their thick, beefy lips, and there was such a contrast between sound and substance, that they attracted my attention more than I should have thought possible. Some of the men, who had heard what we were, entered into conversation with us. I soon discovered that they were all Läsare, and one of them, who seemed to exercise a kind of leadership, and who was a man of considerable intelligence, gave me a good deal of information about the sect. They met together privately, he said, to read the New Testament, trusting entirely to its inspired pages for the means of enlightenment as to what was necessary for the salvation of their souls. The clergy stood between them and the Voice of God, who had spoken not to a particular class, but to all mankind. They were liable to a fine of 200 *rigs* ($52) every time they thus met together, my informant had once been obliged to pay it himself. Nevertheless, he said they were not interfered with so much at present, except that they were obliged to pay tithes, as before. "The king is a good man," he continued, "he means well, and would do us justice if he had the power; but the clergy are all against him, and his own authority is limited. Now they are going to bring the question of religious freedom before the Diet, but we have not the least hope that anything will be done." He also stated—what, indeed, must be evident to every observing traveller—that the doctrines of the Läsare had spread very rapidly, and that their numbers were continually increasing.

The creation of such a powerful dissenting body is a thing that might have been expected. The Church, in Sweden, had become a system of forms and ceremonies. The pure spiritualism of Swedenborg, in the last century, was a natural and gigantic rebound to the opposite extreme, but, from its lofty intellectuality, was unfitted to be the nucleus of a popular protest. Meanwhile, the souls of the people starved on the dry husks which were portioned out to them. They needed genuine nourishment. They are an earnest, reflective race, and the religious element is deeply implanted in their nature. The present movement, so much like Methodism in many particulars, owes its success to the same genial and all-embracing doctrine of an impartial visitation of Divine grace, bringing man into nearer and tenderer relations to his Maker. In a word, it is the democratic, opposed to the aristocratic principle in religion. It is fashionable in Sweden to sneer at the Läsare; their numbers, character, and sincerity are very generally under-estimated. No doubt there is much that is absurd and grotesque in their services; no doubt they run into violent and unchristian extremes, and often merely substitute fanaticism for spiritual apathy; but I believe they will in the end be the instrument of bestowing religious liberty upon Sweden.

There was no end to the desire of these people for knowledge. They overwhelmed us with questions about our country, its government, laws, climate, productions and geographical extent. Next to America, they seemed most interested in Palestine, and considered me as specially favoured by Providence in having beheld Jerusalem. They all complained of the burdens which fall upon a poor man in Sweden, in the shape of government taxes, tithes, and the obligation of supporting a portion of the army, who are distributed through the provinces. Thus Dalecarlia, they informed me, with a population of 132,000, is obliged to maintain 1200 troops. The tax on land corresponded very nearly with the statement made by my female postillion the previous day. Dalecarlia, its mines excepted, is one of the poorest of the Swedish provinces. Many of its inhabitants are obliged to wander forth every summer, either to take service elsewhere, or to dispose of the articles they fabricate at home, in order, after some years of this irregular life, to possess enough to enable them to pass the rest of their days humbly at home. Our fellow-passengers told me of several who had emigrated to America, where they had spent five or six years. They grew home-sick at last, and returned to their chilly hills. But it was not the bleak fir-woods, the oat-fields, or the wooden huts which they missed; it was the truth, the honesty, the manliness, and the loving tenderness which dwell in Dalecarlian hearts.

We had a strong wind abeam, but our little steamer made good progress down the lake. The shores contracted, and the white church of Leksand rose over the dark woods, and between two and three o'clock in the afternoon, we were moored in the Dal River, where it issues from the Sijan. The

Elfdal pedlers shouldered their immense packs and set out, bidding us a friendly adieu as we parted. After establishing ourselves in the little inn, where we procured a tolerable dinner, we called upon the *Domprost* Hvasser, to whom I had a letter from a countryman who made a pedestrian journey through Dalecarlia five years ago. The parsonage was a spacious building near the church, standing upon the brink of a lofty bank overlooking the outflow of the Dal. The Domprost, a hale, stout old man, with something irresistibly hearty and cheering in his manner, gave us both his hands and drew us into the room, on seeing that we were strangers. He then proceeded to read the letter. "Ho!" he exclaimed, "to think that he has remembered me all this time! And he has not forgotten that it was just midsummer when he was here!" Presently he went out, and soon returned with a basket in one hand and some plates in the other, which he placed before us and heaped with fine ripe cherries. "Now it is autumn," said he; "it is no longer midsummer, but we have a little of the summer's fruit left." He presented us to his sister and daughter, and to two handsome young magisters, who assisted him in his parochial duties.

We walked in the garden, which was laid out with some taste along the brow of the hill. A superb drooping birch, eighty feet in height, was the crowning glory of the place. The birch is the characteristic tree of Sweden, as the fir is of Norway, the beech of Denmark, the oak of England and Germany, the chestnut of Italy, and the palm of Egypt. Of nothern trees, there is none more graceful in outline, but in the cold, silvery hue of its foliage, summer can never find her best expression. The parson had a neat little bowling-alley, in a grove of pine, on a projecting spur of the hill. He did not disdain secular recreations; his religion was cheerful and jubilant; he had found something else in the Bible than the Lamentations of Jeremiah. There are so many Christians who—to judge from the settled expression of their faces—suffer under their belief, that it is a comfort to find those who see nothing heretical in the fullest and freest enjoyment of life. There was an apple-tree in the garden which was just bursting into blossoms for the second time. I called the Domprost's attention to it, remarking, in a line from Frithiof's Saga:—"*Hösten bjuder sin thron til varen*" (Autumn offers his throne to the spring). "What!" he exclaimed in joyful surprise, "do you know Tegner?" and immediately continued the quotation.

There was no resisting the hospitable persuasions of the family; we were obliged to take supper and spend the evening with them. The daughter and the two magisters sang for us all the characteristic songs of Wermeland and Dalecarlia which they could remember, and I was more than ever charmed with the wild, simple, original character of the native melodies of Sweden. They are mostly in the minor key, and some of them might almost be called monotonous; yet it is monotony, or rather simplicity, in the notation, which sticks to the memory. The longings, the regrets, the fidelity, and the tenderness of the people, find an echo in these airs, which have all the character of improvisations, and rekindle in the heart of the hearer the passions they were intended to relieve.

We at last took leave of the good old man and his friendly

household. The night was dark and rainy, and the magisters accompanied us to the inn. In the morning it was raining dismally,—a slow, cold, driving rain, which is the climax of bad weather. We determined, however, to push onward as far as Fahlun, the capital of Dalecarlia, about four Swedish miles distant. Our road was down the valley of the Dal Elv, which we crossed twice on floating bridges, through a very rich, beautiful, and thickly settled country. The hills were here higher and bolder than in Westerdal, dark with forests of fir and pine, and swept south-eastward in long ranges, leaving a broad, open valley for the river to wander in. This valley, from three to five miles in width, was almost entirely covered with enclosed fields, owing to which the road was barred with gates, and our progress was much delayed thereby. The houses were neat and substantial, many of them with gardens and orchards attached, while the unusual number of the barns and granaries gave evidence of a more prosperous state of agriculture than we had seen since leaving the neighborhood of Carlstad. We pressed forward in the rain and raw wind, and reached Fahlun towards evening, just in time to avoid a drenching storm.

Of the celebrated copper-mines of Fahlun, some of which have been worked for 600 years, we saw nothing. We took their magnitude and richness for granted, on the strength of the immense heaps of dross through which we drove on approaching the town, and the desolate appearance of the surrounding country, whose vegetation has been for the most part destroyed by the fumes from the smelting works. In our sore and sodden condition, we were in no humour to go sight seeing, and so sat comfortably by the stove, while the rain beat against the windows, and the darkness fell. The next morning brought us a renewal of the same weather, but we set out bravely in our open cart, and jolted over the muddy roads with such perseverance, that we reached Hedemora at night. The hills diminished in height as we proceeded southward, but the scenery retained its lovely pastoral character. My most prominent recollection of the day's travel, however, is of the number of gates our numb and blue-faced boy-postillions were obliged to jump down and open.

From Hedemora, a journey of two days through the provinces of Westerås and Uppland, brought us to Upsala. After leaving Dalecarlia and crossing the Dal River for the fifth and last time, the country gradually sank into those long, slightly rolling plains, which we had traversed last winter, between Stockholm and Gefle. Here villages were more frequent, but the houses had not the same air of thrift and comfort as in Dalecarlia. The population also changed in character, the faces we now saw being less bright, cheerful, and kindly, and the forms less tall and strongly knit.

We had very fair accommodations, at all the post-stations along the road, and found the people everywhere honest and obliging. Still, I missed the noble simplicity which I had admired so much in the natives of Westerdal, and on the frontier of Wermeland,—the unaffected kindness of heart which made me look upon every man as a friend.

The large town of Sala, where we spent a night, was filled with fugitives from Upsala, where the cholera was making great ravages. The violence of the disease was over by the time we arrived; but the students, all of whom had left, had not yet returned, and the fine old place had a melancholy air. The first thing we saw on approaching it, was a funeral. Professor Bergfalk, who had remained at his post, and to whom I had letters, most kindly gave me an entire day of his time. I saw the famous *Codex argenteus*, in the library, the original manuscript of Frithiof's Saga, the journals of Swedenborg and Linnæus, the Botanical Garden, and the tombs of Gustavus Vasa and John III. in the cathedral. But most interesting of all was our drive to Old Upsala, where we climbed upon the mound of Odin, and drank mead out of the silver-mounted drinking horn, from which Bernadotte, Oscar, and the whole royal family of Sweden, are in the habit of drinking when they make a pilgrimage to the burial place of the Scandinavian gods.

A cold, pale, yellow light lay upon the landscape; the towers of Upsala Cathedral, and the massive front of the palace, rose dark against the sky, in the south-west; a chill autumnal wind blew over the plains, and the yellowing foliage of the birch drifted across the mysterious mounds, like those few golden leaves of poetry, which the modern bards of the North have cast upon the grave of the grand, muscular religion of the earlier race. There was no melodious wailing in the wind, like that which proclaimed "Pan is dead!" through the groves of Greece and Ionia; but a cold rustling hiss, as if the serpent of Midgard were exulting over the ruin of Walhalla. But in the stinging, aromatic flood of the amber-coloured mead, I drank to Odin, to Balder, and to **Freja**.

We reached Stockholm on the 22nd of September, in the midst of a furious gale, accompanied with heavy squalls of snow—the same in which the Russian line-of-battle ship "*Lefort*," foundered in the Gulf of Finland. In the mild, calm, sunny, autumn days which followed, the beautiful city charmed us more than ever, and I felt half inclined to take back all I had said against the place, during the dismal weather of last spring. The trees in the Djurgård and in the islands of Mälar, were still in full foliage; the Dalecarlian boatwomen plied their crafts in the outer harbour; the little garden under the Norrbro was gay with music and lamps every evening; and the brief and jovial summer life of the Swedes, so near its close, clung to the flying sunshine, that not a moment might be suffered to pass by unenjoyed.

In another week we were standing on the deck of the Prussian steamer "*Nagler*," threading the rocky archipelago between Stockholm and the open Baltic on our way to Stettin. In leaving the North, after ten months of winter and summer wanderings, and with scarce a hope of returning again, I found myself repeating, over and over again, the farewell of Frithiof:—

> "*Farvål, J fjällar,*
>   *Der åran bor;*
> *J runohällar,*
>   *För väldig Thor;*
> *J blåa sjöar,*
>   *Jag künt så väl;*
> *J skär och öar,*
>   *Farvål, farvål!*"

THE END.